CW00505860

The development
of international law
by the European
Court of Human Rights

The Melland Schill Monographs
in International Law

General editor Gillian M. White

The development
of international law
by the European
Court of Human Rights

J. G. MERRILLS

Professor of Public International Law,
University of Sheffield

MANCHESTER
UNIVERSITY PRESS
Distributed exclusively in the USA and Canada
by St. Martin's Press

Copyright © J. G. Merrills 1993

Published by
Manchester University Press
Oxford Road, Manchester M13 9NR, UK
and Room 400, 175 Fifth Avenue,
New York, NY 10010, USA

Distributed exclusively in the USA and Canada by
St. Martin's Press, Inc.
175 Fifth Avenue, New York, NY 10010, USA
First edition 1988
Second edition 1993

British Library cataloguing in publication data
A catalogue record for this book is available from the British Library

Library of Congress cataloging in publication data
Merrills, J. G.
    The development of international law by the European Court of
Human Rights / J. G. Merrills.
        p.   cm. — (The Melland Schill monographs in international
law)
    Includes index.
    ISBN 0–7190–3737–9 (hbk.)
    1. European Court of Human Rights.   2. Civil rights—Europe.
3. Human rights.   I. Title.   II. Series.
KJC5138.M47   1993
341.4'81—dc20   92-37301
                                                                           CIP

ISBN 0 7190 4560 6 *paperback*

Paperback edition published 1995

Photoset in Linotron Times by
Northern Phototypesetting Co. Ltd., Bolton
Printed and bound in Great Britain by
Biddles Ltd., Guildford and Kings Lynn

CONTENTS

FOREWORD TO FIRST EDITION

The Melland Schill fund was established by the will of the late Miss Olive B. Schill in memory of her brother, Melland, who was killed in the war of 1914–18. The present series of *Melland Schill Monographs in International Law* replaces the earlier series of *Melland Schill Lectures*, published by the University Press. Miss Schill's generous bequest was motivated by her wish to contribute to scholarship and learning as they affect international relations, in the hope, we may surmise, of increasing the role of law and of decreasing the likelihood of further devastating armed conflicts.

It was in the aftermath of the devastation and human suffering brought about by the Second World War and the brutal and inhuman policies of the Nazi regime that the governments of Western Europe concluded the European Convention on Human Rights and Fundamental Freedoms in 1950. The Convention has now been in force for some thirty-five years and has been ratified by all the member countries of the Council of Europe. Most of the Parties have accepted the jurisdiction of the European Court of Human Rights which can decide disputes between them arising out of the Convention and also, and more significantly, can adjudicate in cases brought to it by the European Commission of Human Rights, or by a State concerned, cases which originate in a petition from an individual or group claiming to be the victim of a breach of some provision of the Convention by a State Party.

Professor Merrills's book is certainly not the first study of the jurisprudence of this, the first established court of human rights, nor will it be the last. But, as he makes clear, his purpose has differed from those of previous studies: he has chosen to examine the Court's jurisprudence from the perspective of contribution to the development of international law, or more particularly, its significance for our understanding of the international judicial process generally and of the role of adjudication in developing an international law of human rights. The focus is therefore on the Court, its place in the Strasbourg institutional system, its approach to and methods of interpretation of the unavoidably open-textured language of the human rights provisions, and its resort to some general principles of law. Two concluding chapters take a somewhat wider perspective and consider, respectively, the Convention in the context of general international law and other related treaties, and issues of ideology and international human rights law, including two contrasting ideologies denominated as 'tough conservatism' and 'benevolent liberalism'.

It is surely a happy coincidence that the appearance of the present book should come almost precisely thirty years after the publication of Hersch Lauterpacht's classic study, *The Development of International Law by the International Court* (1958), for it was Lauterpacht's pioneering and challenging work *An International Bill of the Rights of Man* (1945) which strengthened the hands of all those who urged the conclusion of a European Convention to declare and protect fundamental human rights. Sadly, Hersch Lauterpacht did not live to see the European Court of Human Rights deliver its first judgment in 1961. The Court's output since then has been considerable, and its judgments are of crucial importance for the application of the Convention and for the elaboration and refinement of the definitions of the rights protected, their scope and meaning in social and economic circumstances which are very different from those of 1950.

Professor Merrills examines and evaluates this jurisprudence, seeking any lessons which might be drawn from it for other international tribunals, particularly, though not exclusively, tribunals entrusted with the interpretation of other human rights treaties. He is right to warn us that 'the law of the Convention is still developing' and that 'we are therefore dealing with a process as much as a product'. It is also true that there are significant differences between the European Convention and other human rights treaties applying to different parts of the world. Nevertheless, as he maintains, 'the Strasbourg system remains the most developed scheme of international human rights protection, and the Court the most active judicial organ in the field'. The Melland Schill Series is enriched by this contribution to the literature of international judicial law and the international law of human rights.

Gillian White
Professor of International Law
Director of the Melland Schill Fund
Faculty of Law
University of Manchester
February 1988

PREFACE

This is a second edition of a book which first appeared in 1988. Its inspiration, as the title suggests, is to be found in Sir Hersch Lauterpacht's seminal work *The Development of International Law by the International Court*. For it was that book with its penetrating analysis of decisions at The Hague which suggested to me that it might be useful to examine the jurisprudence of the European Court in a similar way.

The preparation of a new edition has provided an opportunity to bring the text up to date in two ways. First, and most important, I have been able to take into account a significant amount of new case law in which the Court has built upon the foundations laid in its earlier jurisprudence and other human rights organs have been influenced by its decisions. Secondly, where relevant, I have noted various actual or anticipated institutional changes such as those contained in the latest Protocols. A full account of the latter, together with other aspects of the Strasbourg system not examined in detail here, may be found in the third edition of Robertson and Merrills, *Human Rights in Europe* (Manchester University Press 1992) which can, in a sense, be regarded as complementary to the present volume.

The key to decision-making in the field of human rights is, I believe, the spirit and philosophy which animate the work of the judge. My aim has therefore again been to show how the judges of the Strasbourg Court approach the task of interpreting human rights as laid down in the European Convention. The Court, like any human institution, can err and it will be clear that certain decisions are in my view open to criticism. The reader will also find, however, that I consider that when taken as a whole the jurisprudence of the Court continues to provide an inspiring example not only to those who may serve at Strasbourg in the future, but also to those responsible for deciding human rights issues elsewhere.

My study of the Court could not have been written had not others prepared the ground with studies of the international judicial process and the European Convention which are mentioned in the text. I am grateful to the Registrar of the European Court for making essential material available to me and to Professor Gillian White, who again read the manuscript and made many helpful suggestions. My thanks are also due to Mrs Jean Hopewell who typed the manuscript of this edition and to my wife Dariel whose encouragement, as always, was invaluable.

J.G. Merrills
Sheffield
November 1992

CHAPTER 1

The Court as an international institution

The European Court of Human Rights was set up in 1959 to ensure the observance of the engagements undertaken by the Parties to the European Convention on Human Rights. The Convention was not the first international instrument to provide an enumeration of rights, but it was the first to do so in treaty form and with institutional machinery for supervision and enforcement. Of course, the protection of human rights does not depend primarily on international guarantees. There are States which provide excellent protection for civil and political rights, but which for various reasons do not subscribe to international arrangements. Conversely, the fact that a State is a party to human rights conventions cannot in itself ensure that these obligations will be respected. But if international law is neither a necessary, nor a sufficient condition of human rights protection, it has been conclusively demonstrated to have a practical part to play.

Arrangements at the national level are the main and certainly the best guarantee of individual rights, but are not always enough. When they prove inadequate for any reason, international guarantees may provide both an incentive to resolve the immediate problem and a salutary reminder for the future. In a more general way, the fact that a State is a party to a human rights treaty means that there is a legal yardstick against which its practice can be measured, while politically the issue of rights will be more prominent than might otherwise be the case. If a human rights treaty contains enforcement machinery the effect is even more pronounced. When governments know that policies must be justified in an international forum an additional element enters their decision-making. Thus, with the State's obligations to the individual as a constant background to official deliberations, the impact of a treaty such as the European Convention is likely to be out of all proportion to the number of cases in which conduct is actually challenged.

The impact of a particular treaty depends upon its substantive content, its enforcement machinery, if any, and the political culture in which it operates. The European Convention on Human Rights, which was signed in 1950, is a striking example of what a well-conceived instrument can accomplish in a propitious environment. As a result of proceedings at Strasbourg individuals can obtain redress for violations of their rights and bring about changes in domestic law and practice which, though some-times long overdue, would be unlikely to be achieved without the Con-vention. Governments know that policies and practices which appear to conflict with the Convention are likely to be challenged and draw the obvious conclusion. Most significant of all, at least to the British observer, is that notwithstanding the doctrine of Parliamentary sovereignty, throughout the area covered by the Convention the proper relation between the citizen and the State is now a legal as well as a political issue.

The success of the European Convention is something for which many can claim credit: the Contracting States which sponsored the Convention and which with rare exceptions have discharged their obligations con-scientiously, the individuals whose patience, tenacity and persistence have generated the ever-increasing flood of case-law, and, not least, the institutions: the Commission, the Court and the Committee of Ministers. What follows is a study of the Court which, as we shall see, plays a key role in the interpretation and application of the Convention. It is not an examination of the Strasbourg system in its entirety, nor an exhaustive review of the application of the Convention. The aim is rather to identify issues of method and function relevant to the international judicial pro-cess generally, and specifically to the role of adjudication in developing an international law of human rights. To set these questions in context, it is useful to begin by considering the Court's place in the scheme of the Convention.

The Court and the Commission

Cases which reach the Court have originated in applications lodged with the European Commission of Human Rights by a State, an individual, a group of individuals, or a non-governmental organisation. The Commis-sion deals first with the admissibility of the application. Any petition may be rejected if domestic remedies have not been exhausted and petitions from applicants other than States may be rejected if they are anonymous or manifestly ill-founded, and on a number of other grounds. Moreover, whereas it is always open to a State to bring a petition against another Contracting Party, the Commission can receive individual petitions only in cases where the respondent has recognised its competence to do so.

If the Commission accepts an application it ascertains the facts and tries to reach a friendly settlement. If this fails, the Commission prepares a report, containing a statement of the facts and an opinion as to whether they disclose a breach of the respondent's obligations under the Convention. This report is transmitted to the Committee of Ministers of the Council of Europe. Provided the jurisdiction of the Court has been accepted, the case may then be brought before the Court within three months by the Commission and/or by any Contracting State concerned. Jurisdiction is accepted by a State making a general declaration that it recognises the Court's jurisdiction as compulsory, or, alternatively, agreeing to the referral of a particular case. Almost all the parties to the Convention have now made declarations and so this requirement, which reflects the consensual basis of international litigation, is not a significant limitation. If, after being dealt with by the Commission, a case is not referred to the Court, the Committee of Ministers decides whether there has been a violation of the Convention.

One of the primary features of the Convention system is that 'the Commission's decision declaring an application admissible determines the object of the case brought before the Court'.[1] That is to say, the Commission has the task of identifying the subject-matter of each case for Convention purposes and its ruling is regarded as definitive. The significance of this process as a way of circumscribing the issues is illustrated by the *Malone* case, where the Court said:

It should be noted from the outset that the scope of the case before the Court does not extend to interception of communications in general. The Commission's decision of 13 July 1981 declaring Mr Malone's application to be admissible determines the object of the case brought before the Court. . . . According to that decision, the present case 'is directly concerned only with the question of interceptions effected by or on behalf of the police' – and not other government services such as HM Customs and Excise and the Security Service – 'within the general context of a criminal investigation, together with the legal and administrative framework relevant to such interceptions'.[2]

In this example the Court was indicating that the treatment of the case by the Commission required it to confine its attention to one aspect of a much broader subject. In other cases the effect has been to restrict the Court's consideration to particular articles of the Convention on which the Commission has held an application admissible, while leaving out of account others on which it has reached the opposite conclusion. Thus in the *Barthold* case, where one of the applicant's complaints concerned Article 11, the Court held that it was unable to examine the point because 'Having been declared inadmissible by the Commission on 12 March 1981 as being incompatible *ratione materiae* with the provisions of the Convention . . . this complaint falls outside the ambit of the case referred to the Court.'[3] And in *Le Compte, Van Leuven and De Meyere*,[4] where the same article was in issue, the Court decided that as the Commission had again ruled this part of the application inadmissible, it could not be examined further.

Thus when a case is referred to the Court, the Commission's processing of it at the admissibility stage has the effect of directing attention to certain aspects, while removing others from consideration. Even more important, it is effectively the Commission which decides whether a case can be considered by the Court at all. The Court cannot choose its cases, but may decide only those which have been referred to it, and although there is nothing to prevent a State from making a reference, it is the Commission's decisions that are important in practice.[5] Neither the Convention nor the Rules of Procedure furnish the Commission with guidance on this point, or provide a basis for predicting the Court's workload. In the light of current practice, however, it is possible to indicate considerations which may be relevant.

Since the Court is the judicial arm of the Convention, it would be natural to expect the Commission to refer to it all cases which raise a new point on the interpretation of the Convention. On the other hand, where the issue is primarily one of fact, one might expect a greater willingness to use the Committee of Ministers. In practice a distinction of this kind appears to be generally observed. It would be thought unusual for a case such as *Marckx*,[6] which raised important questions concerning the scope of Article 8, not to be referred to the Court, while numerous examples can be found of cases where an issue which has already been considered by the Court is not referred again.

Another factor which may be relevant is the extent to which the Commission is divided as to whether the facts disclose a violation of the Convention. Often such cases will raise difficult points of interpretation and so come into the first category. However, even when the law is clear, its application may be controversial. The Convention makes extensive use of standards such as 'reasonable time' which can never be automatic in their application. It is not surprising therefore that despite a substantial amount of jurisprudence, cases involving this concept are still regularly referred to the Court by the Commission.

Finally, it has been suggested that the Commission may be expected to prefer the Committee of Ministers to the Court, where a case has particularly serious political implications. Were a State versus State case, for example, to involve allegations of such gross violations of the Convention that a finding of guilt might lead to expulsion from the Council of Europe, it is possible that this would be so. Without more evidence, however, this can be no more than speculation. The point to grasp, however, is that in these cases, as elsewhere, the Court's field of operations is determined by the decisions of the Commission. Therefore although our concern is the work of the Court, to see its activity in perspective, it must be thought of as a component of an institutional system in which both the size and shape of its case-load are the responsibility of the Commission.

The Commission also has an important part to play in the Court's procedure. The first stage of the procedure before the Court is usually written, though this is not invariable. All documents are filed with the Court's Registry in the order and according to the time limits laid down by the President. When a case is ready for hearing he also fixes a date for the opening of the oral proceedings which normally take place in public. Only the State or States concerned are parties to the case. The Commission therefore is not, although it participates in the proceedings as 'defender of the public interest' and to this end appoints at least one of its members as Delegate to assist the Court. Individual applicants may neither refer cases to the Court nor appear before it as a party. Under the Court's original Rules the Delegates of the Commission could have the assistance of any person they chose. In one of its early judgments[7] the Court held that this could be an applicant's lawyer, or the applicant himself, and this option was exercised on a number of occasions. In new Rules, which came into force on 1 January 1983, an additional option was introduced. As well as the old procedure involving the Commission, whenever a case has been referred to the Court by a Government or the Commission, the applicant may indicate that he wishes to participate in the proceedings. If he does so, he is represented by a lawyer, although technically he is still not a party to the case.

In certain circumstances the views of others, not involved directly in the proceedings, may also be available to the Court. If he deems it necessary for the proper administration of justice, the President may invite or grant leave to a Contracting State which is not a party to submit written comments within a time-limit and on specified issues. He may also extend such an invitation or grant such leave to an individual other than the applicant. This power, which was also conferred by the new Rules, has so far been exercised sparingly and with the ambit of the case, as defined by the Commission, very much in mind. In the *Malone* case, for example, the Post Office Engineering Union requested leave to submit comments on various matters relating to the interception of communications in the United Kingdom, and in the *Ashingdane* case[8] the organisation MIND made a similar request with regard to the treatment of the mentally ill. In both instances the President granted the requests, but specified that the comments submitted should be strictly limited to matters closely connected with the respective cases.

The composition of the Court

The Court consists of a number of judges equal to the number of member States of the Council of Europe (currently twenty-six). The judges are elected for a nine-year term by the Council's Consultative Assembly and no two judges may be nationals of the same State. Elections are staggered to ensure that one third of the Court are elected every three years. At the end of his term, however, a judge may stand for re-election, and if replaced, continues to deal with any case already under consideration.

At the election of the judges each Member of the Council of Europe nominates three candidates of whom at least two must be its nationals. As far as possible the same procedure is followed to fill casual vacancies, or when the admission of new Members of the Council necessitates enlargement of the Court. In accordance with the usual practice in international tribunals, a member of the Court elected to fill a casual vacancy holds office for the remainder of his predecessor's term.

The size of the Court and the election arrangements are designed to ensure that the composition of the Court fully reflects the diversity of the European States. The judges, of course, are in no sense spokesmen for their nominating States and before embarking on their duties must take an oath, or make a declaration, that they will perform their duties impartially and independently. Nevertheless, since those duties concern the obligations of States in a field which is both highly sensitive and genuinely controversial, it is unlikely that governments would be prepared to invest the Court with extensive powers unless they regarded it as adequately representative. In broader perspective the ability of the Court to contribute to human rights law in general is helped when it is seen to have access to a range of different views.

It is important that the judges not only reflect different national cultures and points of view, but are also demonstrably competent as individuals to decide the cases which come before them. Article 39(3) of the Convention requires that candidates for election shall be 'of high moral character and must either possess the qualifications required for appointment to high judicial office or be jurisconsults of recognised competence'. The wording here is similar to that of the European Communities' Treaties and also to the Statute of the International Court, although in contrast with the latter, competence in international law is not specifically required. More surprisingly, the Convention originally contained no reference to the judges' independence. However, this was rectified by Protocol No. 8, and Article 40(7) now requires the judges to sit 'in their individual capacity', adding that 'During their term of office they shall not hold any position which is incompatible with their independence and impartiality as members of the Court or the demands of this office'. As already noted, independence is also emphasised in the oath, while the fact that Article 59 of the Statute provides for members of the Court to enjoy certain privileges and immunities recognises and protects their independent position.

Which activities should be regarded as incompatible with membership of the Court is less straightforward than might be supposed. The Statute of the International Court lays down that 'no member of the Court may exercise any political or administrative function, or engage in any other occupation of a professional nature'. The Statute of the European Court of Justice contains a similar provision. The Court of Human Rights, however, is not in continuous session and its members are remunerated with a daily allowance and an annual retainer. A complete prohibition on work outside the Court would therefore hardly be practicable. There was some discussion of this question before the first elections to the Court in 1959, but no decisions were taken. Eventually, the matter was resolved by a provision in the Rules of the Court, which now lay down that: 'A judge may not exercise his functions while he is a member of a Government or while he holds a post or exercises a profession which is incompatible with his independence and impartiality. In case of need the plenary Court shall decide.'[9]

Subsequently, in 1977, the Parliamentary Assembly of the Council of Europe passed a resolution requesting its members not to vote for candidates 'who, by nature of their functions, are dependent on government' unless they undertake to resign such functions on election.[10]

Though inexact, these directives do not, so far, appear to have created any problems. Candidates for the Court tend to be members of their national judiciary or professors of law, while a smaller number are practising lawyers, politicians or former government officials. In practice, there seems to be no difficulty in maintaining the calibre of the bench and some very distinguished individuals have been, or are, members of the Court.

Because the full Court is so large, Article 43 of the Convention provides that each case shall be heard by a chamber of nine judges.[11] This must include, as *ex officio* members, the President or a Vice-President of the Court and the judge who is a national of any State party concerned. If the 'national' judge is unable to sit or withdraws, or if there is none, the State in question is entitled to appoint a member of the Court (an elected judge of a different nationality), or someone from outside the Court (an *ad hoc* judge). The arrangements for 'national' judges seem less anomalous if one bears in mind the traditional reluctance of governments to entrust international tribunals with important decisions. *Ad hoc* judges, it should be remembered, are regularly appointed for contentious cases in the International Court.

The use of transient chambers, though a sensible and practical way of handling the business of the European Court, means that provision must be made to ensure a continuous and consistent development of its jurisprudence. Accordingly, Rule 51 lays down that wherever a case 'raises one or more serious questions affecting the interpretation of the Convention' the Chamber may relinquish jurisdiction in favour of the plenary Court. Moreover, relinquishment of jurisdiction is obligatory 'where the resolution of such question or questions might have a result inconsistent with a judgment previously delivered by a Chamber or the plenary Court'. On the basis of these provisions a significant number of cases are referred to the plenary Court.

The relation between chambers and the plenary Court differs significantly from that to be found elsewhere. In the European Court of Justice chambers are permanent sections of the Court to which judges are formally assigned and it is the full Court which decides whether a case should be referred to a chamber, and not the other way round. In the International Court, on the other hand, it is for the parties to decide whether they wish their case to be heard by a chamber. If so, they must also be consulted as to its composition, a practice reminiscent of arbitration and which would plainly be out of place at Strasbourg.

The work of the Court

The Court decides all disputes concerning its jurisdiction. However, questions of this kind, which play such a large part in the work of the International Court, are nothing like as significant at Strasbourg. The Court's role as the judicial arm of the Convention ensures that technical questions concerning the manifestation of consent, which are all too frequent at The Hague, are unlikely to arise, while in the rare case where jurisdiction is clearly lacking – because a State has not made the requisite declaration – the Court will never be involved. Nevertheless, cases which present jurisdictional problems do sometimes occur. In the *De Becker* case,[12] for example, the Court had to decide whether it has the power to remove a case from its list without giving judgment; while in the *Ringeisen* case[13] the question was whether it has jurisdiction to interpret a previous judgment, in the absence of any express provision to this effect in the Convention.

Sometimes it is the Commission's jurisdiction that is the issue and here the Court's decision can play a key role in establishing the scope and effectiveness of the Convention. In the *Foti* case[14] Italy argued that the Commission had exceeded its jurisdiction by raising a particular issue on its own initiative instead of adopting the characterisation of the facts put forward by the applicant. Likewise, in *Marckx* and a number of other cases, a respondent government has argued, usually unsuccessfully, that a case should not have been entertained by the Commission because the applicant was not 'claiming to be the victim' of a violation of the Convention, as required by Article 25.

Closely related to jurisdiction are questions of admissibility and what may be termed 'competence in the broad sense', including propriety and various issues calling for the exercise of discretion. Here though the European Court's position is again distinct from that of the International Court, the kinds of issues which arise, and the ways they are resolved shed light on more than one aspect of the judicial function. For example, as a result of its ruling in the *Vagrancy* cases[15] respondents can secure a reconsideration of arguments rejected at the admissibility stage by the Commission, a point which has been particularly important in relation to the obligation to exhaust local remedies contained in Article 26. On a quite different matter, having established that the removal of a case from the list is within its jurisdiction, the Court has had to decide a series of questions concerned with when it is appropriate to do so.

The Court's main work is, of course, the interpretation and application of the substantive provisions of the Convention and its associated protocols, a task which raises a wide range of issues of law and policy. Courts whose function is to apply general international law deal with a relatively narrow range of issues concerned with States' external relations, because this is what the bulk of international law exists to regulate. Obligations in the field of human rights, on the other hand, concern the most intimate aspects of the relations between the citizen and the State. Since there is no aspect of national affairs which can be said to be without implications for one or other of the rights protected by the Convention, there is no matter of domestic law and policy which may not eventually reach the European Court.

In terms of the character of the Court's work this has a double significance. In the first place, it means that the Court is required to investigate and pronounce on many issues which have not hitherto been regarded as appropriate subjects for international adjudication, which in turn raises the question of how far the Court is entitled to go in monitoring the laws and practices of the Contracting States. This is essentially a question about the impact of human rights law on national sovereignty and the role of international adjudication in establishing and enforcing uniform standards. The other way in which the nature of the Court's work is significant is that as a tribunal dealing with human rights, the Court is required to decide difficult and important questions concerning the proper relationship between the individual and the State. The issue here is what it means to have a particular right and how the balance is to be struck between such competing interests as, for example, privacy and national security, or prompt trial and the limitation of public expenditure.

How the Court has handled the question of its role vis-à-vis the Contracting States, and the equally important question of the content of particular rights, are matters we must postpone for later consideration. One point, however, is worth making now. It is that in dealing with both questions the Court has far exceeded what might reasonably have been anticipated in 1950. As a commentator has said of the Strasbourg institutions, 'Conceived as regional international organs with limited jurisdiction and even more limited powers, they have gradually acquired the status and authority of constitutional tribunals'.[16] As we shall see, this transformation of the Convention and its institutions, which is still in progress, is the key to understanding the wider significance of the Court's decisions.

Human rights cases, like other kinds of litigation, often involve argument about the facts as well as the law. However, the Convention makes establishing the facts one of the responsibilities of the Commission, and so the Court has indicated that it is only in exceptional circumstances that it will use its powers in this area. Thus in the *Stocké* case,[17] which concerned an alleged kidnapping by the German police, the Court refused to allow the applicant to call a number of witnesses, observing that as his allegations had been thoroughly investigated by the Commission and the French and German authorities, hearing more evidence would serve no useful purpose. At the same time, however, in this and other cases the Court has emphasised that the Commission's findings of fact are not binding. The Court therefore 'remains free to make its own appreciation in the light of all the material before it'.[18] Thus, although the Court is usually more concerned with the law than with the facts, it has the power to re-examine evidence where necessary.[19]

When considering the kinds of questions which come before the Court it is also important to appreciate that although the Convention is now very influential, it remains ancillary to the protection afforded by the Contracting States' domestic law. Thus the function of the Strasbourg institutions is to apply the Convention and does not usually extend to pronouncing on issues of domestic law. This is sometimes expressed by saying that the Convention institutions are not 'a court of fourth instance' and numerous cases can be found in which the Court has been careful to disclaim this function.

In the *Sramek* case, for example, which was concerned with the decision of a Regional Real Property Transactions Authority, the Court observed in relation to the applicant's claim for compensation under Article 50, that, 'the evidence in the file does not warrant the conclusion that had it been differently composed the Regional Authority would have arrived at a decision in Mrs Sramek's favour and it is not for the Court to inquire whether, under Austrian law, the Regional Authority ought to have given such a decision.'[20] Likewise in the *Foti* case, where the question was whether criminal proceedings involving the applicant had been unduly prolonged, the Court said that it did not consider that it had 'to review the conduct of the investigating judge, that is to say, the question whether he ought to have severed the proceedings against Mr Foti and Mr Aloi. Nor does the Court adjudge it to be within its province to determine whether the Chamber of Deputies ought to have waived Mr Aloi's parliamentary immunity at an earlier date. In all cases what is in issue is the international responsibility of the State.'[21]

Although the Court is careful to avoid trespassing on what it sees as the function of the national authorities, investigating 'the international responsibility of the State' almost always calls for scrutiny of certain aspects of domestic law. Thus another feature of the Court's work is that the very nature of the obligations with which the Court is concerned makes the adequacy of the Contracting States' domestic law a matter for investigation.

The need for the Court to do its duty and enforce the Convention while respecting the jurisdiction of the national authorities is well illustrated by the *Malone* case in which the crucial issue was whether English law provided sufficiently clear guidelines on telephone tapping. Dealing with this issue, the Court found that 'at the very least, in its present state the law in England and Wales governing interception of communications for police purposes is somewhat obscure and open to differing interpretations'. However, recognising the limits of its competence, it went on 'The Court would be usurping the function of the national courts were it to attempt to make an authoritative statement on such issues of domestic law.' It then concluded this part of its judgment by pointing out that, 'The Court is, however, required under the Convention to determine whether, for the purposes of paragraph 2 of Article 8, the relevant law lays down with reasonable clarity the essential elements of the authorities' powers in this domain.'[22]

The scrutiny to which English law was subjected in *Malone* is typical of the way in which the Court must be prepared to analyse domestic law in cases involving particular rights and freedoms. In other situations too, domestic law may need consideration. As already mentioned, Article 26 makes the exhaustion of domestic remedies a condition of admissibility of an individual application, while Article 13 provides for everyone whose rights and freedoms are violated to have 'an effective remedy before a national authority.' Both articles emphasise the priority which the Convention affords to domestic remedies, but, as a corollary, when the adequacy of such remedies is disputed, require this issue to be investigated by the Court.

As well as establishing the scope and meaning of the Convention and dealing, as necessary, with matters of domestic law, the Court may consider requests for the interpretation or revision of judgments and give advisory opinions, although as regards the last, its powers are restrictively defined and have not yet been used. Much more important, Article 50 enables the Court to provide 'just satisfaction' to an applicant who has been the victim of a violation of any article of the Convention. The question of compensation or other recompense is now an issue in the majority of cases in which a claim is upheld and is often dealt with as a separate stage of the proceedings. The Court's final judgments are given by majority vote and their execution supervised by the Committee of Ministers.

The Court's case-law and the development of the law of the Convention

The Court's decisions are binding on the Contracting States, which under Article 53 of the Convention, 'undertake to abide by the decision of the Court in any case to which they are parties'. When the Court concludes that the Convention has been violated, it is therefore incumbent on the respondent to take whatever steps may be needed to put matters right. Thus, following the Court's decision in the *Malone* case in 1984 the British Government introduced legislation to place the law on telephone tapping and interception of communications on a more satisfactory basis and there are many other examples of governments taking action to rectify deficiences which have been identified by the Court or the Commission.

The most dramatic impact of the Court's work is certainly to be found in the changes in domestic law and practice which have been introduced as a result of cases at Strasbourg, together with the consequences for the individuals concerned, who, as we have seen, may be awarded 'just satisfaction' under Article 50. But each ruling is not an isolated episode; it is also a contribution to the jurisprudence of the European Convention. In each decision the Court is not just spelling out the obligations of the State which happens to be involved in the particular case. It is interpreting the Convention for all the States which are parties to it. Naturally, the main impact of a decision will usually be in the State immediately concerned, but every party to the Convention must stay abreast of developments. The common law, advancing from precedent to precedent, has a counterpart, then, in the developing law of the European Convention.

Judgments have this wider significance because the Court consistently seeks to justify its decisions in terms which treat its existing case-law as authoritative. In other words, it follows judicial precedent. Thus in the

Silver case[23] which raised the question whether certain restrictions on prisoners' correspondence could be justified under Article 8 as 'necessary in a democratic society', the Court prefaced its examination of the facts with a summary of the interpretation of this phrase adopted earlier in the *Handyside* case[24] and the *Klass* case.[25] Similarly, when the Court, later in its judgment, turned to the issue of Article 13, which concerns the provision of an effective national remedy, it sought guidance on the interpretation of this article in its previous judgments in *Klass, Van Droogenbroeck*[26] and the *Swedish Engine Drivers Union*[27] case.

The Court adopted the same approach in the *Van der Sluijs* case where it said in relation to Article 5(3): 'The Court has had the occasion in its *Schiesser* judgment of 4 December, 1979 to interpret in detail the expression "officer authorised by law to exercise judicial power". . . . It suffices here to recall the salient principles enunciated in that judgment.'[28] And in the *Ashingdane* case, where it said: 'The Court in its previous case law, has stated three minimum conditions which have to be satisfied in order for there to be "the lawful detention of a person of unsound mind" within the meaning of Article 5 paragraph 1(e).'[29] These are typical of the Court's method of using its own previous decisions to build up a consistent body of jurisprudence on the Convention.

As might be expected, the Court's use of precedent is not confined to the citation of cases supporting its decision, but extends to distinguishing cases which, though arguably relevant to the point in hand, differ in some material particular. Thus in the *Sramek* case in which the applicant argued that her case had not been heard by an 'independent' and 'impartial' tribunal whose membership included civil servants, the Court decided in her favour, saying: 'the present case is distinguishable from the *Ringeisen* case in that the Land Government, represented by the Transactions Officer, acquired the status of a party when they appealed to the Regional Authority against the decision in Mrs Sramek's favour, and in that one of the three civil servants in question had the Transactions Officer as his hierarchical superior'.[30]

Similarly, when Belgium argued in the *De Cubber* case that where appellate proceedings are available it is unnecessary for proceedings at first instance to include the safeguards required by Article 6(1), the Court was at pains to point out that observations in three previous cases which were relied on by the government were to be distinguished because 'The reasoning adopted in the three above-mentioned judgments . . . cannot justify reducing the requirements of Article 6 para 1 in its traditional and natural sphere of application. A restrictive interpretation of this kind would not be consonant with the object and purpose of Article 6 para 1'.[31]

The practice just described, of following or distinguishing previous cases, is not obligatory because the European Court, like the Inter-

national Court, is not bound by its earlier decisions. However, the
practice adopted by the Court, though not formally required, is not
difficult to explain. As a leading writer, who served as a judge of the
International Court, observed, courts follow precedent:

> because such decisions are a repository of legal experience to which it is con-
> venient to adhere; because they embody what the Court has considered in the past
> to be good law; because respect for decisions given in the past makes for certainty
> and stability, which are of the essence of the orderly administration of justice; and
> (a minor and not invariably accurate consideration) because judges are naturally
> reluctant, in the absence of compelling reasons to the contrary, to admit that they
> were previously in the wrong.[32]

These factors which are relevant to the work of courts at both the national
and international levels, are no less prominent at Strasbourg.

Although the Court attaches considerable significance to the role of
precedent, it would be wrong to see this as invariably a decisive element,
or to exaggerate its significance. Like all responsible decision-makers, the
members of the Court want to be able to correct their mistakes and, as
with any tribunal called upon to interpret a basic text over time, the Court
as a whole must be free to revise or adapt the conclusions of the past to
accord with current ideas. Thus when an issue arises for decision the fact
that the Court has already taken a particular view carries weight, but is by
no means conclusive.

Sometimes the Court acknowledges its change of mind and declares
that its current thinking is inconsistent with an earlier treatment of the
point. In the case of *Mathieu-Mohin and Clerfayt*,[33] for example, the
Court repudiated a passage in its judgment in the *Irish*[34] case which
suggested that where the Convention speaks of the Contracting Parties
'undertaking' a certain commitment, it creates obligations between
States which cannot be invoked by individuals. However such recognition
is rather rare. More often, on the occasions the Court has decided to
change its mind it has followed the familiar judicial expedient of adopting
the new approach without mentioning its former view. In the *De Becker*
case, for instance, where it was first presented with the problem of
deciding whether it should strike a case from its list, the Court took what
many regard as a dangerously wide view of this power. In subsequent
cases, as we shall see in chapter 3, its approach to the question was
significantly narrower. There was, however, no acknowledgment of this
as a new departure, and because the move was generally approved, the
modification was not commented on. In *James*,[35] on the other hand,
where the Court interpreted Article 13 in a more limited way than in
certain earlier cases, because the issue was controversial, several members of the Court pointed out this discrepancy and expressed the opinion
either that precedent should have been followed, or that the point needed

further explanation.

The factors which encourage – in the light of what has just been said, one cannot say compel – the Court to follow its own decisions do not apply with anything like the same force when the Court is considering the jurisprudence of the Commission. As the judicial arm of the Convention, the Court has a duty to make its own independent decisions and the arrangements whereby cases can be considered first by the Commission, then by the Court, would obviously be redundant if the latter did no more than endorse the former's rulings. The system, then, is built on the assumption that the Court need not follow the Commission and numerous examples can be found in which this has occurred.

The clearest cases of conflict are those in which the two organs disagree on the question of whether the Convention has been violated. In the *Rees* case,[36] for instance, the Commission concluded that the applicant was the victim of a breach of Article 8 because the United Kingdom had refused to amend his birth certificate to reflect the result of a sex-change operation. The Court, however, held that there was no violation. In the *Feldbrugge* case,[37] on the other hand, which concerned the scope of Article 6(1), the Commission concluded that the Convention was inapplicable, but the Court reached the opposite conclusion and upheld the claim.

In other cases the Commission and Court reach the same conclusion, but adopt quite different reasoning. Thus in the *Irish* case the Court agreed with the Commission that the interrogation of detainees in Northern Ireland had violated Article 3, but whereas the Commission did so on the ground that the practice in question constituted torture, the Court ruled that it should be characterised instead as inhuman and degrading treatment. Conversely, in the *Van der Mussele*[38] case both bodies agreed that there had been no violation of Article 4. The Commission, however, based this conclusion in part on the view that for the purposes of the Convention forced or compulsory labour must be unjust, oppressive or an avoidable hardship, whereas the Court preferred a different approach and held that all the circumstances of the case must be viewed in the light of the underlying objectives of Article 4.

Although the Court is entitled to disagree with the Commission as regards its reasoning or its conclusions, and not infrequently does so, it would be wrong to underestimate the influence which the Commission has exercised on the Court's jurisprudence, or to present the relationship between the two organs as one of antagonism. After all, the Commission and the Court are made up of lawyers interpreting a single text as part of one human rights system. It is therefore hardly surprising that while there is frequently room for differences of opinion, on many matters the two organs reach the same conclusion. When the Court has pronounced on a given matter the Commission will naturally adopt that approach in future cases. More significantly, many developments in the Court's jurisprudence originate with the Commission. The latter, it must be remembered, considers many more cases than the Court and it may be several years before an issue which the Commission has become used to dealing with first reaches the Court. In such a situation the Commission will often have developed its own approach to the matter which it will naturally urge the Court to accept. While the Court is, of course, free to follow a different line of argument, as it did in *Van der Mussele*, it will frequently accept the Commission's approach. Thus the fact that the Convention system is structured in a way which gives the Commission the initial opportunity to develop a *jurisprudence constante* lends its rulings a significant weight as precedents.

The wider significance of the Court's jurisprudence

The primary importance of the European Court's activity is to be found in the impact of individual decisions on domestic law and practice and the progressive elaboration of States' obligations under the Convention. There is, however, another way in which the work of the Court may be significant – as contributions to international law. Article 38 1(d) of the Statute of the International Court of Justice refers to judicial decisions as 'subsidiary means for the determination of rules of law' and places them alongside 'the teachings of the publicists of the various nations' as source material subordinate to customary rules, international conventions and general principles of law. Clearly, then, although the European Court's decisions have very considerable force as precedents within the Strasbourg system, their significance elsewhere should not be exaggerated. The Court has taken the view that its function is 'not only to decide those cases brought before [it] but, more generally, to elucidate, safeguard and develop the rules instituted by the Convention'.[39] This is, however, something very different from a mandate to construct a code of human rights law for Europe, let alone the world, and expectations of what the Court can achieve must be adjusted accordingly. But, though a court is not a legislature and international law-making is primarily a matter for States, not judges, if the right conditions are present, a tribunal such as the Court can have a constructive part to play.

One condition is an appropriate amount of work. A court which is scarcely used cannot make much of a mark. A full docket, on the other hand, though not the only requirement, provides a tribunal with a series of opportunities to display its potential. It has often been pointed out that the International Court is under-used and that this has restricted its achievements. At one time this was true also of the European Court, but the same cannot be said today. After a very slow start in which for the first decade of its existence cases averaged only one a year, business doubled in the next five years and doubled again in the five after that. Even so, up to the end of 1979 the Court had given only thirty-six judgments. Then, however, there was a dramatic acceleration, with no less than fifty-eight judgments in the next five-year period. The one hundredth judgment of the Court was given in May 1985 and the two hundredth in November 1989. The annual output of decisions has thus increased sharply and seems set to rise still further.

In assessing these figures it should be noted that virtually all the Court's cases originate in individual rather than State applications and in several the Court has given more than one judgment, while in others what are recorded as separate judgments relate to essentially similar facts. It is true, nevertheless, that in a relatively short period of time the European Court has built up a substantial jurisprudence and that for the foreseeable future lack of business is unlikely to inhibit its contribution to the law.

Another requirement is that the Court's work should involve legal subject-matter capable of general application. At first sight it might be thought that the Court's brief – the interpretation and application of the European Convention – is too specific to satisfy this requirement. On further reflection, however, it is evident that there are several ways in which the scope and character of the Court's work may be appropriate to this function.

As already indicated, a substantial part of the Court's work is taken up with issues of jurisdiction, admissibility and procedure. Some of these, naturally, are concerned exclusively with the operation of the European human rights system; others, however, are not so limited. The local remedies rule, for example, which the Commission and Court are called upon to apply under Article 26 of the Convention, is a part of general international law. The same is true of estoppel, which is a general principle of law and the doctrine of judicial propriety which, as we shall see in chapter 3, is concerned with the circumstances in which a tribunal should decline to deal with a case on the ground that the matter is academic or insubstantial. All these, and similar issues, many of which are of particular significance for human rights tribunals, are regularly dealt with by the Court and provide an opportunity to develop principles of general applicability.

The Human Rights Committee (HRC) has stated that the reference to domestic remedies in the Optional Protocol to the International Covenant on Civil and Political Rights 'should be interpreted and applied in accordance with the generally accepted principles of international law with regard to the exhaustion of local remedies as applied in the field of human rights'.[40] This certainly points up the relevance of the Court's case-law and is fully borne out by the Committee's practice. Similarly, the Committee, like the Court, has had to determine who can be considered a 'victim' for the purposes of admissibility, leading a scholarly commentator to see this too as 'an area of the HRC's work where the experience with regard to the ECHR may be instructive'.[41] Other areas in which the Committee has had to deal with problems similar to those which have been encountered by the Court include interpretative declarations and estoppel.[42]

The influence of the Court's decisions can also be seen in the work of the Inter-American Court of Human Rights which referred to its jurisprudence at three successive stages of the *Velasquez Rodriguez* case. In the proceedings on the merits, in 1988, it referred to the *Handyside* case as authority for the principle that 'a court has the power and the duty to apply the juridical provisions relevant to a proceeding, even when the parties do not expressly invoke them'.[43] The following year, in the proceedings concerning compensation, the American Court discussed the question of its jurisdiction to provide indemnification for violations of human rights in the light of the European Court's practice under Article 50 of the Convention.[44] Then, when it was required to consider the power of an international tribunal to interpret a judgment, at the last stage of the case in 1990, the American Court referred to the way in which this issue had been treated by the European Court in the *Ringeisen* case.[45]

Even more important is the Court's potential contribution to what may be termed the law of human rights, meaning the substantive obligations which States are increasingly assuming in other regional conventions and general international law.[46] The European Convention is the most highly developed scheme of international human rights protection, but no longer stands alone. In 1976 the two United Nations Covenants on Human Rights, which were opened for signature in 1969, came into force. In 1969 the American Convention on Human Rights was signed by twelve Latin American States and in 1981 the Heads of State of the Organisation of African Unity unanimously adopted the African Charter on Human and Peoples' Rights. The African Charter came into force in 1986 and the American Convention in 1978 and its court, the Inter-American Court of Human Rights, was inaugurated in 1979.

These various conventions are not framed in identical terms. They differ to a considerable extent in the ground they cover, and, even when they are concerned with the same right – the right to a fair trial, for example – they are frequently couched in different terms.[47] In spite of these differences, however, there is a great deal of overlap, especially in the area of civil and political rights and it is here that the interpretations and, more crucially, the basic approach of the European Court can be important generally. The influence of the European Court's decisions is something which will vary a good deal from case to case, not just because there is no formal obligation to follow its rulings, but also because local conditions, or other considerations, may dictate a different result. The practice which is on record under the European Convention is nevertheless significant because through the work of the Court the scope and meaning of so many concepts in human rights law and indeed the whole function of adjudication in this area, are now regularly considered.

The value of the Court's jurisprudence has already been demonstrated in a number of cases on the American Convention. In its advisory opinion in the *Proposed Amendments* case[48] the Inter-American Court adopted the approach to discrimination put forward in the *Belgian Linguistics* case,[49] and in the same opinion observed that it was fully mindful of the 'margin of appreciation' reserved to States in this area. Subsequently, in both the *Habeas Corpus* case[50] and the *Judicial Guarantees* case[51] the Court emphasised the obligation to provide effective judicial guarantees, something which, as we shall see in chapter 5, has been very prominent in the European case-law. In the *Licensing of Journalism* case[52] the Court referred to the treatment of permissible limitations to freedom of expression in the *Sunday Times*[53] and *Barthold* cases[54] and held that the European Court's analysis of 'necessary' limitations was 'equally applicable' to the corresponding provision of the American Convention. And in the *Interpretation of Laws* case[55] the Court again mentioned the *Sunday Times* case when it discussed the relation between the principle of legality, democratic institutions and the rule of law.

The influence of Strasbourg can also be seen in the work of the Human Rights Committee. In the *Hertzberg* case,[56] which concerned the scope of freedom of expression, the Committee referred to the State's 'margin of discretion' in matters of morality and adopted a similar view as regards the protection of family life in the *Mauritian Women* case.[57] In its analysis of the concept of 'inhuman or degrading treatment or punishment' in the *Vuolanne* case[58] the Committee emphasized the relevance of the degree of humiliation or debasement and in the *Estrella* case[59] sought evidence of a 'practice' of inhuman treatment, although this concept does not appear in the Covenant. When reviewing the issue of discrimination, the Committee, like the American Court, has followed the *Belgian Linguistics* case in holding that 'a differentiation based on reasonable and objective criteria does not amount to prohibited discrimination'.[60] In its case-law concerning the issue of a fair trial the Committee has emphasised both the concept of 'equality of arms' and the obligation to provide the accused with guarantees of his rights which are effective.[61] All of the above, as we shall see in later chapters, echo the approach of the Court to similar issues under the European Convention.

It should be noted, moreover, that the European Court of Justice has held that fundamental rights and general principles of law analogous to fundamental rights are part of Community law.[62] Since both have their origin in the European Convention, as well as the constitutions of the Member States of the Community, this is another way in which the interpretation and application of human rights law by the Strasbourg institutions may have wider significance. In the *Rutili* case,[63] for example, the Court of Justice held that restrictions on residence in the interests of national security or public safety are limited to those 'necessary in a democratic society' and justified its decision by reference to Articles 8 to 11 of the Convention, while the general principles recognised by the Court have included the right to legal representation, protected by Article 6, the prohibition of retroactive punishment, embodied in Article 7 and the principle of non-discrimination to be found in Article 14. The Court of Justice is, of course, not bound to follow the Human Rights Court's treatment of these and other principles.[64] However, since the latter sees its role as that of a constitutional tribunal, which is essentially the basis on which the Court of Justice treats these issues, not only decisions, but also the philosophy emanating from Strasbourg, are bound to be influential.

European Convention case-law can also be used by domestic courts. This is so not only within Europe, where the Convention is, of course, part of many States' internal law,[65] but also elsewhere, because many domestic courts become concerned with issues of human rights when interpreting constitutions or applying customary international law. Thus in the *Hussainara Khatoon* case[66] and in a number of other decisions the Supreme Court of India has referred to Article 5 of the European Convention when interpreting the guarantee of personal liberty in the Indian Constitution. Likewise, in the case of *Filartiga v Penã-Irala*,[67] a United States Court of Appeals used the European Court's decision in the *Irish* case along with other material to show that the prohibition against torture is part of customary law. Further evidence of the Court's influence may be seen in two recent cases from Zimbabwe. In the *Ncube* case,[68] where the question was whether the corporal punishment of an adult constituted 'inhuman or degrading punishment', the Supreme Court decided that it did, and supported its decision by referring to the European Court's decision in the *Tyrer* case. Then, in a case in 1989 involving the caning of a juvenile,[69] the Supreme Court again decided that the punishment was unconstitutional, relying once more on *Tyrer* and also on the *Campbell and Cosans* case.[70]

Just as the procedural side of the Court's work involves some issues of general significance and others specific to the European Convention, so in its treatment of substantive matters the Court is generally dealing with questions of human rights law, but sometimes may be called upon to address wider issues. This is therefore another way in which the Court's work is significant. Since the Convention is a treaty, and the Court's task is to decide its scope, one would expect to find in its case-law discussion of theories and techniques of treaty interpretation.[71] Similarly, since the Court is concerned with defining the rights of individuals and the corresponding duties of governments, it would be natural to find decisions dealing with issues of state responsibility. The resolution of these questions is, of course, within the context of the European Convention and must be viewed as such. But as treaty interpretation, state responsibility and a number of other topics are part of general international law, it cannot be assumed *a priori* that pronouncements on such matters by the European Court are without wider significance.

The final factor and the one which will ultimately determine the importance of the European Court's contribution is the quality of its work. 'The potency of ideas', it has been said, 'is in direct proportion to the efficacy of the means employed for their realisation'.[72] This means that an appropriate range and scale of activity are not enough; the development of an influential jurisprudence calls for convincing judgments, and responsible decision-making in accordance with the highest traditions of judicial craftsmanship. For a judgment to carry conviction it must be seen to have a firm grounding in principle – for that is what justice according to law means. Judgments which have such a basis are thus jurisprudentially significant by virtue of what has been felicitously termed 'the law behind the cases'.[73] In this respect the European Court is in much the same position as the International Court, or any other tribunal, because in the last analysis its contribution to the development of the law depends on the technique to be found in its decisions. What it does and how well it does it are the concern of the rest of this book.

Notes

1 *Irish* case, Series A, No. 25 para. 157.
2 Series A, No. 82 para. 63.
3 Series A, No. 90 para. 61.
4 Series A, No. 43.
5 Under Protocol No. 9, which was opened for signature in 1990, individuals will be able to refer cases to the Court after they have been declared admissible and examined by the Commission. Thus the role of the Commission in regulating the Court's case-load will change. However, the new Protocol requires ratification by ten Contracting States and is not yet in force.
6 Series A, No. 31.
7 *Vagrancy* cases (*Questions of Procedure*), Series A, No. 12. For discussion of the significance of this ruling see chapter 8.
8 Series A, No. 93.
9 Rule 4. An earlier version referred to 'a profession likely to affect confidence

in his independence'.

10 Resolution 655 (1977), quoted in P. Van Dijk and G. J. H. Van Hoof, *Theory and Practice of the European Convention on Human Rights* (2nd ed.), Kluwer, Deventer, 27 (1990). The same Resolution requests members not to vote for candidates 'who have not given a formal undertaking to retire from the office of judge during the year in which they reach the age of 75'.

11 Until 1990 chambers consisted of seven judges. Protocol No. 8, which came into force in that year, raised the number to nine to reflect the increase in the size of the plenary Court.

12 Series A, No. 4.

13 Series A, No. 16.

14 Series A, No. 56.

15 Series A, No. 12. For discussion of this ruling see chapter 3.

16 T. Buergenthal, *American Journal of International Law*, LXXXI, 280 (1987).

17 Series A, No. 199.

18 *Cruz Varas* case, Series A, No. 201 para. 74.

19 See, for example, the *Müller* case, Series A, No. 133, in which the Court viewed a number of allegedly obscene paintings at a special session *in camera* in order to enable it to decide whether by punishing the artist the Swiss authorities had violated Article 10.

20 Series A, No. 84 para. 46.

21 Series A, No. 56 para. 63.

22 Series A, No. 82 para. 79.

23 Series A, No. 61.

24 Series A, No. 24.

25 Series A, No. 21.

26 Series A, No. 50.

27 Series A, No. 20.

28 Series A, No. 78 para. 41.

29 Series A, No. 93 para. 37.

30 Series A, No. 84 para. 41.

31 Series A, No. 86 para. 32.

32 H. Lauterpacht, *The Development of International Law by the International Court*, Stevens, London, 14 (1958).

33 Series A, No. 113. For a more recent example see the *Borgers* case, Series A, No. 214A discussed in chapter 8.

34 Series A, No. 25.

35 Series A, No. 98.

36 Series A, No. 106. See also the *Cossey* case, Series A, No. 184 where the decision in *Rees* was followed and compare *B v France*, Series A, No. 232C in which the two earlier cases were distinguished and the Commission's opinion was endorsed.

37 Series A, No. 99.

38 Series A, No. 70.

39 *Irish* case, Series A, No. 25 para. 154.

40 Doc. A/33/40, para. 586, and see D. McGoldrick, *The Human Rights Committee*, Clarendon Press, Oxford, 187–97 (1991).

41 McGoldrick, *ibid.*, 177.

42 See McGoldrick, *ibid.*, 138–9 and 193–4, respectively.

43 *Velasquez Rodriguez* case, Judgment of 29 July 1988, para. 163, *Human Rights Law Journal*, IX, 212 (1988).

44 Judgment of 21 July 1989, para. 28, *Human Rights Law Journal*, XI, 127

(1990).
45 Judgment of 17 August 1990, para. 26, *Human Rights Law Journal*, XII, 14 (1991).
46 See A. H. Robertson and J. G. Merrills, *Human Rights in the World*, 3rd ed., Manchester U.P., Manchester (1989).
47 For a comprehensive review see P. Sieghart, *The International Law of Human Rights*, Clarendon Press, Oxford (1983).
48 Advisory Opinion, No. OC–4/84 of 19 January 1984, Series A, No. 4 paras. 56 and 62, *Human Rights Law Journal*, V, 161 (1984). In the same case Judge Rodolfo E. Piza Escalante referred to 'the need to interpret and integrate each standard of the Convention by utilising the adjacent, underlying or overlying principles in other instruments, in the country's own internal regulations and in the trends in effect in the matter of human rights' (separate opinion, para. 2). This approach is consistent with Article 29 of the American Convention and is also encouraged in Articles 60 and 61 of the African Charter, which instruct the African Commission to draw inspiration 'from international law on human and peoples' rights' and a number of specific sources, including 'legal precedents and doctrine'.
49 Series A, No. 6.
50 Advisory Opinion, No. OC–8/87 of 30 January 1987, Series A, No. 8 para. 29, *Human Rights Law Journal*, IX, 94 (1988).
51 Advisory Opinion, No. OC–9/87 of 6 October 1987, Series A, No. 9 para. 24 *Human Rights Law Journal*, *ibid.*, 204.
52 Advisory Opinion, No. OC–5/85 of 13 November 1985, Series A, No. 5 para. 46, *Human Rights Law Journal*, VII, 74 (1986).
53 Series A, No. 30.
54 Series A, No. 90.
55 Advisory Opinion, No. OC–6/86 of 9 May 1986, Series A, No. 6 para. 20, *Human Rights Law Journal*, VII, 231 (1986).
56 Doc. A/37/40, p. 176
57 Doc. A/36/40, p. 134.
58 Doc. A/44/40, p. 249.
59 Doc. A/38/40, p. 150.
60 See McGoldrick, *The Human Rights Committee*, 283.
61 McGoldrick, *ibid.*, 416–29.
62 See M. H. Mendelson, 'The European Court of Justice and human rights', *Yearbook of European Law*, I, 125 (1982); and M. B. Akehurst, 'The application of general principles of law by the Court of Justice of the European Communities', *British Year Book of International Law*, LII, 29 (1981).
63 1975 ECR, 1219.
64 For a different view see W. Ganshof van der Meersch, 'L'ordre juridique des Communautés Européennes et le droit international', *Hague Recueil*, 148, 176–80 (1975).
65 For a recent survey of the impact of the Convention within Europe see M. Delmas-Marty (ed.), *The European Convention for the Protection of Human Rights*, Nijhoff, Dordrecht, 101–278 (1992).
66 *Hussainara Khatoon and Others v Home Secretary, State of Bihar* (1980) 1 SCC 81. See also *Mullin v Administrator, Union Territory of Delhi and Others* (1981) 1 SCC 608 and *Olga Tellis v Bombay Municipal Corporation* (1986) AIR 180.
67 630 F. 2d 876 (1980). For discussion of this and other American cases see T. Meron, *Human Rights and Humanitarian Norms as Customary International*

Law, Oxford University Press, Oxford, 122–30 (1989). On the approach of courts in the United States see also R. B. Lillich, 'The Constitution and human rights', *American Journal of International Law*, LXXXIII, 851 (1989).

68 *Ncube, Tshuma and Ndhlovu v The State* (1988) 2 S.Afr. L.Rep. 702.

69 *Juvenile v The State*, Judgment No. 64/89, Crim. App. No. 156/88. See H. Hannum, Case note, *American Journal of International Law*, LXXXIV, 768 (1990). For further discussion of the position of domestic courts see M. D. Kirby, 'The role of the judge in advancing human rights by reference to international human rights norms', *Australian Law Journal*, LXII, 514 (1988); and A. F. Bayesky, 'The judicial function under the Canadian Charter of Rights and Freedoms', *McGill Law Journal*, XXXII, 791 (1987).

70 Series A, No. 48.

71 See I. Sinclair, *The Vienna Convention on the Law of Treaties*, 2nd ed., Melland Schill Monographs in International Law, Manchester U.P., Manchester, 128–35 (1984).

72 Lauterpacht, *Development*, 70.

73 Lauterpacht, *ibid*.

CHAPTER 2

The Court's judgments

Our review of the Court's work in the preceding chapter indicates that its role in the development of international human rights law is a potentially significant one. The fact that the Court is almost entirely concerned with individual applications and has frequently declared that in such proceedings 'it has to confine itself as far as possible, to an examination of the concrete case before it'[1] in no way prevents its decisions from contributing to a developing jurisprudence on the Convention. Moreover, while the Court is exclusively concerned with the European Convention, and in this respect has a more specialised remit than some international tribunals, its decisions are often capable of wider application. There is, however, nothing inevitable about these consequences. Whether they occur depends on how well the Court uses the opportunities presented by the cases which come before it, that is to say on its judgments. How these are prepared and the factors which determine their scope and impact are the subject of the present chapter.

The form and content of a judgment

In the European Court, as in the International Court, the decision is expressed in the form of a single judgment, representing the Court's verdict, accompanied by separate opinions in which judges may state their individual views. This arrangement, which is provided for in the Convention and the Rules, is thus a compromise between, on the one hand, the practice of the Court of Justice of the European Communities and many continental courts of issuing a single collective judgment with no expression of individual views and, on the other, the practice of courts in the common law world of requiring every judge to indicate his decision.

The content of a judgment of the European Court is laid down in the Convention and the Rules of the Court. The Convention says only,

'Reasons shall be given for the judgment of the Court' (Article 51(1)). The Rules are much more elaborate and state, in Rule 53:

The judgment shall contain:
(a) the names of the President and the judges constituting the Chamber, and also the names of the Registrar and, where appropriate, the Deputy Registrar;
(b) the dates on which it was adopted and delivered;
(c) a description of the Party or Parties;
(d) the names of the Agents, advocates or advisers of the Party or Parties;
(e) the names of the Delegates of the Commission and of the persons assisting them;
(f) the name of the applicant;
(g) an account of the procedure followed;
(h) the final submissions of the Party or Parties and, if any, of the Delegates of the Commission and of the applicant;
(i) the facts of the case;
(j) the reasons in point of law;
(k) the operative provisions of the judgment;
(l) the decision, if any, in respect of costs;
(m) the number of judges constituting the majority;
(n) where appropriate, a statement as to which of the two texts, English or French, is authentic.

Article and Rule are closely modelled on the corresponding provisions of the Statute and Rules of the International Court and like them provide for the right of any judge who has taken part in the consideration of the case to deliver a concurring or dissenting opinion, or a bare statement of dissent.

Although the various elements in the judgment are not equally important each in its own way is significant. Describing the history of the case provides the essential background and relates the Court's decision to the report of the Commission without the need for the reader to have the latter available. Giving the judges' names establishes responsibility for the decision, and since the majority of cases are handled by chambers, permits conclusions to be drawn as to whether a judgment reflects the views of the Court as a whole. The statement of the facts and the provisions of domestic law supply the necessary context for the point or points of law involved, but also enable the Court to satisfy the litigants that it has understood the situation. The same functions are fulfilled by the Court's summary of the final submissions, while the reasoning provides the justification for the decision and the *dispositif*, the statement of what it is the Court has decided.

In accordance with Rule 53 the Court's judgments always follow the same pattern. The relevant names and dates, together with an outline of the procedural history of the case are followed by a full statement of the facts and an equally detailed description of the relevant provisions of domestic law. After a summary of the proceedings before the Commission and the final submissions, the Court reviews the position under the Convention, discussing each article and each issue separately, and giving its conclusion. Then, in the final paragraph the Court summarises its ruling and indicates the voting on each question. The heart of the judgment is, of course, the penultimate section in which the Court explains its reasoning. For here is to be found the material which will determine whether the decision itself is convincing and a different, but related point, the extent to which the case can be regarded as a contribution to the law. As we shall see, the fact that the judgment is a collective formulation has a crucial bearing on both issues.

Formulating the collective pronouncement

After the oral proceedings the judges spend some time studying the arguments and the relevant documentation. The case is then discussed and the process of drafting the judgment begins. The Court's deliberations are not referred to in the Convention, but are provided for in Rule 19 in the following terms:

Deliberations

1 The Court shall deliberate in private. Its deliberations shall remain secret.
2 Only the judges shall take part in the deliberations. The Registrar or his substitute, as well as such other officials of the registry and interpreters whose assistance is deemed necessary, shall be present. No other person may be admitted except by special decision of the Court.
3 Each judge present at such deliberations shall state his opinion and the reasons therefor.
4 Any question which is to be voted upon shall be formulated in precise terms in the two official languages and the text shall, if a judge so requests, be distributed before the vote is taken.
5 The minutes of the private sittings of the Court for deliberations shall remain secret; they shall be limited to a record of the subject of the discussions, the votes taken, the names of those voting for and against a motion and any statements expressly made for insertion in the minutes.

Because the members of the Court are drawn from only one part of the world they reflect legal traditions which, though not identical, have a great deal in common. Moreover, the decisions they are called upon to make relate to a single instrument, the Convention, which was produced for the express purpose of consolidating those traditions in key respects. The fact that the Court's judges share a common outlook and are engaged on a single enterprise does not mean that they will always agree on what to do and how to do it. It does, however, appreciably narrow the scope for disagreement. In this respect therefore the Court's affinities as a corporate institution are with the Court of Justice of the European

Communities, another homogeneous tribunal with a specific brief, rather than the International Court, where the absence of common cultural reference points and the diverse issues for adjudication often makes accommodation extremely difficult.[2]

Producing an agreed judgment will clearly tend to be easier in a case which raises only one or two points than in one which ranges over a wider area. Similarly, the fact that the majority of cases are handled by chambers again places the Court in a more favourable position than the International Court where chambers are the exception and fifteen or more judges are usually involved. Of course, neither the complexity of the case nor the size of the Court is necessarily decisive. A case which raises a single highly controversial issue will always be difficult, while finding a form of words which a majority of a chamber can support may sometimes be no less taxing than framing a judgment for the plenary Court.

A judge of the International Court once said that at the discussion stage the draft judgments of that Court suffered 'the fate of a whale attacked by a school of killer-whales which tear big chunks of flesh from its body'.[3] This may perhaps be something of an exaggeration, at least as regards the European Court, but it is certainly true that constructing a judgment involves the members of the Court in a kind of bargaining over words and phrases, with the result that in difficult cases key passages may go through many formulations until an acceptable version is found. Although the Court must ensure that each case is considered properly, its time is not unlimited. If, therefore, it is to achieve the aim of giving judgment within a few months of the close of the oral proceedings there is pressure on individual judges to compromise, rather than to insist on the inclusion of particular words. In this respect the possibility of delivering a separate opinion is probably beneficial, since observations which are unacceptable to the majority and cannot be included in the judgment may be preserved in an individual opinion.

In view of the need to reconcile divergent points of view it is not surprising that once the Court has found a way of expressing a point which commands agreement, it will tend to repeat the talismanic words, often verbatim, in later cases. An example is the constantly reiterated principle that for an interference with a Convention right to be 'prescribed by law' 'the interference must have some basis in domestic law, which itself must be adequately accessible and be formulated with sufficient precision to enable the individual to regulate his conduct, if need be with appropriate advice'.[4] Another, equally familiar, is the Court's ruling that 'whilst the adjective "necessary", within the meaning of Article 10 para 2 of the Convention is not synonymous with "indispensable", neither does it have the flexibility of such expressions as "admissible", "ordinary", "useful", "reasonable" or "desirable"; rather, it implies a "pressing social need" '.[5] These and similar phrases become very well known indeed to students of the Court, and recur like *leitmotifs* in its judgments.[6]

The above practice not only makes the Court's judgments less interesting than they might be, but also ensures that they rarely display either the forcefulness or the depth of juridical analysis characteristic of the best individual opinions.

Moreover, we shall see later that the need to reconcile divergent views means that the Court has a tendency to focus its judgment on issues essential to the case, leaving those that are less central to be discussed in the separate opinions. Thus the fact that the Court gives a collective judgment is important because it has a bearing on both the manner and the content of its pronouncements. As these are matters which also relate to the Court's development of the law, they now call for closer examination.

The Court's style of judgment

In its early years the Court adopted the practice of the higher continental courts and drafted the section of the judgment dealing with the law as a single long sentence with the various steps in its reasoning set out in a series of subordinate clauses, culminating in the main sentence 'the Court decides . . .'. Thus the Court's main judgment in the *Lawless* case features forty-seven paragraphs of reasoning, occupying nineteen pages, each paragraph introduced by the word 'whereas' (*considérant que*), before the short final ruling that Ireland had made a valid derogation under Article 15 and was therefore not in breach of the Convention.

This style was used for the four judgments the Court gave between 1960 and 1962 and for its preliminary ruling in the *Belgian Linguistics* case in 1967. Then, for its judgment on the merits of that case in 1968 the Court abandoned the single sentence form and drafted its judgment in a grammatically conventional way. The new style of judgment, which is certainly more convenient when a case raises many separate issues, as the *Belgian Linguistics* case did, has been employed for all subsequent cases.

The Court's style of judgment has a significant bearing on its ability to develop the law. For one thing, there is a close relation between style and substance, that is to say how the Court expresses itself has a direct influence on what it can do. The single-sentence style is something of a strait-jacket and as well as being cumbersome, makes it difficult to support a conclusion with different kinds of arguments. Abandoning that form and substituting conventional sentences may not guarantee that the Court will always support its decisions with adequate reasons, but at least removes one of the obstacles to its doing so.

Another reason style is important is that no court can work successfully unless its decisions are accepted by those whom we may term its audience. In the case of the European Court the audience comprises not only the parties to the Convention, but also the Commission, the individual applicants, members of the legal profession and the general public. If the judgment is seen as the way in which the Court communicates with this audience, the significance of its style is obvious. Whereas good style enables the Court to turn formal into effective authority, poor, or inappropriate style acts as a barrier to acceptance and has the opposite effect.

The criteria of good judicial style have long been a matter of debate, but in essence are not really controversial. The first requirement is that the judgment is successful in communicating the point or points being made. It must be clear and expressed in language which the audience can understand. Here again the advantage of abandoning the 'whereas' form of judgment is evident. The judgments of a court are never likely to make easy reading. However, those unaccustomed to the single-sentence style would be alienated by what is so clearly an esoteric technical form, a reaction which is much less likely now that the Court uses ordinary language.

Communication is enhanced if points can be made in a striking way which sticks in the memory. Every English law student knows that the doctrine of promissory estoppel is a shield and not a sword[7] and it is therefore a pity that felicitous expression is not conspicuous in the European Court. Indeed, the tone of the Court's judgments is usually rather flat. This, of course, is a reflection of the way they are produced which, as we have seen, is almost guaranteed to eliminate excitement, humour or the telling phrase. For these one must turn to the individual opinions where we find: 'One is not bound to regard torture as only present in a mediaeval dungeon';[8] 'The war on poverty cannot be won through broad interpretations of the Convention';[9] and this in relation to Article 14, 'If I choose to help my neighbour tidy up his garden, does this mean that, either in law or in ethics, I must do the same for all the other residents of the street?'[10]

The second feature of a good judicial style is that it is persuasive. As a leading authority puts it:

Convincing a very large part of the audience is the hallmark of an effective judgment . . . . In order to convince, the judge must properly identify the audience and familiarise himself with it. He must use arguments which are appropriate to that audience. Where the audience is comprised of diverse elements he must carefully consider all its segments.[11]

The European Court has a relatively homogeneous audience all of whom can be assumed to subscribe both to the idea of human rights and to most of the specific concepts involved. Moreover, as we have seen, this outlook is shared by the judges, whose work is largely concerned with establishing the scope of those rights in particular contexts. In terms of writing persuasive judgments all this means that the Court starts with an enormous advantage. Not only is there likely to be substantial agreement within the Court on many matters, but also in justifying its conclusions, the Court can appeal to a common set of cultural values.

Many courts use this technique. In the *Corfu Channel* case the International Court invoked 'elementary considerations of humanity, even more exacting in peace than in war' to establish Albania's international responsibility.[12] However, in that court whose audience, membership and work are all conspicuously varied, finding a persuasive premise is often extremely difficult. In the European Court, on the other hand, it is much more straightforward. Thus in the *Delcourt* case the Court said 'In a democratic society within the meaning of the Convention, the right to a fair administration of justice holds such a prominent place that a restrictive interpretation of Article 6(1) would not correspond to the aim and purpose of that provision'[13] and, as we shall see in later chapters, this kind of appeal to shared values features prominently in its judgments.

Another way in which a court can seek to make its judgments more persuasive is to take care to avoid offending the sensibilities of its audience. In both the *Neumeister*[14] and *Stögmüller*[15] cases the Court cushioned the impact of its ruling that Austria had violated the Convention by stating expressly that no blame attached to the Austrian authorities. Similarly, a court can go out of its way to draw attention to the best points of the unsuccessful argument so as to indicate that it is aware of both sides of the question. The European Court makes extensive use of this technique which enables it to present a balanced judgment and to demonstrate that points to which one side attaches particular importance are fully appreciated. Thus in the *De Cubber* case the Court responded to Belgium's argument concerning the compatibility of different judicial functions with the observation that 'This reasoning no doubt reflects several aspects of the reality of the situation . . . and the Court recognises its cogency',[16] and stated that it had arrived at its conclusion that the Convention had been violated 'without underestimating the force of the Government's arguments'.[17]

The persuasiveness of a judgment is also enhanced if a court can support its conclusion with cumulative reasons instead of resting the decision on a single point. This technique is especially useful in cases where there are factual as well as legal issues and it is possible to deal with both in the judgment. In the *Colak* case,[18] for example, the applicant complained that he had been denied a fair trial on the ground that the presiding judge had given his lawyer certain assurances in a conversation outside the courtroom and these had subsequently been dishonoured. The Court rejected the claim (a) because the applicant could not prove that a conversation had ever taken place, (b) because if there had been a conversation, there was no way of establishing its content, and (c) because even if (a) and (b) had been proved, there would still have been no infringement of the right to a fair trial, since the applicant's lawyer knew that the president had no authority to speak on behalf of his fellow judges. Each reason would have been enough to support the conclusion on its own. Combining them, however, made for a much more persuasive judgment.

The point just considered brings us to the third and last criterion of a good judicial style – completeness. By this we mean that the judgment should address every essential point and deal with each point fully. It is not difficult to see how this requirement is bound up with those already discussed. A judgment which is incomplete because it omits essential considerations, or fails to consider arguments to which the litigants attach importance is unlikely to be very persuasive. Likewise, if issues are passed over or treated cursorily, the Court's reasoning may be unclear, or the import of the judgment actually unintelligible. Completeness, however, is more than a matter of justifying a decision in terms that are persuasive and intelligible, but goes to the heart of the international judicial process. How this relates to the work of the Court, and in particular to its part in developing the law, consequently requires separate consideration.

The process of judicial justification

Writing on the need for the International Court to provide full reasoning in support of its decisions, Sir Hersch Lauterpacht observed that:

Experience has shown that governments as a rule reconcile themselves to the fact that their case has not been successful – provided the defeat is accompanied by the conviction that their argument was considered in all its relevant aspects. On the other hand, however fully they may comply with an adverse decision, they do not find it easy to accept it as expressive of justice – or of law – if they feel that their argument was treated summarily, that it was misunderstood, or that dialectics have usurped the place of judicial reasoning.[19]

Exactly the same may be said of the work of the European Court. Since the Convention system depends for its success on the support of governments, it is essential that the Court should be able to support its conclusions with adequate reasons.

The Court's jurisdiction, like that of other international tribunals, derives from the consent of the State or States concerned. Consequently, before considering the merits the Court must examine any objections to its jurisdiction or to admissibility which may have been raised. Questions of jurisdiction, as already noted, are relatively uncommon, but when they do arise must be and are fully examined in order to demonstrate that the Court is competent. Questions of admissibility, and in particular the application of the local remedies rule under Article 26, are more frequent, although the Court's conclusion will often be that the respondent is estopped from raising the issue, or that the Commission was correct to reject it. Nevertheless it is clear that one of the advantages to flow from the ruling in the *Vagrancy* cases[20] has been that with the respondent able to raise its objections to admissibility in the Court as well as in the Commission, if and when the Court gets as far as deciding the merits, there can be no doubt that it is competent to do so. Since it is essential that the Contracting States should be satisfied that the Court has the authority which it claims, the importance of the Court's dealing fully with issues of jurisdiction and admissibility cannot be exaggerated.

The lengths to which the Court is prepared to go to demonstrate that its authority is well-founded are illustrated by the *Axen* case.[21] The case concerned Article 6(1) and specifically the right to a public hearing and to a judgment pronounced publicly. It was referred to the Court by the Commission, but not by the German Government, a point which was underlined when the latter in its oral pleadings, contested the expediency of the reference. Although this was not a preliminary objection in the formal sense, the Court considered that a response was necessary and prefaced its treatment of the merits with a reminder of some elementary features of the Convention.

Explaining that it is no part of its function to evaluate the expediency of the decision to bring a case to the Court, it stressed that in this respect the Commission and the Contracting States are autonomous. To the claim that the Commission's goal was to secure an abstract review of the relevant provisions of German law the Court made the point that in proceedings originating in an individual application it must confine itself, as far as possible, to an examination of the concrete case. Finally, the Court explained that no weight could be attached to the fact that the Act under which Mr Axen's case had been dealt with was no longer in force, nor that the applicant might be more concerned with securing a variation of the domestic decision, than with the interpretation of the Convention. The change in the law did not have the effect of restoring the applicant's rights, while the object of the proceedings was to obtain a ruling on the applicant's complaints. In accordance with the Court's established jurisprudence, there were therefore no grounds on which its competence could be challenged.

While the Court is anxious to deal fully with the issue of competence and may be prepared to consider points which are not raised as formal preliminary objections, it will not, indeed it cannot, examine issues which fall outside its province merely to satisfy the respondent. Thus in *Axen* it refused to examine the Commission's decision to refer the case, while in the *Foti* case, it rejected an unusual request from the Italian Government that it should confirm and amplify the Commission's decision that certain complaints were inadmissible, with the curt observation that 'it is not within the province of the Court to take cognisance of a request of this kind, for complaints rejected by the Commission fall outside the compass of the case'.[22]

As far as the treatment of substantive issues is concerned, the need for its judgments to be fully reasoned is no less pressing. Unlike the matters with which most international tribunals are concerned, human rights questions impinge directly on a State's internal affairs and call for a close scrutiny of its internal law and practice. As a body of judges who, being foreigners, begin with no special knowledge of the domestic arrangements or circumstances of the individual Contracting States, the Court must be especially careful to demonstrate that it understands the case and is therefore in a position to give an informed decision. The danger here is not so much that a failure may lead to accusations of bias or lack of objectivity, as that judgments which do not explore the position fully will appear ill-informed and arbitrary, neither of which is conducive to confidence in the Court.

The character of the Court's work is such as to require the fullest justification of its decisions in another way also. As a charter of human rights the Convention, like all such instruments, sets out principles rather than rules. The application of the Convention therefore leaves the Court with, and indeed requires it to exercise, a wide measure of discretion. To the extent that those with the responsibility of interpreting the Convention support their decisions with reasons, they can justify the decisions in particular cases and provide their successors with guidance in the future. In view of the Convention's character it is of the greatest importance that this process occurs. Because human rights obligations are clearly open to more than one interpretation, if the Court failed to justify its decisions it would again seem to, and might actually be, acting arbitrarily. Both risks can, however, be avoided by decisions which are properly reasoned.

To these more or less pragmatic considerations may be added a point, or it would be more accurate to say the point of principle. The Court should support its decisions with adequate reasons because the provision of a reasoned decision is the *raison d'être* of a court of law. Courts, that is, exist not just to give decisions, but to give decisions by reference to the particular criteria which constitute the law. It is therefore not merely a matter of convenience that a decision should be properly justified. It is the duty of the Court to explain how it has arrived at its decision and from this it follows that those who created the Court and those who are subject to its jurisdiction have a right to expect that it will do so.

Finally there is the point that only by giving judgments which are fully reasoned can the European Court, or any court, develop the law. For only decisions which are properly grounded in legal principle can constitute precedents for the future. While this facet of the Court's activity is the one with which we are particularly concerned, in comparison with the points made earlier, it must be regarded as a secondary consideration. The first duty of any court is not to develop the law but to decide the cases which come before it. To do this, a court must support its decisions with judgments which, if they are fully reasoned, will incidentally develop the law. Of course, a court may choose to go further and make the development of the law a deliberate aim. Such a policy will no doubt assist the process further. But whether it adopts such a policy or not, if a court's judgments are fully reasoned, such development will occur. Thus, while the argument for exhaustiveness in judicial reasoning has deeper foundations than the value of legal development, the latter can certainly be numbered among its advantages.

Without anticipating the discussion of specific features of the Court's approach which will be found in later chapters, it can be said that, as with the treatment of jurisdictional issues, the Court normally seeks to support its substantive conclusions with reasoning calculated to consolidate its authority. Thus, in addition to precedent, which has already been discussed, the Court takes into account a variety of considerations, including as we shall see, general principles of law and international law, as well as considerations with a direct bearing on the Convention such as the values of a democratic society. In interpreting the Convention, as will be seen in chapter 4, the Court does not rely only on a literal approach, but has regard to the object and purpose of the agreement, the impact of social change and many other factors, including the preparatory work. As already noted, the Court does seek to respond to the parties' arguments and this not simply as a way of making the judgment more persuasive, but also as a technique for making points of substance. Thus in the *Malone* case where the question was whether certain arrangements were 'in accordance with the law', the Court said: 'Undoubtedly, as the government rightly suggested, the requirements of the Convention, notably in regard to foreseeability, cannot be exactly the same in the special context of interception of communications for the purposes of police investigations as they are where the object of the relevant law is to place restrictions on the conduct of individuals.'[23] Similarly, in relation to the practice of 'metering' the Court said, 'As the government rightly suggested, a meter check printer registers information that a supplier of a telephone service may in principle legitimately obtain.'[24] In both instances having made these points, the Court went on to explain why in the circumstances there had been a breach of the Convention.

In certain respects, however, this picture of the Court calls for some qualification. Judgments, it will be recalled, are collective acts and as such subject to the limitations of any negotiated pronouncement. One result of this – the Court's tendency to focus on issues essential to its decision – will be discussed in the next section. But the same factor has a bearing on the completeness of the Court's treatment of the issues which are dealt with in the judgment. This is because the need for the judgment to represent as many opinions as possible can lead to the more controversial arguments being omitted, tempt the Court to use imprecise language and discourage stringent reasoning. The tendency of the Court to build its judgments around certain almost ritualistic formulae has already been noted. Although it would sometimes be refreshing to have a fresh analysis, this tendency is not objectionable provided that in the remainder of the judgment the Court is careful to ensure that the principle, as formulated, is scrupulously applied to the particular facts and its relevance carefully explained. Regrettably, this has not always been the case. While the explanation for such deficiency is no doubt to be sought in the compromises necessary to produce an agreed decision, these and comparable lapses do occasionally result in judgments which, as regards reasoned justification, are not all that they might be.

Limitation of the scope of the decision

Although it is desirable for a decision to be fully reasoned, it does not follow that a judgment must deal with every point which has been raised in argument. Indeed, it will be rare for it to do so and whether the verdict is that the Convention has been violated or that it has not, the Court will usually concentrate its attention on matters which it regards as essential to the decision.

Thus when the Court has identified a violation of one article of the Convention, it may hold that it has no need to deal with alleged violations of other articles arising out of the same facts. In the case of *Campbell and Fell*,[25] for example, the Court decided that by preventing confidential consultation between one of the applicants and his solicitor, the United Kingdom had infringed Article 6(1). In view of this decision it agreed with the Commission that it was unnecessary to examine the claim that this also constituted a breach of the applicant's right to respect for his private life under Article 8. Similarly, in the *Malone* case, having identified various violations of Article 8 arising out of the arrangements for controlling official interception of communications, the Court decided that it had no need to decide whether there was also a violation of Article 13 because there was no domestic remedy for such violations.

In the same way, when the Court finds that a particular article of the Convention has been violated in one respect, it may decide that it is unnecessary to consider whether it has been violated in other respects. In the *Sramek* case,[26] for example, the applicant alleged that there had been an infringement of the right to a fair trial guaranteed by Article 6(1) because she had been granted neither a 'fair' nor a 'public' hearing before a tribunal which, according to the applicant, also lacked independence. Having upheld her complaint on this last ground, the Court held that it was unnecessary to rule on her other complaints.

Similarly, if the Court finds that one part of an article has been violated, it may hold that alleged violations of other parts of the article need not be considered. This can leave the Court open to criticism if used with respect to a provision like Article 5, which contains a number of separate guarantees within a single article,[27] but is not out of place in relation to a provision like Article 6 which covers the right to a fair trial both generally and specifically. Thus in the *Pakelli* case, where the applicant complained that the authorities had deprived him of an effective defence contrary to Article 6(1) and Article 6(3) (c), the Court recalled that:

the provisions of Article 6 para 3(c) represent specific applications of the general principle of a fair trial stated in paragraph 1 . . . . Accordingly, the question whether paragraph 1 was observed has no real significance in the applicant's case; it is absorbed by the question whether paragraph 3(c) was complied with. The finding of a breach of the requirements of paragraph 3(c) dispenses the Court from also examining the case in the light of paragraph 1.[28]

The same economy of reasoning is found in cases in which the decision is that the Convention has not been violated. If, for example, the Court decides that the respondent has a conclusive answer to the claim, it will not usually regard it as necessary to discuss every other objection which may have been raised. Thus in the *Van der Mussele* case[29] the Court held that there had been no imposition of 'compulsory labour' contrary to Article 4(2) and decided that it was therefore unnecessary to determine whether the work in question could be justified as part of 'normal civic obligations' under Article 4(3) (d). Likewise in the *Klass* case[30] and the *Ashingdane* case,[31] both of which raised points concerning Article 6(1), the Court decided that it was unnecessary to rule on the respondent's argument that the article was inapplicable because in any event nothing amounting to a violation had been shown.

When a claim is rejected on the basis of one of the qualifying provisions of the Convention, the Court's treatment often exhibits a similar pattern. Thus in the *Barthold* case,[32] the Court upheld the respondent's argument that certain injunctions were issued 'to protect the rights of others' in accordance with Article 10(2) and in view of this decided that it was unnecessary to consider whether they could also be justified to protect 'health' or 'morals'. Likewise in the *Rasmussen* case,[33] having held that the respondent was justified in treating spouses differently and had therefore not transgressed Article 14 in conjunction with Article 8, the Court decided that it had no need to decide whether in relation to paternity proceedings husbands and wives were to be regarded as in analogous situations.

The Court's desire to avoid ruling on matters not essential to the decision means that it is not uncommon for the judgment to leave open some major question concerning the interpretation or application of the Convention. In the *Barthold* case, for example, which concerned an injunction designed to prevent a veterinary surgeon from obtaining press publicity, the Court decided that the facts were such as to raise the issue of freedom of speech under Article 10, without the need to decide whether, as a matter of principle, Article 10 covers commercial advertising. Similarly in the *Luedicke* case[34] the Court decided that the Federal Republic of Germany had violated Article 6(3) (e) by requiring the applicant, who had been convicted of a criminal offence, to pay for the costs of a court interpreter. However, it left open the question whether, or to what extent, the costs associated with compliance with Articles 6(3) (c) and 6(3) (d) may be passed on to an accused on conviction. Likewise in the case of *Albert and Le Compte* the Court held that in the particular circumstances disciplinary proceedings against two Belgian doctors involved a dispute over 'civil rights and obligations' and therefore fell within Article 6(1). It declined to go further, however, observing that 'It is not for the Court to go beyond the facts submitted for its consideration and determine whether, for the medical profession as a whole, this right [to practise] is a civil right, within the meaning of Article 6 paragraph 1.'[35]

The Court, then, like most judicial bodies, will not go out of its way to address broad issues of principle when it is possible to decide a case on some narrower ground. As a result, in terms of exploring the law of the Convention, the judgment of the Court is invariably more circumscribed than the arguments presented.

Separate opinions

Where a judgment does not represent in whole or in part the unanimous opinion of the judges who heard the case, Article 51(2) of the Convention provides that each member of the Court is entitled to deliver a separate opinion. There is a similar provision in the Statute of the International Court (Article 57) and although judges of the European Court have made less use of the opportunity to express an individual point of view, enabling them to do so has already proved a wise decision.

The Court, as we have seen, consists of more than twenty judges from a variety of backgrounds. Given the diversity of the Court and the nature of its work, disagreement is inevitable. The fact that the Convention is based on the common cultural heritage of the Contracting States is no guarantee that at the level of specific application, or on quite basic issues of interpretation there will be general agreement. In practice, as we shall see, the Court exhibits a remarkably high degree of unanimity, but if the United States Supreme Court and other domestic courts charged with the task of adjudicating upon issues of civil and political rights are frequently divided, it is hardly surprising that the European Court which is dealing with similar issues, with the complication that it is an international tribunal, regularly encounters the same problem.

By authorising the delivery of separate opinions, Article 51 permits any differences of opinion to be articulated. From the perspective of legal development this is important in two ways. First, in the case of a dissenting opinion it can throw the judgment into sharp relief by indicating the argument which was rejected. This leads to a better understanding of what was decided and of the wider implications of the case. Secondly, any separate opinion generally presents an alternative line of analysis, which may inspire or invite second thoughts about the matter in the future.

An example of first point is the long-running controversy over the meaning of the phrase 'civil rights and obligations' in Article 6(1). So, in *Albert and Le Compte* Judge Matscher and others used their dissenting opinions to demonstrate that despite the Court's disclaimers, the clear implication of its interpretation of the phrase is that the Convention protects the right to practise medicine and any other profession. An example of the second point was the unusual three-way division of opinion on a different aspect of Article 6(1) in the *Sramek* case. The Court held that the presence of a particular civil servant, one of three on an Austrian land tribunal, meant that it failed to qualify as an 'independent' tribunal for the purposes of the Convention. However, in a dissenting opinion two members of the Court held that the civil servant's membership did not have this effect, while in an individual opinion two other judges held that any civil servant's membership was a fatal defect. All three schools of thought claimed to be consistent with the Court's treatment of a similar issue in the *Ringeisen* case.[36] In subsequent cases on this issue there have therefore been three approaches, with varying degrees of judicial support, for the Court to consider.

Another advantage of separate opinions is the opportunity they provide for a review of issues which for one reason or another have not been examined in the main judgment. As noted above, the Court, while not always inclined to decide cases on the narrowest possible ground, will often avoid examining issues which are not strictly necessary to the decision, and generally refrains from excursions into issues of legal policy. Individual members of the Court are naturally less inhibited and in relation to both types of issues can through their separate opinions broaden the range of questions which are discussed.

Convenient illustrations are provided by two opinions of Judge Pettiti. In the *Barthold* case, where, it will be recalled, the Court declined to examine the scope of Article 10 of the Convention, he delivered a thoughtful separate opinion in which he explained his belief that this provision is broad enough to embrace advertising. Similarly, in the *Malone* case,[37] where the Court held that it had no need to decide whether the interferences with the applicant's rights under Article 8 were 'necessary in a democratic society', Judge Pettiti gave a well-argued separate opinion explaining why in the light of current developments in the technology of surveillance, this aspect of the case really should have been considered.

Separate opinions also have a part to play in maintaining the confidence of the Court's clientele. In most law suits there must be a winner and a loser, but the unsuccessful party should at least have the satisfaction of seeing his case fully considered and to the extent that his contentions are sound, having them upheld. The responsibility for seeing that this is achieved rests, of course, primarily on the Court. But the tendency to confine the judgment to a limited number of issues, together with the somewhat terse explanations characteristic of its reasoning mean that, as in the International Court,[38] there is room here for a valuable contribution from individual judges.

The effect of separate opinions in rendering unpalatable decisions acceptable – in sweetening, as it were, the bitter judicial pill – can be especially important when the unsuccessful litigant is a government. An individual who has failed to persuade the Court may be able to take comfort from indications that his case was not entirely without merit, but the effectiveness of the Convention depends ultimately on the support of governments. It is therefore they who must be satisfied that in accepting its obligations, along with the jurisdiction of the Court and the right of individual petition, they are subscribing to a system whose object and effect are the protection of rights, and not national humiliation. Separate opinions which go into issues passed over in the judgment, or which demonstrate that there is something to be said for the government's position (as there usually is) can do much to maintain the correct perspective. That the subjection of national decisions to international scrutiny is such a delicate matter is, then, another aspect of the Convention system which can justify the writing of separate opinions.

There is, of course, a price to be paid for allowing separate opinions.

Indeed, it was an awareness of this which caused those responsible for drafting the Statute of the Permanent Court to hesitate before including a provision allowing them. One problem is that a proliferation of individual opinions tends to undermine the judgment of the Court and weaken its authority. To some extent this is unavoidable because the whole purpose of the separate opinion is to enable differences to be articulated and a case in which the judges themselves are divided can never carry the weight of a unanimous or near-unanimous decision. On the other hand, there is a very considerable difference between allowing judges to express a personal point of view and encouraging them to append a discursive individual essay to every judgment. In the second situation, what the Court has actually decided can easily become submerged beneath a torrent of idiosyncratic views. In the International Court of Justice this is now a serious problem. However, in the European Court, where there is greater judicial reticence and certainly less disagreement, it is not a source of difficulty. Separate opinions are fewer and much shorter and where several judges wish to make the same point, joint opinions are very common.

A related objection is that even a single separate opinion, if argued forcefully and at length, may present a more persuasive analysis of the legal issues than the judgment. This is unquestionably the case and it must be acknowledged that the quality, as much as the quantity of separate opinions, is directly relevant to the authority of the Court's judgments.

In the practice of the European Court cases can be readily identified in which the reasoning to be found in the judgment left something to be desired and was exposed by the argument of a dissenting judge. In the *Tyrer* case,[39] for example, the Court may have reached the right result, but Sir Gerald Fitzmaurice, who alone dissented, produced much the more convincing and well-argued judgment. Likewise in the *Golder* case,[40] where the same judge again dissented, the Court arrived at an interpretation of the Convention which has been generally accepted, but one is compelled to agree with the comment that 'As between the somewhat meagre judgment of the majority, and the deeply reasoned judgment of Sir Gerald, there can be no doubt which is the more satisfying to the mind of any English lawyer. Here was the true product of the common law system.'[41]

The question these cases pose is which is more important: the preservation of the Court's authority, or the exposure of deficiencies in its reasoning? The question answers itself. However inconvenient it may be for the Court to face criticism in an individual case, in the longer term, its authority will not be maintained by silencing dissent, but by the quality of its judgments. Criticism, provided that it is courteous and within the bounds of judicial convention, should therefore be welcomed, as a way of maintaining the proper standard. No doubt the product of a single out-standing intellect will always outstrip in vigour and persuasiveness judgments of the Court which must be constructed so as to reflect the highest common factor of agreement. Allowance can be made for that and so it is unimportant. What matters is that the Court is encouraged to achieve the best that is attainable in its judgments. Any separate opinion which does that has more than fulfilled its purpose.

The last, and perhaps the most serious reservation is that the opportunity to voice disagreement which the right to produce a separate opinion provides, may make it more difficult for the members of the Court to arrive at a collective view. Like the International Court, the European Court can only discharge its function if the individual judges, or at least a majority of them, are prepared to sink their differences and agree to support a judgment. However, each judge knows that if he is so minded, he may expound his own views at whatever length he considers appropriate. Clearly, this could lead to a situation in which formulation of a majority view became difficult, or even impossible, because of an unwillingness on the part of too many judges to subscribe to a judgment with which they were not wholly in agreement.[42]

Whether separate opinions have this stultifying effect depends in the end on the judges themselves and the way they view the Court. It helps, of course, that the cases we are dealing with concern a subject – human rights – on which there is a large measure of agreement. By itself, however, this is not enough because, as we shall see, there is also disagreement, sometimes over quite fundamental matters. If the differences, great and small, which will always exist among those who ponder upon the more problematic issues of human rights are not to impede the judicial process, what is needed is a recognition that the Court is more than the sum of its parts, or, to put it in a slightly different way, a sense of collegiality. Without this no court will function well, whether separate opinions are allowed or not. With it (and it is clearly present at Strasbourg), such opinions have a properly constructive role to play in the application, interpretation and development of the law.

Notes

1 *Axen* case, Series A, No. 72 para. 24.
2 For an excellent treatment of this issue see L. V. Prott, *The Latent Power of Culture and the International Judge*, Professional Books, Abingdon, 1979.
3 S. Petren, 'Forms of expression of judicial activity', in L. Gross (ed.), *The Future of the International Court of Justice*, Oceana, New York, 450–1 (1976).
4 *Barthold* case, Series A, No. 90 para. 45.
5 *Ibid.*, para. 55.
6 Cf. L. N. Brown and F. G. Jacobs, *The Court of Justice of the European*

The Court's judgments 43

Communities, 2nd ed., Sweet and Maxwell, London, 41 (1983).
7 See *Combe* v. *Combe* [1951] 2 K. B., 215 at 224 (Birkett L. J.).
8 *Irish* case, Series A, No. 25 p. 106, separate opinion of Judge O'Donoghue.
9 *Airey* case, Series A, No. 32, dissenting opinion of Judge Thór Vilhjálmsson.
10 *National Union of Belgian Police* case, Series A, No. 19, separate opinion of Judge Sir Gerald Fitzmaurice, para. 26.
11 Prott, *Power of Culture*, 184.
12 *Corfu Channel* case, Merits, [1949] I. C. J. Rep., 4 at 22.
13 Series A, No. 11 para. 25.
14 Series A, No. 8.
15 Series A, No. 9.
16 Series A, No. 86 para. 29.
17 *Ibid.*, para. 30.
18 Series A, No. 147.
19 H. Lauterpacht, *The Development of International Law by the International Court*, Stevens, London, 39 (1958).
20 Series A, No. 12.
21 Series A, No. 72, see para. 24.
22 Series A, No. 56 para. 41.
23 Series A, No. 82 para. 67.
24 *Ibid.*, para. 84.
25 Series A, No. 80.
26 Series A, No. 84.
27 See on this point the dissenting opinion of Judge Bernhardt in the *Koendjbiharie* case, Series A, No. 185B.
28 Series A, No. 64 para. 42.
29 Series A, No. 70.
30 Series A, No. 28.
31 Series A, No. 93.
32 Series A, No. 90.
33 Series A, No. 87.
34 Series A, No. 29.
35 Series A, No. 58 para. 28.
36 Series A, No. 13. The dissenting judges in *Sramek* were Judges Sir Vincent Evans and Gersing; the concurring judges were Judges Ganshof van der Meersch and Evrigenis.
37 Series A, No. 82.
38 See J. G. Merrills, 'Sir Gerald Fitzmaurice's contribution to the jurisprudence of the International Court of Justice', *British Year Book of International Law*, XLVIII, 183 at 186 (1976–7).
39 Series A, No. 26.
40 Series A, No. 18.
41 W. Dale, 'Human rights in the United Kingdom – international standards', *International and Comparative Law Quarterly*, XXV, 292 at 302 (1976); and I. Sinclair, *The Vienna Convention on the Law of Treaties*, 2nd ed., Melland Schill Monographs in International Law, Manchester U.P., Manchester, 132 (1984). The standard set by Sir Gerald has been maintained by some of his successors on the Court; see, for example, the powerful dissenting opinions of Judge Martens in the *Cossey* case, Series A, No. 184 and the *Borgers* case, Series A, No. 214A.
42 See Lauterpacht, *Development*, pp. 69–70.

CHAPTER 3

The Court's conception of the Strasbourg system

The primary concern of any court is with the interpretation and application of the substantive law within its particular area of concern. Thus, the bulk of the European Court's work is concerned with establishing the scope of the rights guaranteed in the Convention and its protocols. But if this work, which is, of course, the Court's *raison d'être*, occupies a central place in its activity, it would be wrong to think of it as its only concern. As we saw in chapter 1, the Court is regularly called upon to consider questions relating to its own competence and the functioning of the whole human rights system. Though less dramatic than some of the cases involving substantive rights, these decisions are important because they require the Court to define the place of adjudication in the Convention and to answer basic questions about the scope of its protection.

The issues with which we are presently concerned arise in a variety of situations. In some cases the Court has been called upon to consider the standing, or procedural capacity of an individual applicant. In others, the scope of its own jurisdiction has been in issue. Sometimes, on the other hand, the question has been not whether the Court is competent, but whether a problem can be the subject of a complaint to the Commission. These may appear to be very different issues. Yet they are linked by the fact that they all raise questions about the nature of the Strasbourg system. In resolving them, as we shall see, the Court has provided an object lesson in judicial development of the law by consistently employing the principle of effectiveness. That is, adopting the solution which gives the provisions of the Convention the maximum effect commensurate with its language and underlying aim.

The position of the applicant

According to Article 44 of the Convention only the Contracting Parties or the Commission have the right to refer a case to the Court. An individual applicant, therefore, does not and, if his case is referred, is not a party to the proceedings.[1] A question which arose in the first case to be decided by the Court was whether as a result of these disabilities, an individual applicant is denied access to the Court altogether.

The *Lawless* case, which was referred to the Commission in 1957, raised substantive issues concerning Articles 5 and 15 of the Convention. In 1960 the Commission adopted its Report in which it expressed the opinion by a narrow majority that there had been no violation of the Convention by the respondent, the Republic of Ireland. Subsequently, the Commission decided to refer the case to the Court which was given a copy of the Report. As already noted, the Commission's role in the Court's proceedings is that of 'defender of the public interest' which requires it to be objective and impartial. This does not prevent it from expressing an opinion, but does mean that it cannot act as advocate for an individual applicant. The question in *Lawless* was whether there was any way in which the applicant's views could legitimately be put before the Court.

To deal with this problem the Commission had adopted Rule 76 of its Rules of Procedure. This provided that if an application lodged by an individual was subsequently referred to the Court, the Commission would normally give him a copy of its Report and invite him to submit his written observations on it. Although it was not stated in the Rule, the purpose of the procedure was to enable the Commission to transmit the applicant's views to the Court, thereby obviating the consequences of his lack of standing. In accordance with the Rule the Commission transmitted its Report to *Lawless* and invited his observations.

Not surprisingly, the Irish Government took strong exception to this procedure and lodged a number of preliminary objections challenging the Commission's actions and intentions. The Commission entered a no less vigorous defence and so it was necessary for the Court, before considering the merits of the case, to deal with these matters as preliminary objections. Deciding how they should be handled provided the Court with the first opportunity to consider the effectiveness of its jurisdiction.

In the light of the parties' final submissions, the Court decided that it was being asked to decide three questions, which it described as follows:

(i)   Is Rule 76 of the Rules of Procedure of the Commission in general contrary to the terms of the Convention?

(ii) Could the Commission, after bringing the case before the Court, communicate its Report to G. R. Lawless, the applicant, in the manner described by the Commission's delegate, without infringing the terms of the Convention?

(iii) Should the Court, either at the instance of the Commission acting on its own authority, or through the Commission after authorisation by the Court, receive the written observations of G. R. Lawless, the applicant, on the Commission's Report or on points arising during the proceedings?[2]

In dealing first with the issue of Rule 76 the Court was careful to distinguish between its jurisdiction to answer questions pertaining to the Convention in general and its responsibility for ensuring that improprieties do not occur. As regards the first, it recognised that its powers are limited to dealing with specific cases. For after distinguishing the functions of the Court from those of the Commission, it said 'it follows from the whole body of rules governing the powers of the Court that it cannot interpret the Convention in an abstract manner, but only in relation to such specific cases as are referred to it.' From this it followed that 'the Court is not competent to take decisions such as that to delete a rule from the Commission's Rules of Procedure – a step which would affect all Parties to the Convention – since this would amount to having power to make rulings on matters of procedure or to render advisory opinions'.[3] Consequently, the Court decided that it had no power to answer the first question asked.

On the other hand, by virtue of its authority to supervise the working of the Convention, the Court held that it could answer the second question. It said 'it is the duty of the Court, in the exercise of its functions, to ensure that the Convention is respected and, if need be, to point to any irregularities and to refuse to apply in such a case any provisions or regulations which are contrary to the Convention',[4] an observation which not only indicates the way in which its institutional effectiveness was uppermost in the Court's thinking, but also demonstrates the subtle power of the principle. For, of course, the answer to the second question would implicitly either validate or invalidate the Commission's Rule. As soon as the Court recognised that it had the authority to review the Commission's action in *Lawless*, its failure to address the general question was no longer important.

In its submissions to the Court on the second question the Commission made specific reference to the principle of effectiveness, arguing that the Contracting States had conferred on it 'the necessary powers to fulfil effectively the functions entrusted to it by Article 19 of the Convention' and that as a result it was entitled to transmit its Report to Lawless because it had judged this to be necessary. The government, in contrast, maintained that since the Convention requires the Contracting Parties to keep the Report secret, the Commission was similarly bound. The Court's approach was to point out that whereas the Commission's proceedings are confidential, the Court's are public. Consequently, the fact that permission is required to publish the documents in a case does not mean they cannot be communicated on a confidential basis to interested parties. Here the applicant was such a party. Emphasising that 'it must be borne in mind that the applicant instituted the proceedings before the Commission and that, if the Court found that his complaints were justified, he would be directly affected by any decision', the Court drew attention to its authority under the Rules to hear any person 'whose depositions seem to it useful in the fulfilment of its task'.[5] In the light of these considerations the Court concluded that the Commission possessed the power it was claiming, to communicate its Report, in whole or in part, to an applicant when it considered this appropriate.

Before considering the significance of this decision it is convenient to deal with the Court's treatment of the third question, namely the present-ation by the Commission of the applicant's observations. The Court approached this matter in the same spirit as the earlier issues. Again, the government maintained that the action proposed was contrary to the Convention, pointing out that an individual applicant cannot appear before the Court and arguing that to submit his observations as a Com-mission document would inevitably prejudice the latter's objectivity. The Commission, on the other hand, cited a number of precedents from international judicial practice to demonstrate that transmission of an individual's observations need not connote *locus standi*, and suggested that it was not the intention of the Convention to dissociate individual applicants from proceedings in the Court entirely.

The Court decided that, as on the previous issue, the answer was to be found in its duty to the applicant and, specifically, its need to know his point of view. In a passage which is worth quoting in full, the Court's reasoning was as follows:

according to Article 44 of the Convention, Contracting States and the Commis-sion are alone empowered to bring a case before the Court or to appear in Court . . . nevertheless, the Court must bear in mind its duty to safeguard the interests of the individual, who may not be a party to any court proceedings . . . the whole of the proceedings in the Court, as laid down by the Convention and the Rules of Court, are upon issues which concern the applicant. . . . Accordingly, it is in the interests of the proper administration of justice that the Court should have knowledge of and, if need be, take into consideration, the applicant's point of view.

How was this to be done? The Court identified three sources of informa-tion:

to this end the Court has at its disposal: in the first place, and in any event, the Commission's Report, which of necessity sets out the applicant's allegations with regard to the facts and his legal arguments, even if it does not endorse them; secondly, the written and oral observations of the delegates and Counsel of the Commission which, as the defender of the public interest, is entitled of its own accord, even if it does not share them, to make known the applicant's views to the Court as a means of throwing light on the points at issue; and thirdly, the Court may also hear the applicant in accordance with Rule 38 of the Rules of Court, and, as part of the enquiry, may invite the Commission *ex officio*, or authorise the Commission at its request, to submit the applicant's observations on the Report or on any specific point arising in the course of the debates.[6]

Although the Court thus held that it had the power to receive the applicant's observations, it reserved its decision on the particular facts until it had examined the merits.

How the Court finally resolved the issue of the applicant's observations will be examined in chapter 8, where the consequences of *Lawless* will be considered in the context of the Court's implementation of the principle of equality of arms. To appreciate the significance of the case in the shaping of the Strasbourg system one need only reflect on what the effect of a contrary decision would have been. If the Court had decided that the applicant could not see the Commission's Report, or that he could not comment on it, a barrier would have been created between the individual and the Court's proceedings which would become, as it were, the private affair of the government and the Commission. By rejecting this in its very first case, the Court not only laid the foundation for a number of later developments, but also demonstrated that it was committed to a conception of its own role in which the function of the Convention in protecting individual rights takes priority over jurisdictional and procedural objections reflecting the traditional attitudes of governments.

The competence of the Court to examine issues of admissibility

In the *Belgian Linguistics* case[7] and the *Vagrancy* cases the Court decided that it is competent in certain circumstances to review rulings of the Commission concerned with issues of admissibility. These decisions, the second of which was controversial, are another striking example of the Court developing the law by giving an effective interpretation to those articles of the Convention which lay down its jurisdiction.

In the *Belgian Linguistics* case the Belgian Government put forward an elaborate preliminary objection in which it argued that the Court should dismiss the case for lack of jurisdiction on the ground that the right to receive education in one's own language, which was the basis of the applicants' claim, fell completely outside the Convention. In the proceedings before the Commission the government had sought to make the same point in support of the submission that the case should be dismissed as 'manifestly ill-founded', but its argument had been rejected. The case therefore presented the Court with the question of whether it had jurisdiction to rule on an issue of competence which had already been dealt with by the Commission. It decided that it had and proceeded to dismiss Belgium's objection.

At first sight the issue here may not seem particularly important. As the Court indicated, the substantive question which Belgium wished to raise, namely the extent to which the Convention protects linguistic minorities, would be considered in any case when the Court came to examine the merits. Thus whether the Court was prepared to review it in a preliminary way as an issue of jurisdiction, or postpone it for later consideration, may not appear to be very significant. This is deceptive, however, for most issues of admissibility do not pertain to the merits. Consequently by suggesting that the Court might be prepared to review any matter already dealt with by the Commission, including the various requirements of Articles 25, 26 and 27, the *Belgian Linguistics* case paved the way for the Court's more controversial decision in the *Vagrancy* cases.

The question in the *Vagrancy* cases was whether the Court is competent to examine issues which have already been decided by the Commission if they are not related to the merits. In those cases Belgium submitted that the three applications which were before the Court were inadmissible because local remedies had not been exhausted, as required by Article 26, and, in one case, for the further reason that the application was out of time. The Commission opposed the submission on the ground that consideration of these issues was outside the Court's jurisdiction, questions of admissibility being exclusively within the province of the Commission.

The Court decided that it was competent to consider Belgium's objections and justified its conclusions by referring to Article 45 of the Convention, which provides that the jurisdiction of the Court *ratione materiae* 'shall extend to all cases concerning the interpretation and application of the present Convention'. Pointing out that this phrase 'is remarkable for its width'[8] the Court held that a literal interpretation was confirmed by the reference in Article 46(1) to declarations accepting the Court's jurisdiction in 'all matters' concerning the interpretation and application of the Convention. It went on to say that:

This conclusion is in no way invalidated by the powers conferred on the Commission under Article 27 of the Convention as regards the admissibility of applications. The task which this Article assigns to the Commission is one of sifting; the Commission either does or does not accept the applications. Its decisions to reject applications which it considers to be inadmissible are without appeal as are, moreover, also those by which applications are accepted; they are taken in complete independence. . . . The decision to accept an application has the effect of leading the Commission to perform the function laid down in Articles 28 to 31 of the Convention and of opening up the possibility that the case may be brought before the Court; but it is not binding on the Court any more than the Court is bound by the opinion expressed by the Commission in its final report 'as to whether the facts found disclose a breach by the State concerned of its obligations under the Convention' (Article 31).[9]

The *Vagrancy* cases presented the Court with a choice between two views of its relationship to the Commission. For the four judges who dissented, the Commission was correct in maintaining that there was a clear separation of functions between the two institutions with the Commission responsible for admissibility, fact-finding and conciliation and the Court concerned solely with authoritative rulings on alleged violations. On this view the competence of the Court was limited to the questions in issue in the Commission's report, which would concern only the merits of the application. For the majority, on the other hand, the Commission and the Court were not separate and equal institutions 'each sovereign within its own sphere',[10] but the primary responsibility for interpreting and applying the law of the Convention rests with the Court.

An important advantage of the majority's approach is that there is now a single institution competent to handle all questions of interpretation arising out of the Convention and that institution is the Court which, as the judicial arm of the Strasbourg system, is the most appropriate body to perform this function.[11] It must be remembered, however, that as regards the further consideration of points raised before the Commission there is a crucial distinction to be drawn between the respective fates of admitted and rejected applications. In the case of the former, objections to admissibility rejected by the Commission may be reconsidered, as happened in the *Vagrancy* cases; rejected applications, on the other hand, will never reach the Court and consequently objections which the Commission has accepted cannot be reconsidered.

For the dissenting judges in the *Vagrancy* cases the above point constituted a further objection to the Court's decision and was particularly anomalous in a human rights context because the only decisions which may be reconsidered are those which have been given against the respondent State. Too much should not be made of this, however. Although there is certainly no question of the Court being able to consider an application which has been wholly rejected, if an application is partly admitted the ruling in the *Vagrancy* cases can work to the advantage of the applicant. In the *Handyside* case,[12] for example, the Court held that it was competent to consider a claim by the applicant under Article 14, notwithstanding the fact that the Commission had ruled that it was inadmissible, because it was based on facts identical to those underlying other claims which the Commission had admitted.

It should not be supposed that as a result of its ruling in the *Vagrancy* cases the work of the Court now duplicates that of the Commission. As noted earlier, the latter's decision on admissibility establishes the ambit of the case and will exclude certain issues from reconsideration. Moreover, the *Vagrancy* judgment itself laid down a further important limitation. Having established its competence to review Belgium's submissions as to admissibility, the Court held that they must be rejected. This was because 'objections to jurisdiction and admissibility must, in principle, be raised first before the Commission to the extent that their character and circumstances permit'.[13] And Belgium's failure to raise either of its objections earlier meant that it was estopped from doing so now.

The doctrine of estoppel, which is discussed further in chapter 8, is a way in which the Court has sought to recognise and protect the special role of the Commission. Like the principle that the Commission establishes the ambit of the case, it has the effect of limiting the issues for the Court's consideration. However, even when these qualifications are taken into account, the judgment in the *Vagrancy* cases can be seen to have had a very significant impact on the Court's activity. Instead of being limited to substantive issues, and the occasional issue of jurisdiction, the Court regards itself as competent at least in principle, to consider 'all questions of fact and law', arising out of the case at any stage. Armed with this broad remit the Court has been able to develop its jurisprudence on the local remedies rule, the question of who may be considered a 'victim' for the purposes of Article 25 and a number of other questions. The Court has not so much usurped the functions of the Commission, as reserved to itself the right to be the ultimate arbiter of the Convention's scope. As a result, its decisions cover a much wider range of legal issues than if the narrower view of its competence had prevailed.

Effectiveness and the right of individual petition

Individuals are able to take cases to Strasbourg by virtue of Article 25(1) of the Convention which provides that the Commission may receive petitions from individuals or groups claiming to be the victim of a violation by one of the Contracting States, provided that the State concerned has made a declaration recognising the competence of the Commission to receive such petitions. The same article goes on to provide that 'Those of the High Contracting Parties who have made such a declaration undertake not to hinder in any way the effective exercise of this right'. In the *Cruz Varas* case it was necessary for the Court to consider the meaning of these words and the decision, which is so far the only one on this aspect of Article 25, provided another opportunity to shape the Convention system.

The case arose out of a decision on the part of the Swedish authorities to deport a man, his wife and their son from Sweden to Chile. Shortly before the expulsion was due to take place, the family, all of whom were Chilean nationals, made an application to Strasbourg in which they claimed that as the husband ran the risk of political persecution if he were returned, the applicants' deportation would violate Sweden's obligations under Article 3 of the Convention. The Commission, using a power contained in Rule 36 of its Rules, indicated to the Swedish Government that it was desirable not to deport the applicants until the Commission had had an opportunity to examine their application further. Notwithstanding this communication, the husband was expelled to Chile on the same day. His wife and son, who had gone into hiding, remained in Sweden.

When the case reached the Court one of several questions which had to be decided was whether it was open to Mr Cruz Varas to invoke Article 25(1) and claim that Sweden had hindered the effective exercise of his right of individual petition. In a ruling which specifically relied on the principle of effectiveness the Court decided that it was, saying:

In its ordinary meaning Article 25(1) imposes an obligation not to interfere with the right of the individual effectively to present and pursue his complaint with the Commission. Such an obligation confers on an applicant a right of a procedural nature distinguishable from the substantive rights set out under Section 1 of the Convention or its Protocols. However it flows from the very essence of this procedural right that it must be open to individuals to complain of alleged infringements of it in Convention proceedings. In this respect also the Convention must be interpreted as guaranteeing rights which are practical and effective as opposed to theoretical and illusory . . . .[14]

Having established this important point of principle, the Court went on to decide that the applicant's expulsion had not in fact hindered the effective exercise of his right of individual petition or violated Article 25(1). It recognised that allowing Mr Cruz Varas to remain in Sweden would have facilitated the presentation of the case to the Commission, but found that following the applicant's return to Chile, he was at liberty and counsel was able to represent the family fully before the Commission. Nor did it appear that the applicant's inability to confer with his lawyer had hampered the gathering of additional material. The Court therefore considered that there was no evidence of hindrance to a significant degree and decided that there had been no violation of the Convention.

The decision that Sweden had complied with its obligations was arrived at by the narrow majority of 10 votes to 9 and the dissenting judges adopted a quite different approach to Article 25(1). Whereas the majority were content to ask whether the applicant's access to the Commission had been hindered in fact, the minority regarded the issue more broadly and saw the case as concerned with the very purpose of the Strasbourg system. As their argument rested on the powers of the Commission under Rule 36, which were also reviewed by the majority, it is worth examining this issue more closely.

Rule 36 provides:

The Commission, or where it is not in session, the President may indicate to the parties any interim measure the adoption of which seems desirable in the interest of the parties or the proper conduct of the proceedings before it.

Unlike other international instruments, the Convention contains no provision specifically empowering its organs to order interim measures.

The Court decided that in the absence of such a specific power, a Rule 36 indication could not give rise to a binding obligation. Furthermore, it decided that such an obligation could not be derived from Article 25(1) because, although individuals can complain of violations of this provision, in the absence of a specific power to indicate interim measures, it would 'strain the language of Article 25'[15] to infer an obligation to comply with a Rule 36 indication. The Court recognised that in practice there is almost total compliance with Rule 36 indications, but held that while subsequent practice is relevant on issues of interpretation, it could not be used to create new rights and obligations and was thus no more than 'a matter of good faith cooperation with the Commission'.[16]

The nine dissenting judges took a very different view. Appreciating perhaps that it would be a bold step to hold that Rule 36 indications are binding *per se*, they maintained that Article 25(1) had been violated in this case because in their view it was 'implicit in the Convention that in cases such as the present one, the Convention organs have the power to require the parties to abstain from a measure which might not only give rise to serious harm but might also nullify the result of the entire procedure under the Convention'.[17] They were not saying that every complaint under Article 25 should inhibit extradition or expulsion; rather, their argument was that in cases where the possibility of irreparable harm leads to a request by the Commission under Rule 36, a State is obliged to comply.

In answer to the argument that the Convention contains no provision expressly authorising provisional measures, a point on which, as we have seen, the judgment placed great weight, the dissenting judges made the following revealing observation:

It is true that, unlike some other international instruments, the Convention does not contain any express provision as to the indication of provisional measures. But this does not exclude an autonomous interpretation of the European Convention with special emphasis placed on its object and purpose and the effectiveness of its control machinery. In this context too, present day conditions are of importance. Today the right of individual petition and the compulsory jurisdiction of the Court have been accepted by nearly all the member States of the Council of Europe. It is of the essence that the Convention organs should be able to secure the effectiveness of the protection they are called on to ensure.[18]

The division of opinion in *Cruz Varas* was not over the relevance of the effectiveness principle, which was acknowledged on all sides, but over whether it was proper to employ the principle to extend the scope of Article 25(1) and, as a corollary, the powers of the Commission, without express authorisation in the Convention. As the quotation demonstrates, almost half the members of the Court were prepared to use the principle in this way, while their colleagues were more cautious. The obligation not to hinder the right of individual petition is thus a matter on which the Court's present conception of the Strasbourg system is less radical than many of its members would wish, but where the ground has already been prepared for a further step forward.

Jurisdiction ratione personae

As regards the kinds of complaints which the Strasbourg institutions may consider, an important distinction is drawn between cases brought by States and those brought by individuals. Article 24 of the Convention enables States to refer to the Commission 'any alleged breach of the provisions of the Convention by another High Contracting Party'. Article 25, on the other hand, allows petitions from individuals only where they are 'claiming to be the victim' of a violation of the Convention. In this respect it resembles Article 1 of the Protocol to the United Nations Covenant on Civil and Political Rights, which is in similar terms. The aim of these limitations is clear: it is to prevent an individual from challenging the validity of a law *in abstracto*. Their application, however, can sometimes be a source of difficulty. In the various cases in which the scope of Article 25 has been considered, the tendency already noted, for the Court to resolve issues of admissibility and jurisdiction by reference to the effectiveness principle, receives further confirmation.

In the *Klass* case the question was whether the applicants could challenge the various methods of secret surveillance employed in the Federal Republic of Germany, despite the fact that, for obvious reasons, they were unable to prove that such measures had been applied to them personally. To answer it the Court made a detailed analysis of Article 25. An individual could not institute an *actio popularis* and complain against a law *in abstracto:* 'In principle it does not suffice for an individual applicant to claim that the mere existence of a law violates his rights under the Convention, it is necessary that the law should have been applied to his detriment.'[19] On the other hand, the right of individual petition was 'one of the keystones' in the Convention machinery and was designed to provide a means of challenging alleged violations. In the Court's view the need to make that right effective pointed to the solution:

The question arises in the present proceedings whether an individual is to be deprived of the opportunity of lodging an application with the Commission because, owing to the secrecy of the measures objected to, he cannot point to any concrete measure specifically affecting him. In the Court's view, the effectiveness (*l'effet utile*) of the Convention implies in such circumstances some possibility of having access to the Commission. If this were not so, the efficiency of the Convention's enforcement machinery would be materially weakened. The procedural provisions of the Convention must, in view of the fact that the Convention and its institutions were set up to protect the individual, be applied in a manner which serves to make the system of individual applications efficacious.[20]

The Court therefore concluded that under certain conditions an individual may claim to be the victim of a violation occasioned by the mere existence of legislation providing for secret surveillance. In the light of the facts, which disclosed that the legislation in question could be applied to any member of the public, the applicants were held entitled to bring their claim.

Was the Court saying here that the applicants could be regarded as victims because it was possible that they had been subject to secret surveillance, although they could not prove it, or was it laying down the broader proposition that their status as victims derived from the risk that the legislation might be applied to them in the future? On the particular facts the distinction was unimportant, but matters a great deal where the element of risk is the only basis for the claim. This was the situation in the *Marckx* case which concerned the Belgian legislation on illegitimacy.

The government argued that since on the facts the legislation in question had not actually been applied to the applicants, their challenge was actually directed to the law *in abstracto* and as such was inadmissible. The Court, however, rejected the argument. Citing the *Klass* case, it ruled that 'Article 25 of the Convention entitles individuals to contend that a law violates their rights by itself, in the absence of an individual measure of implementation, if they run the risk of being directly affected by it.'[21] Since the Court found that this was the case here, it rejected the government's submission.

The ruling in *Marckx* confirms the broader reading of *Klass* and is consistent with the Court's declared aim of making the right of individual petition effective. Subsequent cases, moreover, have taken the concept of the notional victim somewhat further. Thus in *Corigliano*, which raised the issue of trial within a reasonable time, the Italian Government argued that the applicant could not be regarded as a 'victim' because his aim in invoking the Convention was not to speed the course of the prosecution but simply to avoid conviction. In support of this submission the government cited the fact that following his acquittal in 1980 the applicant had sought to withdraw his application on the ground that the object of the dispute had disappeared, and had changed his mind only when further proceedings (not relevant to the present application) had been instituted against him. The Court decided that this objection could not be accepted. Explaining that according to its previous decisions 'the word "victim" in Article 25 denotes the person directly affected by the act or omission in issue, the existence of a violation being conceivable even in the absence of prejudice',[22] the Court held that since the duration of the proceedings against Mr Corigliano directly affected him, it was irrelevant that this was not his major concern.

Similarly in *de Jong, Baljet and van den Brink*,[23] which concerned pre-trial detention, the Court rejected a submission from the Netherlands Government that certain of the applicants could not be regarded as victims, because time spent in remand had been deducted in its entirety from their sentences. In this case the Court indicated that its decision might have been different if the mitigation of the applicants' sentences had been based on an acknowledgement that the Convention had been violated. This, it is suggested, is the key to understanding the Court's approach in *Marckx* and the other cases involving Article 25. While the Convention clearly precludes an *actio popularis*, the Court sees itself as much more than a provider of remedies for isolated complaints. In the interests of the effectiveness of the Convention as a whole it is prepared to use individual applications as an opportunity to make points which it considers need to be made and interprets the concept of 'victim' accordingly.

Propriety

Closely related to the issue considered in the previous section is the question of when a case may be struck out on the ground that the object of the application has disappeared. This issue was one of the earliest matters to be discussed at Strasbourg and has been considered in numerous subsequent cases.

There is no provision in either the Convention or the Rules of the Court which expressly deals with the possibility of removing a case on the broad ground that the object of the application has disappeared, although, as we shall see, there is provision in the Rules for the removal of a case following a friendly settlement or other solution. In the cases with which we are concerned, however, the respondent has relied not on that provision, but on general considerations of propriety, which in 1963 prompted the International Court to decline to decide a case because, as one judge put it:

courts of law are not there to make legal pronouncements *in abstracto*, however great their scientific value as such. They are there to protect existing and current legal rights, to secure compliance with existing and current legal obligations, to afford concrete reparation if a wrong has been committed, or to give rulings in relation to existing and concrete legal situations.[24]

As a succinct statement of principle, this cannot be faulted. The question for the European Court and the aspect of its activity which is of particular interest as regards the functioning of the Strasbourg system is its relevance to the adjudication of human rights.

The issue has most frequently been raised when at some point after the lodging of the application, the respondent has adopted, or promised to adopt, measures directed towards the underlying problem. In this situation, although a violation of the Convention may have occurred, it can be argued that the matter is being attended to; the respondent is therefore likely to suggest that the case should be removed from the Court's list on the ground that its object has disappeared. If, as has happened in a number of cases, the applicant has also indicated that he has no further interest in pursuing the claim, the respondent will naturally use this to buttress its argument. Almost invariably, the Court has proved unreceptive to submissions of this kind. It has taken the position that even if it has the power to remove a case on grounds of propriety, in the particular circumstances it has no reason to do so. Indeed, so far from the case being one which should be discontinued, a proper understanding of the Court's function indicates that it should proceed.

In some cases the point which the Court has emphasised is that whatever changes the respondent may have made in its law or practice for the future, the applicant is entitled to a ruling as to whether his rights were violated at the salient time. This entitlement does not depend on whether the applicant is claiming financial or other compensation which can only be obtained through a judgment. If such a claim is outstanding, this is an additional reason for retaining the case, but it is not essential. For whether the applicant is claiming concrete reparation or not, he is entitled to know his rights. In short, he is entitled to a judgment, because, as the Court stated in the *Guzzardi* case, 'proceedings under the Convention frequently serve a declaratory purpose'.[25]

A convenient example of the Court's emphasis on the individual interest in the continuation of proceedings is the *Tyrer* case which concerned a birching which the applicant had suffered in the Isle of Man and raised a number of issues under Article 3. The respondent submitted that the case should be struck out because legislation was envisaged to abolish corporal punishment for certain types of offences, including the offence for which it had been inflicted on the applicant. This was opposed by the Commission and rejected by the Court, which explained that:

There is no certainty as to whether and when the proposal will become law and even, if adopted, it cannot erase a punishment already inflicted. What is more, the proposed legislation does not go to the substance of the issue before the Court, namely whether judicial corporal punishment as inflicted on the applicant in accordance with Manx legislation is contrary to the Convention.[26]

The view that a case must be retained so long as the individual's rights still have to be determined is a clear example of the Court making the effectiveness of the Convention and its own jurisdiction the basis of its decision. But the applicant's position is not the only factor. For as well as this, the Court has taken into account broader considerations.

In the *Irish* case, for example, one of the findings of the Commission was that in certain respects the treatment of detainees by the British authorities in Northern Ireland violated Article 3 of the Convention. Before the case reached the Court, the United Kingdom announced that it would not be contesting the adverse findings of the Commission, gave an unqualified undertaking that the notorious 'five techniques' of interrogation would not in any circumstances be reintroduced and took a number of measures designed to prevent a recurrence of the acts complained of. The government argued that in view of these actions the case had become moot, that there was no point in the Court ruling on allegations that were now uncontested and that since the proceedings had ceased to have any worthwhile object, the Court should exercise its discretion and decline to adjudicate.

The Court rejected the British argument and proceeded to consider the merits. As its justification for doing so it relied on the broad proposition that 'The Court's judgments . . . serve not only to decide those cases brought before the Court but, more generally, to elucidate, safeguard and develop the rules instituted by the Convention, thereby contributing to the observance by States of the engagements undertaken by them as Contracting Parties.'[27] In other words, to discharge its functions effectively, the Court must have regard both to the significance of its decision for the particular applicant and to its wider role as guardian of the Convention. This does not mean that it can deal with purely hypothetical points, or furnish interpretations of the Convention *in abstracto*. However, it does mean that provided an issue of interpretation needs to be resolved, it is no objection to the Court's deciding a case that the precise issue will not arise again, or that the judgment will have no 'forward reach'.

The above review, which does not purport to be exhaustive, demonstrates that decisions as to whether a case should be struck out because the object has disappeared, have provided the Court with a further opportunity to explore and develop its conception of the Strasbourg system as an effective scheme of human rights protection. It is in the light of this approach that the Court's early decision in the *De Becker* case must now be mentioned.

This case, only the second to be referred to the Court, was decided in 1962. The applicant complained that certain restrictions imposed on him as a criminal penalty infringed the right to freedom of expression guaranteed by Article 10. While the case was before the Court, Belgium, which was the respondent in the case, amended its legislation on the point to which the complaint related and then submitted that the matter had been resolved. When Belgium asked the Court to strike the case out of its list neither the applicant, nor the Commission, objected. In these circumstances the Court decided that although it would be entitled to proceed with the case, it had no need to do so, since the question of whether De Becker had been the victim of a violation of the Convention was now of only historical interest, and the Court had no power to examine the compatibility of the new law with the Convention *in abstracto*. Accordingly, the Court agreed to strike the case off.

One member of the Court dissented from this conclusion. For Judge Ross two questions needed to be distinguished. First, there was the question of whether new legislation was relevant in this kind of situation. He considered that it was not, on the grounds that it seemed:

to follow from the spirit of the Convention that the Applicant is entitled to a decision on the question which the Commission has brought before the Court. Whatever changes may occur after the case is brought before the Court, the Applicant may, should he, for example, wish to bring a suit for damages, have a legitimate interest in a decision relating to the legal situation prevailing before the legislative changes.[28]

The second question was the effect of the withdrawal of the application. Here Judge Ross considered the answer was to be found in the role of the Court, which was not to enforce private claims, but to supervise observance of the Convention.

This question could have been answered in the positive if the function of this Court had been to enforce private claims, which a claimant may, if he wishes, modify during proceedings. This is not, however, the case here. According to the Convention, the function of the Court is 'to ensure the observance of the engagements undertaken by the High Contracting Parties in the present Convention' (Article 19 of the Convention). In view of this the Applicant is not recognised as a Party before the Court. His Application can only cause the Commission to make investigations; and, if the result of these investigations substantiates to a reasonable extent the complaint and a friendly settlement is not achieved, the Commission may bring the question for final decision before the Committee of Ministers or before the Court. When the proceedings have gone that far, the public interest requires that the question whether a violation has or has not taken place shall be decided regardless of whether the Applicant is or is not interested in the continuance of proceedings.[29]

It is clear that at some point between *De Becker* and the cases considered earlier a profound reorientation of judicial perspective occurred. As regards both the interests of the applicant and the public interest, the views of Judge Ross, who alone saw the significance of these matters in 1962, now represent the approach of the Court. It would be hard to find a more striking example of the value of the separate opinion as an institution nor, more generally, of the influence of considerations of effectiveness in the current work of the Court.

Friendly settlement

A similar tendency to ensure that the Convention functions effectively is found in the cases in which the Court has been called upon to decide another issue of general importance: whether a case which is on its list should be struck out on the grounds that the dispute has been settled.

Rule 49(2) of the Rules of the Court provides that: 'When the Chamber is informed of a friendly settlement, arrangement or other fact of a kind to provide a solution of the matter, it may, after consulting, if necessary the Parties, the Delegates of the Commission and the applicant, strike the case out of the list.' It will be noted that the removal of a case is discretionary. The way the Court has exercised its discretion in the various situations which have arisen demonstrates the extent to which it has been guided by the principle of effectiveness.

When the Court is informed of a friendly settlement it will strike the case off if it is satisfied that it is appropriate to do so having regard to the applicant's interest and the general interest. The first is usually straightforward. The Court will look to the Commission to certify that the settlement recognises the applicant's rights and has been accepted. As regards the general interest, however, there can be difficulty.

In the *Can* case the applicant complained of violations of Article 5(3) and 6(3)(c) and his complaints were upheld by the Commission. Subsequently, a friendly settlement was negotiated with the Austrian Government. Within the framework of the comprehensive reform of the Code of Criminal Procedure which was in preparation the government would propose new rules on the supervision of consultations between a suspect in detention on remand and his lawyer and these would take into account the Commission's observations on this matter. The government also undertook to pay the applicant 100,000 schillings by way of compensation, together with a reimbursement of his costs and expenses.

In the light of the settlement the government requested the Court to strike the case off its list in accordance with the Rules. The Commission had no objection and the applicant clearly regarded the settlement as in his interests. Therefore the only question was whether considerations of public policy necessitated a continuation of the proceedings. The Court ruled that they did not. Explaining that in several previous cases it had decided issues analogous to those arising in the present case under Article 5(3), it noted that the same could not be said of the question concerning Article 6(3)(c). However, there were, the Court found, 'certain indications'[30] in its case-law as to the relevance of this part of the Convention at the stage of preliminary investigations. In view of this, and the government's undertaking to put forward proposals for reform taking into account the unanimous report of the Commission on the point, the

Court considered that in all the circumstances it was appropriate to strike the case from its list.

Two members of the Court expressed only qualified support for this approach. In their view when a settlement satisfies the individual interest in the case the Court needs merely to satisfy itself that the cause of the problem will be eliminated. Thus:

there is no room in a judgment striking a case out of the list for the inclusion of any observations on what the Court's opinion might have been if it had had to determine the merits of the case, or on the opinion it had expressed in similar cases, the existence of any established case-law of the Court on the issue in question being a matter that is totally irrelevant for a decision to strike out.[31]

Clearly the issue here is one of considerable importance. Is the Court entitled to retain a case because it raises a point of interpretation which would otherwise go unresolved? In answering this question positively, the Court was confirming a view of its role that we encountered earlier, that to discharge its function effectively, it must look beyond the resolution of individual cases, and take into account development of the law of the Convention.

A rather different issue of effectiveness was raised in the *Skoogström* case.[32] Like the previous case this involved a period of pre-trial detention which the Commission found excessive. Here the terms of the settlement between the applicant and the Swedish Government provided for the introduction of legislation to amend the Code of Judicial Procedure, publication to the judiciary and prosecutors of a summary of the Commission's report and reimbursement of the applicant's costs.

In view of the settlement the government requested the Court to strike the case off its list. The applicant stated that he had no objection to this and the Commission's Delegate acknowledged that the settlement satisfied the individual interest in the case. He pointed out, however, that neither the content nor the timing of the proposed legislation had been indicated and that publication of the Commission's report, whatever its effect on practice would not in itself change the law. The Commission therefore proposed that the Court should not strike the case from its list, but should adjourn it until details of the legislative programme were available.

The Court disagreed. Taking formal note of the friendly settlement, it examined the applicant's position and held that as far as the general interest was concerned, there was no reason to defer judgment, or proceed to the merits of the case. It therefore concluded that it would be appropriate to strike the case off its list. Three judges dissented from this conclusion and went somewhat further than the Commission's recommendation, maintaining that in the general interest the Court should proceed immediately to the merits of the case. This was because the intended reforms were unclear and because the main issue in the case – whether the district prosecutor could be regarded as an 'officer authorised by law to exercise judicial power' – raised an important question of principle.

Although the Commission and the dissenting judges proposed different alternatives, they shared the belief that when a breach of the Convention has been identified, a friendly settlement should not be approved unless it is absolutely clear that steps to correct any systemic deficiences are being taken. Such a view has much to commend it. Whilst it would not be appropriate for the good faith of a Contracting State to be called into question, once a case has reached the threshold of the Court, it seems reasonable to require a guarantee that the Convention will be respected before removing it from the list.

Where there is no friendly settlement an application to strike out a case will rarely succeed. For the Court, having regard to the effectiveness of the Convention, is likely to take the view that there is still judicial work to be done. This is so even if the applicant indicates a wish to withdraw his application because here, as elsewhere, there are factors other than the individual's interest to be taken into account. In the *Tyrer* case, for example, the applicant indicated that he wished to withdraw his application while it was before the Commission, but the latter decided that it could not accede to the request since the case raised questions of a general character affecting the observance of the Convention. When the case reached the Court, the respondent argued that it should be struck off. The Court, however, explained that it had received no indication that the applicant's withdrawal was 'a fact of a kind to provide a solution of the matter' and on this ground decided to retain the case.

A rather different situation had to be considered in the *Luedicke* case. This case involved the Federal Republic of Germany and the right to a free interpreter under Article 6(3)(e) of the Convention. By the time the case reached the Court one of the applicants, Koç, had returned to an unknown address in Turkey. On account of this the domestic courts had decided not to pursue the recovery of costs against him and the government had indicated that even if he returned to Germany, he would not be asked to pay.

The Court nevertheless refused to strike the case from its list. There was no friendly settlement and the action of the government and the courts were not a 'fact of a kind to provide a solution of the matter' for the purposes of the Rules, because, as the Court put it:

In point of fact, the waiver of recovery of the sums due by Mr Koç is not prompted by reasons deriving from Article 6(3)(e) of the Convention; the waiver results simply from the practical difficulties and cost of recovery, as well as from consideration of the applicant's family and financial situation. Furthermore, the waiver of recovery does not remove the applicant's legal interest to have established the incompatibility with the Convention of the Cologne Court of Appeal's judgment ordering him to pay the interpretation costs. The government do not, by their above-mentioned declaration, admit that the German law and its application to Mr Koç contravene Article 6(3)(e). On the contrary, they maintain that the law and its application comply with the Convention. Since Mr Koç has requested reimbursement of the ancillary costs incurred by him in the present proceedings, the retention of his case on the Court's list is also justified for the purposes of the possible application of Article 50 in this respect.[33]

Of course, there are circumstances in which unilateral action of the kind involved in *Koç* may be enough to justify the removal of a case. The test is whether it can be regarded as providing a solution. In the *Rubinat* case[34] the applicant had been tried and convicted while abroad, extradited to Italy, imprisoned following an unsuccessful attempt to challenge his conviction, then pardoned. At the time of the proceedings he was abroad again and all attempts to contact him had failed. In this situation the Court considered that the pardon could be regarded as a 'fact of a kind to provide a solution of the matter', since the applicant had been released well before the expiry of his sentence and appeared to have no further interest in the proceedings. Although the case raised issues of principle which transcended the applicant's interests and could therefore be retained if desired, the Court saw no reason to adopt this course. Having just examined analogous legal issues in the *Colozza* case,[35] the Court decided that it would be appropriate to strike the case from its list, subject only to its right to restore it in the event of fresh circumstances justifying such a course.

The power to award compensation

Some of the most revealing indications of the Court's conception of the Strasbourg system are to be found in a series of early cases in which it established the meaning and significance of Article 50 which provides for the award of what the Convention terms 'just satisfaction' if the internal law of a State in breach of the Convention allows only partial reparation to be made.

At the final stage of the *Ringeisen* case in 1972 the Austrian Government argued that the judgment of July 1971, in which the Court upheld the applicant's claim that he had been the victim of an excessive period of pre-trial detention contrary to Article 5(3), had closed the proceedings in the case. Consequently, the Court could only entertain a claim for compensation under Article 50 if it was filed with the Commission as a fresh complaint, investigated by the Commission in the usual way and ultimately referred to the Court. The government relied in this connection on Article 52 of the Convention which states that the judgment of the Court is final.

The obvious objection to the argument is that requiring an applicant to go through the whole Convention procedure twice would frustrate the purpose of Article 50 which is to provide an effective remedy for violations. In an unanimous judgment rejecting the government's argument the Court relied on this when it described the purpose of Article 50 as 'to enable the Court to afford without further delay just satisfaction to the person who is a victim of a violation',[36] and explained that Article 52 had no bearing on the case because its purpose is merely to indicate that the Court's judgments are not subject to appeal.

A different means of delaying recourse to Article 50 was put forward by Belgium in the *Vagrancy* cases. The government argued that the applicants' request for just satisfaction was inadmissible on the ground that they had not exhausted their domestic remedies. In the government's submission Article 26 applied not only to the original application but also to any claim for compensation under Article 50. The Court rejected this argument with reasoning analogous to that in the *Ringeisen* case. The applicants' claims were not new petitions, but related solely to the reparation to be awarded for the violations identified earlier. Since the claims under Article 50 had nothing to do with the initiation of proceedings under Article 25, there was no call to exhaust domestic remedies.

In support of its plea of inadmissibility the Belgian Government put forward a second argument based on the terms of Article 50: because the applicants had not exhausted domestic remedies, they had not established that Belgian law allowed 'only partial reparation' for the consequences of the violation, as the Convention requires. Again the Court rejected the argument. In its view if the Convention had been intended to incorporate the domestic remedies requirement in Article 50 it would have said so. In the absence of such an explicit indication there was no room to read in such a limitation as an inference.

In arriving at this conclusion the Court attached considerable importance to the effectiveness of the Convention. For after noting that the inspiration for Article 50 was to be found in earlier treaties which have no connection with the domestic remedies issue, it explained that:

if the victim, after exhausting in vain the domestic remedies before complaining at Strasbourg of a violation of his rights, were obliged to do so a second time before being able to obtain from the Court just satisfaction, the total length of the procedure instituted by the Convention would scarcely be in keeping with the idea of the effective protection of Human Rights. Such a requirement would lead to a situation incompatible with the aim and object of the Convention.[37]

A third attempt to restrict the scope of Article 50 was made – and repulsed – in the *Neumeister* case. Here the question was the relation between the Court's power to award just satisfaction and Article 5(5) which lays down that 'Everyone who has been the victim of arrest or detention in contravention of the provisions of this Article shall have an enforceable right to compensation.' The Austrian Government argued that Article 5(5) was *lex specialis* and provided a special rule for compensation in cases involving freedom of the person. If this was correct, a claim for reparation for a violation of Article 5, such as that in the present case, could not be dealt with in the usual way by a continuation of the proceedings culminating in a decision under Article 50, but required a new application under Article 25, alleging a violation of Article 5(5).

The Court unanimously rejected the government's argument. Observing that Article 5(5) and Article 50 are placed on different levels, the former laying down a rule of substance, the latter a rule of competence, it held that:

while paragraph 5 of Article 5 carefully specifies that 'everyone who has been the victim' of such a breach 'shall have an enforceable right to compensation', it in no way follows therefrom that the Court cannot apply Article 50 when it has found that there has been a breach, for example, of paragraph 3; what does follow, and no more, is that in the exercise of the wide competence conferred upon it by Article 50, the Court must take into consideration among other factors the rule of substance contained in paragraph 5 of Article 5.[38]

As in the cases already considered, the Court regarded the effectiveness of its jurisdiction and specifically of Article 50, as a major consideration. For, the Court stated, acceptance of the Austrian Government's argument:

would lead to consequences incompatible with the aim and object of the Convention. In order to obtain just satisfaction over and above mere recognition of his entitlement to his rights, the victim of a violation of liberty of the person might find himself obliged to lodge two successive petitions with the Commission on each of which the Court or the Committee of Ministers would be called upon, if need be, to rule after a lapse of several years. The system of safeguards set up by the Convention would therefore operate only at an extremely slow pace in the case of Article 5, a situation which would scarcely be in keeping with the idea of the effective protection of human rights.[39]

Passages such as this call to mind the decisions of the International Court in the case concerning *Certain German Interests in Upper Silesia*[40] and the *Corfu Channel* case,[41] in both of which jurisdiction to decide questions of liability was held to carry with it jurisdiction to award compensation. There, too, effectiveness was an important consideration. In this context and elsewhere the International Court has often emphasised that formal or technical considerations must yield to the overriding principle of effectiveness. It is therefore interesting to find the same point being made in the cases on Article 50, in two of which the Court said that 'it would be a formalistic attitude alien to international law to maintain that the Court may not apply Article 50 save on condition that it either rules on the matter in the same judgment which found a violation or that this judgment has expressly kept the case open'.[42]

As regards the Convention specifically, those early decisions on Article 50 are important not for their immediate results, for only in *Ringeisen* was the applicant ultimately successful, but because they removed a number of potential obstacles to victims of violations, thereby creating a possibility of both redress and development of the substantive law. As the extensive case-law on Article 50 now demonstrates,[43] the Court has taken full advantage of this opportunity.

The interpretation of judgments

A final illustration of how the Court's concern for the principle of effectiveness has governed its approach to the Convention system is to be found in the first, and so far the only, case in which it was asked to interpret a judgment. In its second decision in the *Ringeisen* case, as we have just seen, the Court held that it was competent to deal with the applicant's case under Article 50 and awarded him DM 20,000 by way of compensation. The question then arose whether the money should be paid directly to Ringeisen, or whether it might be paid to his trustee in bankruptcy. This was dealt with ambiguously in the judgment and so the Commission requested a further judgment by way of interpretation, asking in particular what the Court's intentions were with respect to the currency and place of payment and the position of other claimants.

The Austrian Government objected to the request, claiming that since the interpretation of judgments is not mentioned in the Convention, it was outside the Court's jurisdiction and inconsistent with Article 52 which lays down that judgments are final. The Court unanimously rejected this submission. Explaining that the object of Article 52 is to exclude the possibility of appeals, it pointed out that a request for the interpretation of a judgment is not an appeal, being addressed to the Court itself. Moreover, 'In considering the request the Court is exercising inherent jurisdiction: it goes no further than to clarify the meaning and scope which it intended to give to a previous decision which issued from its own deliberations, specifying, if need be, what is thereby decided with binding force.'[44] Since such competence was 'in no way irreconcilable' with the Convention, the Court saw no reason why it should not entertain the request. This it then proceeded to do, holding that its earlier judgment meant that the compensation was to be paid to the applicant in German marks, in the Federal Republic of Germany and 'personally and free from attachment'.

However carefully the Court's decisions are drafted, problems of interpretation are bound to arise from time to time. Since a request for
interpretation is the only way in which such problems can be satisfactorily
resolved, use of the concept of inherent jurisdiction to make this possible
is a significant contribution to the Convention's effectiveness. The
decision was a bold one because it ran counter to the widely held view that
an international tribunal has no power to interpret its judgments in the
absence of an express authorisation. The Inter-American Court of
Human Rights, the International Court of Justice and a number of other
tribunals have such an authorisation which reduces the immediate
significance of the decision. It should be noted, however, that the Inter-
American Court referred to the decision in *Ringeisen* when it recently had
to interpret one of its own previous decisions.[45] Moreover, that court has
no express authority to revise a decision. Like the interpretation of
judgments, this is provided for in the Rules of the European Court, and
not the Convention. However, should a request for revision one day be
received, this will no doubt also be treated as an inherent power.

Notes

1 As noted in chapter 1, this situation will change when Protocol No. 9 comes
   into force.
2 Series A, No. 1, p. 10.
3 *Ibid.*, p. 11.
4 *Ibid.*, pp. 11, 12.
5 *Ibid.*, p. 14.
6 *Ibid.*, pp. 15, 16.
7 Series A, No. 5, p. 19.
8 Series A, No. 12 para. 48.
9 *Ibid.*, para. 51.
10 See D. J. Harris, *British Year Book of International Law*, XLVI, 469
   (1972–3).
11 In the *Pine Valley Developments Ltd* case, Series A, No. 222, the Court
   rejected a suggestion from the Commission that it should depart from the
   principle in the *Vagrancy* cases and no longer review the latter's decisions on
   admissibility. Support for the Commission's position was, however, expressed
   by Judges Martens and Morenilla in their dissenting opinions in the *Cardot*
   case, Series A, No. 200, and earlier by Judge Martens in his separate opinion
   in the *Brozicek* case, Series A, No. 167. In the case of *B v France*, Series A,
   No. 232C the *Pine Valley* ruling was confirmed by the plenary Court, although
   on this occasion five judges supported the contrary view.
12 Series A, No. 24.
13 Series A, No. 12 para. 54.
14 Series A, No. 201 para. 99.
15 *Ibid.*
16 *Ibid.*, para. 100.
17 *Ibid.*, dissenting opinion, para. 3.

18 *Ibid.*, para. 5.
19 Series A, No. 28 para. 33.
20 *Ibid.*, para. 34.
21 Series A, No. 31 para. 27. See also the *Norris* case, Series A, No. 142. On the treatment of this issue under the United Nations Covenant see P. R. Ghandhi, 'The Human Rights Committee and the right of individual communication', *British Year Book of International Law*, LVII, 201 at 218–19 (1986).
22 Series A, No. 57 para. 31.
23 Series A, No. 77.
24 *Northern Cameroons* case, [1963] I.C.J. Rep., 3 at 98, 99, separate opinion of Judge Sir Gerald Fitzmaurice.
25 Series A, No. 39 para. 85.
26 Series A, No. 26 para. 26.
27 Series A, No. 25 para. 154.
28 Series A, No. 4, dissenting opinion of Judge Ross, para. 5.
29 *Ibid.*, para. 6.
30 Series A, No. 96 para. 17.
31 *Ibid.*, separate opinion of Judges Matscher and Pinheiro Farinha.
32 Series A, No. 83.
33 Series A, No. 29 para. 36.
34 Series A, No. 89. See also the *Owner's Services Ltd* case, Series A, No. 208.
35 *Ibid.*
36 Series A, No. 15 para. 16.
37 Series A, No. 14 para. 16.
38 Series A, No. 17 para. 30.
39 *Ibid.*
40 *Certain German Interests in Polish Upper Silesia*, Merits, P.C.I.J. Series A, No. 7 (1926).
41 *Corfu Channel*, Assessment of Amount of Compensation, [1949] I.C.J. Rep., 244; and see H. Lauterpacht, *The Development of International Law by the International Court*, Stevens, London, 245–8 (1958).
42 See Series A, No. 17 para. 31.
43 See P. Van Dijk and G. J. H. Van Hoof, *Theory and Practice of the European Convention on Human Rights* (2nd ed.), Kluwer, Deventer, 171–85 (1990); C. D. Gray, 'Remedies for individuals under the European Convention on Human Rights', *Human Rights Review*, VI, 153 (1981); and Christine Gray, *Judicial Remedies in International Law*, Clarendon Press, Oxford, 153–60 (1990).
44 Series A, No. 16 para. 13.
45 *Velasquez Rodriguez* case, Judgment of 17 August 1990, para. 26, *Human Rights Law Journal*, XII, 14 (1991).

CHAPTER 4

The Court's methods of interpretation

The Court's approach to the interpretation and application of the European Convention is the product of two forces. In part it reflects general beliefs about the proper judicial approach to treaty interpretation, a topic of central importance in international law and which, quite apart from the work of the Strasbourg Court, has always featured prominently in the case-law of judicial tribunals. In part, however, the Court's approach stems from a specific conception of the nature of the European Convention and, as a corollary, a particular conception of the judicial role in relation to it. This combination makes the Court's jurisprudence of great interest as a contribution to treaty interpretation in general and human rights law in particular.

The textuality principle

In its judgment in the *Golder* case in 1975 the Court said that it was 'prepared to consider . . . that it should be guided by Articles 31 to 33 of the Vienna Convention of 23 May 1969 on the Law of Treaties. That Convention has not yet entered into force and it specifies, at Article 4, that it will not be retroactive, but its Articles 31 to 33 enunciate in essence generally accepted principles of international law to which the Court has already referred on occasion.'[1] This comment, though directed specifically to the issue with which *Golder* was concerned, describes the Court's treatment of interpretation generally. Though its decisions have been very much influenced by certain characteristics of the European Convention, the Court's approach to interpretation has its basis in the Vienna Convention. Here the starting point is the principle of respect for the text.

The general rule of interpretation, as stated in Article 31(1) of the Vienna Convention, begins 'A treaty shall be interpreted in good faith in accordance with the ordinary meaning to be given to the terms of the treaty in their context and in the light of its object and purpose.' The context is then defined in Article 31(2) as including the text 'including its preamble and annexes' and certain other material. The interpreter is directed to take into account subsequent agreements, subsequent practice and any relevant rules of international law (Article 31(3)). Finally, Article 31(4) of the Convention provides that 'A special meaning shall be given to a term if it is established that the parties so intended.'

In international law, then, the interpretation of a treaty begins with the text of the agreement and the ordinary meaning of its terms. Not surprisingly, therefore, on numerous occasions the Court has employed the concept of ordinary meaning to elucidate the provisions of the Convention. In the *Johnston* case, for example, the Court said that to determine whether the applicants could derive a right to divorce from Article 12, it would 'seek to ascertain the ordinary meaning to be given to the terms of this provision in their context and in the light of its object and purpose',[2] and concluded that it agreed with the Commission that 'the ordinary meaning of the words "right to marry" is clear, in the sense that they cover the formation of marital relationships but not their dissolution'.[3] Similarly in the *Lithgow* case the Court rejected a wide reading of the phrase 'the general principles of international law' in Article 1 of Protocol No. 1 on the ground that 'the words of a treaty should be understood to have their ordinary meaning . . . and to interpret the phrase in question as extending the general principles of international law beyond their normal sphere of applicability is less consistent with the ordinary meaning of the terms used.'[4]

Usually, as in these cases, the Court tends to treat the ordinary meaning of a word or phrase as more or less self-evident and does not elaborate upon it. Occasionally, however, it deals with the matter in detail. In the *Leudicke* case, for instance, which concerned the right to 'the free assistance of an interpreter' in Article 6(3)(e), the judgment includes the following passage:

The Court finds, as did the Commission, that the terms *'gratuitement'*/'free' in Article 6(3)(e) have in themselves a clear and determinate meaning. In French, *'gratuitement'* signifies *'d'une manière gratuite, qu'on donne pour rien, sans rétribution'* (Littré, *Dictionnaire de la langue française*), *'dont on jouit sans payer'* (Hatzfeld *et* Darmesteter, *Dictionnaire général de la langue française*), *'à titre gratuit, sans avoir rien à payer'*, the opposite of *'à titre onéreux'* (Larousse, *Dictionnaire de la langue française*), *'d'une manière gratuite; sans rétribution, sans contrepartie'* (Robert, *Dictionnaire alphabétique et analogique de la langue française)*. Similarly, in English, 'free' means 'without payment, gratuitous' (*Shorter Oxford Dictionary*), 'not costing or charging anything, given or furnished without cost or payment' (Webster's *Third New International Dictionary*). Consequently, the Court cannot but attribute to the terms *'gratuitement'* and 'free' the unqualified meaning they ordinarily have in both of the Court's official languages: these terms denote neither a conditional remission, nor a temporary exemption, nor a suspension, but a once and for all exemption or exoneration.[5]

In this case and many others the ordinary meaning of the crucial term has been a major plank in the Court's reasoning. But although the Court has made extensive use of the concept of ordinary meaning, in respect of some of the most important terms used in the Convention it has gone beyond what might be considered the ordinary meaning and treated them as having a special meaning. This, of course, is in accordance with Article 31(4) of the Vienna Convention, which has already been mentioned. Terms given such a special meaning by the Court are known as 'autonomous concepts' and the process as giving the Convention an 'autonomous interpretation'.

The reasoning which lies behind this approach, and some of its implications, can be seen in the *Engel* case. The applicants were conscripts in the Netherlands' armed forces who had been subject to various penalties for offences against military discipline. In their applications to the Commission they complained *inter alia* that the proceedings against them had been conducted in violation of Article 6, which lays down the procedural requirements in cases involving a 'criminal charge'. Did the proceedings here fall within the article? In the law of the Netherlands the offences concerned were classified as disciplinary, not criminal, but the question, as the Court pointed out, was whether this classification was decisive from the standpoint of the Convention.

The Court held that it was not, and that the term 'criminal charge' must be given an autonomous interpretation. This was because:

If the Contracting States were able at their discretion to classify an offence as disciplinary instead of criminal, or to prosecute the author of a 'mixed' offence on the disciplinary rather than on the criminal plane, the operation of the fundamental clauses of Articles 6 and 7 would be subordinated to their sovereign will. A latitude extending thus far might lead to results incompatible with the purpose and object of the Convention. The Court therefore has jurisdiction under Article 6 and even without reference to Articles 17 and 18, to satisfy itself that the disciplinary does not improperly encroach upon the criminal.[6]

Having decided that the concept of a 'criminal charge' is an autonomous one, the Court then had to establish its own criteria. It decided that the respondent's classification, though not conclusive, was relevant, but that greater importance attached to the nature of the offence and the severity of the penalty. These criteria the Court then applied to the various charges against the applicants, some of which it decided were such as to engage Article 6 while others were not.

To say that a concept such as 'criminal charge' exists independently of its classification in a particular legal system does not mean that such classification, along with those of the other Contracting States, has no bearing on its meaning. Indeed, it is difficult to see how an autonomous meaning can be arrived at in a case like *Engel* except by reference to national systems of classification and the Court has often made this point in its decisions. On the other hand, as one judge has noted, 'reliance on this method of interpretation raises problems of legal hermeneutics which are far more complex than one might at first suppose'.[7] Involving, as it does, a degree of judicial initiative, it is a method which can easily lay the Court open to criticism. The difficulties encountered in giving an autonomous interpretation to another aspect of Article 6 illustrate this situation.

The protection of Article 6 is not limited to cases involving a criminal charge, but also covers those involving 'the determination of civil rights and obligations'. Here also the Court has chosen to treat the concept as autonomous and again has had to formulate its own criteria. This has produced very considerable problems. In the *König* case, for example, the applicant's complaint concerned his unsuccessful attempt to challenge the withdrawal of his right to run a clinic. His case was heard by a West German administrative court and the European Court had to decide whether the proceedings in question had related to civil rights and obligations.

The Court decided that they had, essentially on the ground that in the Federal Republic a doctor's relations with his patient are of a private law character, being contractually based. Judge Matscher, however, disagreed with this conclusion which he considered ignored the public law aspect of the issue of professional status which he saw as the heart of the case. Agreeing that an autonomous interpretation of 'civil rights and obligations' was called for, Judge Matscher suggested that the Court's wide interpretation of the phrase might be regarded as going beyond autonomous interpretation and 'venturing into the field of legislative policy'.[8] This, it is suggested, points to the true significance of these cases. Detaching the Convention's concepts from those of domestic law is a major step. Autonomous interpretation is a kind of judicial legislation and as such calls for a decision as to how far the Court will go.[9]

Interpretation of the Convention as a whole

When the Court interprets the Convention by employing the concepts of ordinary or autonomous meaning, it does not treat the words in question in isolation, but considers them in context and against the background of the object and purpose of the treaty. This again is what the Vienna Convention requires: respect for the text and an awareness of the usual signification of the words used without prejudice to other aids to interpretation. Or, as the Court has put it: 'In the way in which it is presented in the "general rule" in Article 31 of the Vienna Convention, the process of interpretation of a treaty is a unity, a single combined operation; this rule, closely integrated, places on the same footing the various elements enumerated in the four paragraphs of the Article.'[10]

Interesting issues of contextual interpretation are raised by cases in which the Court has to consider the relation between different parts of the Convention. For the Court often has to decide whether a matter should be regarded as covered by one provision exclusively, or whether, in addition, other articles may be relevant. In handling this kind of case the Court has been guided by the principle that 'the Convention and its Protocols must be read as a whole.' From this it has drawn the conclusion that 'a matter dealt with mainly by one of their provisions may also, in some of its aspects, be subject to other provisions thereof'.[11] Thus in the *Abdulaziz*[12] case, which concerned British immigration legislation, the Court rejected the government's argument that immigration matters are governed exclusively by Protocol No. 4 and accepted the applicants' argument that where there is interference with the right to respect for family life, the case can also be considered under Article 8. Similarly, in the *Rasmussen*[13] case, which concerned the right to contest paternity under Danish law, the Court held that the case fell within Article 8 because it concerned the applicant's private life, notwithstanding the fact that the rights of parents with regard to their children are expressly provided for in Article 5 of Protocol No. 7.

The relation between different parts of the Convention can give rise to problems in relation to any of its articles, but is particularly critical in cases like *Rasmussen* and *Abdulaziz* where the subject-matter is governed by a protocol which the respondent has still to accept. The State will argue that the matter is governed exclusively by the protocol. The applicant, naturally, will try to find an article by which the respondent is bound and then argue that the matter is governed by both provisions.

A case which demonstrates the difficulties of this situation is *Guzzardi*[14] which raised the question of the relation between Article 5(1), which guarantees the right to liberty, and Article 2(1) of Protocol No. 4, which guarantees freedom of movement. The applicant was a member of the Mafia with a substantial criminal record. In 1973 he was arrested, charged with various criminal offences and placed in detention on remand. Under Italian law the maximum period of such detention is two years, but particularly dangerous persons can be ordered to live in a specified district under police supervision. Accordingly, in January 1975, on the application of the local Chief of Police, the Milan Regional Court ordered Guzzardi to reside on the small island of Asinara, where he was compelled to stay until he was returned to the mainland in July of the following year. He was eventually convicted of terrorist offences and sentenced to eighteen years' imprisonment.

The question for the European Court was whether Guzzardi's confinement on Asinara was a breach of the Convention. Since Italy had not accepted Protocol No. 4, this turned on whether there was a violation of Article 5(1) which proved to be contentious. Though prepared to acknowledge that to constitute an infringement of Article 5(1) there must be something over and above a mere restriction on liberty of movement, the Court eventually decided that taken cumulatively and in combination the circumstances of the applicant's confinement were indeed such as to deprive him of his right to liberty. From this conclusion, which was supported by a majority of eleven to seven, the Court went on to decide by different majorities that the said deprivation of liberty could not be justified. A majority of the Court thus found that Guzzardi had been denied his rights under the Convention and ordered the Italian Government to pay him one million lire by way of compensation.

Sir Gerald Fitzmaurice, who was one of the dissenting judges, disagreed with this result and held that the Court had interpreted Article 5(1) too broadly. In his view the cardinal point was that liberty of movement and freedom to choose one's residence are the subject of express guarantees in Article 2(1) of Protocol No. 4. The inclusion of that provision, said Fitzmaurice, indicated that Article 5 was intended to have a limited scope, providing protection against imprisonment or very close confinement, but not against restrictions on movement or place of residence falling short of that. Thus it was necessary to reject the broad interpretation of Article 5, proposed by the applicant, because it would create an unnecessary overlap with the protocol and supply an improper means of subjecting the Italian Government, and others which had not accepted the protocol, to an obligation they were not yet ready to assume.

The difference between this narrow reading of Article 5 and the broader reading of the majority rests on different conceptions of the purpose of the Convention. Whereas the majority was prepared to treat the relevant provisions of the Convention and protocol as almost coextensive, thereby enhancing the applicant's protection, Fitzmaurice, always an advocate of restraint, had no doubt that when the circumstances of confinement produced a borderline case, the government should be given the benefit of the doubt.

In general it can be said that when the question is whether a particular article is applicable, the presence of another article dealing with the subject is not a conclusive objection. Because the Convention must be read as a whole, the same subject may sometimes fall to be considered under more than one rubric. Two qualifications to this policy, stemming from the self-same principle of contextual interpretation, must now be mentioned.

The first is that the Court will not permit one article of the Convention to be used in a way which undermines or neutralises the effect of another. In other words, where a matter is covered by one provision, the Court may be prepared to recognise that another has a bearing on the matter, but not if such an interpretation would render the main provision nugatory. A good example of this kind of situation is to be found in the *Leander* case. The applicant, who was refused employment near a Swedish naval base on the basis of information held in a secret police register, argued unsuccessfully that he had been the victim of a breach of Article 8. He then sought to argue that because the crucial information had been withheld from him, he had been denied an effective remedy before a national authority as required by Article 13. The Court, however, rejected the argument, on the following reasoning:

The Court has held that Article 8 did not in the circumstances require the communication to Mr Leander of the information on him released by the National Police Board . . . . The Convention is to be read as a whole and therefore, as the Commission recalled in its report, any interpretation of Article 13 must be in harmony with the logic of the Convention. Consequently, the Court, consistently with its conclusion concerning Article 8, holds that the lack of communication of this information does not, of itself and in the circumstances of the case, entail a breach of Article 13.[15]

The second situation, in which the Court may be expected to decide that a matter is, in effect, governed exclusively by one article, is a corollary of the first. It is the situation which arises when it is clear that a particular right was omitted from one article of the Convention, but the Court is pressed with the argument that it should be given protection elsewhere. This question arose in the *Johnston* case, where it was argued that although the right to obtain a divorce might not be covered by Article 12, it could nevertheless be read into Article 8. The Court rejected the argument on the ground that 'the Convention must be read as a whole' and observed that 'the Court does not consider that a right to divorce, which it has found to be excluded from Article 12 . . . can, with consistency, be derived from Article 8, a provision of more general purpose and scope.'[16]

The conclusion in *Johnston* is in no way surprising. It would have really been a very radical step to read the right in question into Article 8. Moreover, although the Court may be expected to reach the same conclusion whenever it is sought to read rights which were deliberately omitted from one article into another, the principle here should not be over-stated. In the *Kosiek* case, for example, which concerned the dismissal of a civil servant in the Federal Republic of Germany, the Court pointed out that the Convention does not confer a right of recruitment to the civil service and found this to be a deliberate omission from the Convention. Observing, however, that 'it does not follow that in other respects civil servants fall outside the scope of the Convention',[17] the Court proceeded to consider whether the circumstances were such as to raise an issue under Article 10.

Object and purpose

Because the Convention makes unique inroads into States' domestic jurisdiction, some have argued that it requires a very cautious interpretation. Thus a leading exponent of the cautious approach maintained that the factors which distinguish the Convention from other treaties:

> could justify even a somewhat restrictive interpretation of the Convention but, without going as far as that, they must be said, unquestionably, not only to justify, but positively to demand, a cautious and conservative interpretation, particularly as regards any provisions the meaning of which may be uncertain, and where extensive construction might have the effect of imposing upon the contracting States obligations they had not really meant to assume, or would not have understood themselves to be assuming. . . . Any serious doubt must therefore be resolved in favour of, rather than against, the government concerned.[18]

However, this view has not been endorsed and the Court has adopted a much less restrictive view.

In its judgment in the *Wemhoff* case in 1968 the Court said that it was necessary 'to seek the interpretation that is most appropriate in order to realise the aim and achieve the object of the treaty, not that which would restrict to the greatest possible degree the obligations undertaken by the Parties'.[19] This policy, which has been consistently reflected in the Court's practice, is a further indication of the way in which its approach to interpretation seeks to follow the Vienna Convention. This, it will be recalled, lays down in Article 31(1) that a treaty is to be interpreted in accordance with the ordinary meaning of the terms in their context and in the light of its object and purpose. Interpreting a text therefore involves more than looking up the meanings of words in a dictionary. Treaties are drawn up with certain purposes in mind and a responsible interpreter must have regard to those purposes when deciding what the treaty means.

Although the relevance of object and purpose to treaty interpretation is generally recognised, how these may be established is a matter of some controversy.[20] One school of thought, who for convenience may be termed teleologists, asserts that the terms of a treaty may be both interpreted and supplemented by reference to its object and purposes as ascertained by the interpreter from the treaty itself or other evidence. The other school of thought, whom we may call textualists, takes a stricter view. To them the source of the interpreter's authority is the text and while the object of the treaty is a relevant consideration, it must be presumed to be reflected in the words used and may not be sought elsewhere. It follows that on this view there can be no question of supplementing the text by, as it were, adding words which might improve it, or more truly reflect what the parties had, or might have had, or ought to have had, in mind.

The difference between the teleological school and the textualist school is important but should not be exaggerated. It has been pointed out that the teleological approach is an application in extended form of a principle of interpretation which all textualists would accept, namely the principle of effectiveness. This states that 'particular provisions are to be interpreted so as to give them their fullest weight and effect consistent with the normal sense of the words and with other parts of the text, and in such a way that a reason and a meaning can be attributed to every part of the text'.[21] Thus the question here is essentially one of emphasis: whether, as the textualists assert, an effective interpretation must always proceed from the text, or as the teleologists maintain, the interpreter is authorised to engage in a measure of judicial legislation and in order to make an agreement effective can take into account object and purpose in a wider way.

Between these two approaches the Court has sought to steer something of a middle way. On the one hand, it has consistently emphasised that it is interpreting a text and, as we have seen, regularly relies on the ordinary meaning of the Convention's terms in their context. On the other, it has emphasised that the object of the Convention should be seen as the protection of individual rights and through autonomous interpretation and in other ways has sought to give it an effective interpretation in accordance with that broad aim.

The point may be illustrated by the Court's adoption of the principle that because the object of the Convention is to protect individual rights, where an article provides for the limitation or qualification of a right, such restrictions are to be narrowly construed. In the *Klass* case, for example, where the question was whether arrangements for secret surveillance could be justified under Article 8(2), the Court ruled that 'This paragraph since it provides for an exception to a right guaranteed by the Convention is to be narrowly construed.'[22] Similarly, in the *Sunday Times* case, where the question was whether an injunction restraining publication of a newspaper report could be justified under Article 10(2) as 'necessary . . . for maintaining the authority . . . of the judiciary', the Court held that it was 'faced not with a choice between two conflicting principles but with a principle of freedom of expression that is subject to a number of exceptions which must be narrowly interpreted'.[23] The significance of this ruling is made clear in the joint dissenting judgment in which nine members of the Court held that the case did require a balance to be struck between conflicting principles and on this basis exonerated the British

Government. To the majority, on the other hand, the individual interest was paramount, the limited exception did not apply and so the Convention had been violated.

In addition to the reference in Article 31(1), another reference to object and purpose is to be found in Article 33 of the Vienna Convention. This deals with the interpretation of treaties authenticated in two or more languages and is relevant because the French and English texts of the European Convention are equally authentic. Article 33(4) provides for the situation in which a comparison of the authentic texts discloses a difference of meaning which the application of Articles 31 and 32 does not remove. In such a case the interpreter is instructed to adopt 'the meaning which best reconciles the texts, having regard to the object and purpose of the treaty'.

The Court has made use of Article 33(4) on a number of occasions. In the *James* case, for example, it adopted a broad interpretation of the phrase 'in the public interest' in Article 1 of Protocol No. 1, which it justified by saying 'The Court, like the Commission, considers that such an interpretation best reconciles the language of the English and French texts, having regard to the object and purpose of Article 1 . . . which is primarily to guard against arbitrary confiscation of property.'[24] Similarly, in the *Sunday Times* case when called upon to interpret the phrase 'prescribed by law' in Article 10(2), the Court considered the French text and cited the Vienna Convention as authority for the proposition that when 'confronted with versions of a law-making treaty which are equally authentic but not exactly the same, the Court must interpret them in a way that reconciles them as far as possible and is most appropriate in order to realise the aim and achieve the object of the treaty'.[25]

The Convention as a living instrument

Article 3 of the Convention provides that 'No one shall be subjected to torture or to inhuman or degrading treatment or punishment.' A question which arises in interpreting this, and many other provisions, is what criteria are relevant in deciding whether the Convention's prohibition has been violated? How, for example, is the Court to decide whether a person has been subjected to 'degrading' punishment?

Two approaches to the interpretation of such provisions are possible. One view is that when the text of the Convention was adopted in 1950 the governments concerned had a particular idea of what could constitute degrading punishment and intended Article 3 to embody that conception. The other view is that although governments doubtless had their own ideas on the subject, they included a general reference to the concept of degrading punishment so that when the time came to interpret the Convention, the Commission and the Court would be able to look beyond the particular conceptions of 1950 and take into account contemporary ideas.[26]

In the *Tyrer* case in 1978 the Court expressly endorsed the view that Article 3 is to be interpreted as embodying the concept of inhuman and degrading punishment, rather than any conception which may have been held in 1950 and, more importantly, indicated that it would be prepared to take a similar approach to other parts of the Convention. The question in *Tyrer* was whether the birching of a juvenile in the Isle of Man violated Article 3 and specifically whether it constituted degrading punishment. In deciding this question the Court said it must:

recall that the Convention is a living instrument which, as the Commission rightly stressed, must be interpreted in the light of present-day conditions. In the case now before it the Court cannot but be influenced by the developments and commonly accepted standards in the penal policy of the member States of the Council of Europe in this field. Indeed, the Attorney-General for the Isle of Man mentioned that, for many years, the provisions of Manx legislation concerning judicial corporal punishment had been under review.[27]

In the light of these factors and taking account of the nature and context of the punishment and the manner and method of its execution, the Court had no hesitation in concluding that birching did violate Article 3.

Whatever one's opinion of the actual decision in *Tyrer*, the view that the Convention should be interpreted by reference to current conditions is clearly well justified. Where those who drafted the Convention intended it to embody a particular conception, as with the right to a fair trial in Article 6, the conception is elaborated so as to make this clear. Where, on the other hand, the Convention is in general terms, it is plainly the concept which is referred to with the scope for judicial development which that entails. Thus, to take another example, Article 5(1)(e) of the Convention provides that one of the cases in which deprivation of liberty is permitted is the lawful detention of 'persons of unsound mind'. In the absence of a definition of this term the Court rightly concluded in the *Winterwerp* case that:

This term is not one that can be given a definitive interpretation: as was pointed out by the Commission, the Government and the applicant, it is a term whose meaning is continually evolving as research in psychiatry progresses, an increasing flexibility in treatment is developing and society's attitude to mental illness changes, in particular so that a greater understanding of the problems of mental patients is becoming more widespread.[28]

Although the principle that the Convention must be interpreted as a 'living instrument' is now generally accepted, deciding what interpretation is appropriate in modern conditions can raise difficult questions of judicial policy. The decision, of course, must not be arbitrary, or a reflection of the judge's personal preferences, but as the cases already mentioned indicate, is supposed to reflect current conceptions of the matter in hand. In this respect judicial corporal punishment and mental illness seem relatively straightforward. Other cases, however, may be much more difficult.

One danger is that the Court may find itself anticipating developments before they have occurred. Thus, the Court may rule that a particular interpretation is needed to reflect the current situation, but critics may argue that its real motive is to encourage or promote a tendency which has yet to become firmly established. In the *Marckx* case, for example, the Court had to decide whether Belgian legislation which drew certain distinctions between legitimate and illegitimate children contravened the right to respect for family life guaranteed by Article 8. The Court held that it did, on the ground that although such a distinction was traditional, the 'Convention must be interpreted in the light of present-day conditions'. In this respect, said the Court, it could not 'but be struck by the fact that the domestic law of the great majority of the member States of the Council of Europe has evolved and is continuing to evolve, in company with the relevant international instruments, towards full juridical recognition of the maxim *"mater semper certa est"* '.[29] But, as we shall see in chapter 9, reference to the international instruments in question suggests that the Court's identification of the trend described may have been premature.

There is, however, also the possibility of making the opposite mistake and refusing to recognise that changes have occurred which make an evolutive interpretation necessary. The Court was faced with this kind of criticism in the *Cossey* case. Here the applicant was a male-to-female transsexual who claimed that as English law put her at a disadvantage in various ways, she had suffered a violation of her rights under Articles 8 and 12. The Court decided that neither provision had been infringed, but eight judges dissented on the issue of Article 8 and four as regards Article 12. Emphasising that 'the status of transsexuals is one where legal solutions necessarily follow medical, social and moral developments in society',[30] the dissenting judges maintained that since the Court's earlier decision in the *Rees* case,[31] there had been 'clear developments' in the laws of the Contracting States which demanded a fresh approach. The majority, on the other hand, pointed to the continuing diversity of national practice, which they considered favoured a wide margin of appreciation for States in relation to Article 8, and as regards Article 12 found that 'the developments which have occurred to date . . . cannot be said to evidence any general abandonment of the traditional concept of marriage'.[32]

Conscious of the problem of reconciling continuity with the need for change, which is essentially the challenge in cases on evolutive interpretation, the Court has sometimes sought to accommodate both points of view in its judgments. Thus in the *Marckx* case, although the Court held that Belgian law violated Article 8, it acknowledged that:

differences of treatment between 'legitimate' and 'illegitimate' children, for example, in the matter of patrimonial rights, were for many years regarded as permissible and normal in a large number of Contracting States. . . . Evolution towards equality has been slow and reliance on the Convention to accelerate this evolution was apparently contemplated at a rather late stage.[33]

In these circumstances the Court held that Belgium was not required to reopen legal acts or situations antedating the Court's judgment.

Conversely, in the *Rees* case the Court decided that the position of transsexuals under the law of the United Kingdom did not violate Article 8; but then added that it was:

conscious of the seriousness of the problems affecting these persons and the distress they suffer. The Convention always has to be interpreted and applied in the light of current circumstances. . . . The need for appropriate legal measures should therefore be kept under review having regard particularly to scientific and societal developments.[34]

This observation, repeated in *Cossey*, was a strong hint that while British practice currently satisfied Article 8, the Court's duty to interpret the Convention as a living instrument may lead it to a different conclusion in the future.

Subsequent practice

Closely related to the idea of the Convention as a living instrument is the possibility of interpreting its provisions by reference to the Contracting States' subsequent practice. Article 31(3)(b) of the Vienna Convention authorises an interpreter to take into account, together with the context, 'any subsequent practice in the application of the treaty which establishes the agreement of the parties regarding its interpretation'. This is therefore a well-recognised aid to interpretation and, as might be expected, has been relied on in argument before the Court on a number of occasions.

One of the issues in the *Soering* case was whether in view of evolving practice in Western Europe the death penalty could be held to constitute an inhuman and degrading punishment, contrary to Article 3 of the Convention, despite the fact that Article 2(1), which protects the right to life, expressly permits judicial executions. After observing that the Convention must be read as a whole, the Court noted that 'On this basis Article 3 evidently cannot have been intended by the drafters of the Convention to include a general prohibition of the death penalty since that would nullify the clear wording of Article 2(1)'. However, it then went on:

Subsequent practice in national penal policy, in the form of a generalised abolition of capital punishment, could be taken as establishing the agreement of the Contracting States to abrogate the exception provided for under Article 2(1) and hence to remove a textual limit on the scope for evolutive interpretation of Article 3.[35]

Did this mean that the death penalty must now be held to violate Article 3? The answer was no, because a further factor had to be taken into account. Protocol No. 6 expressly provides for the abolition of the death penalty in time of peace and enables States which wish to do so to renounce capital punishment as a legal obligation. It followed, said the Court that:

the intention of the Contracting Parties . . . was to adopt the normal method of amendment of the text in order to introduce a new obligation . . . . In these conditions, notwithstanding the special character of the Convention . . . Article 3 cannot be interpreted as generally prohibiting the death penalty.[36]

Although the Court decided that subsequent practice had not had the effect of modifying the Convention, the suggestion that without Protocol No. 6 it might have done so is a striking and somewhat questionable view of the power of subsequent practice. While there is no objection in principle to the idea of a provision such as Article 2(1) being abrogated by subsequent practice, before such a conclusion could be drawn there would have to be evidence, firstly that all Contracting States had abolished the death penalty (which was not the case in 1989) and secondly that they had not only abolished it, but also recognised that they had no right to reintroduce it, should they ever wish to do so. Since this second requirement, like the first, was clearly not fulfilled at the time of *Soering*, the conclusion must be that the Court's *obiter dictum* on abrogation went beyond anything which can be justified under the Vienna Convention.

In the *Cruz Varas* case, which was decided less than two years after *Soering*, the Court had to consider the significance of subsequent practice in a procedural context and on this occasion adopted a more cautious view. As noted in chapter 3, the Commission is entitled under Rule 36 of its Rules of Procedure to indicate 'any interim measure the adoption of which seems desirable in the interests of the parties or the proper conduct of the proceedings before it'. One of the questions in *Cruz Varas* was whether such measures could be regarded as binding when the Convention itself is silent on the matter. The applicants and the Commission maintained that they could, at least in certain circumstances, and relied *inter alia* on the fact that whenever the Commission has exercised this power the Contracting States have almost always complied with the Commission's indications. To decide this point the Court had therefore to decide what weight should be given to subsequent practice.

The Court acknowledged that 'The practice of Contracting States in this area shows that there has been almost total compliance with Rule 36 indications'. There was consequently no doubt that the practice in question had been established. It also recognised that in principle 'Subsequent practice could be taken as establishing the agreement of Contracting States regarding the interpretation of a Convention provision' and relied, as authority for this proposition, on the Vienna Convention and its own observations in the *Soering* case. However, the Court again rejected the applicants' argument, giving as its reason here the maxim that subsequent practice cannot 'create new rights and obligations which were not included in the Convention at the outset'.[37]

This restrictive view sits uneasily with the Court's view in *Soering* that subsequent practice is capable of abrogating a power expressly reserved in the Convention, for the latter plainly has the effect of creating new obligations. It should be pointed out, however, that in *Cruz Varas* the Court said that it found its view confirmed by discussions of the issue of interim measures in the Council of Europe which, in its opinion, demonstrated that 'the practice of complying with Rule 36 indications cannot have been based on a belief that these indications gave rise to a binding obligation'.[38] This, it is suggested, is a more convincing point. There should be no question of identifying new obligations on the basis of practice in the absence of *opinio juris* and *a fortiori* where there is evidence of *opinio non juris*. In *Soering*, as we have seen, the Court recognised this when it emphasised the significance of Protocol No. 6. In *Cruz Varas*, similarly, it meant that practice alone carried little weight.

In the cases considered so far the subsequent practice relied on was quite general and so the issue was whether it could be regarded as legally significant. In the final case to be mentioned the subsequent practice was more limited. In the *Belilos* case the Court was required to decide as a preliminary issue whether a declaration purporting to limit Switzerland's obligations under Article 6(1) of the Convention satisfied the requirements of Article 64(2) which provides that reservations must contain 'a brief statement of the law concerned'. The Swiss declaration contained no such statement and *prima facie* violated this requirement. However, the government maintained that this was unimportant because a very flexible practice 'had evolved with the tacit consent of the depository and of the other Contracting States'.[39] In this connection it referred to a reservation by Ireland to Article 6(3)(c) and a declaration by Malta in respect of Article 6(2), neither of which contained the statement mentioned in Article 64(2).

The government's argument relied on various other considerations, but was clearly based in part on subsequent practice. The Court, however, rejected it and, as we shall see in the next chapter, insisted on a strict application of the conditions laid down in the Convention. As the Court did not address the issue of subsequent practice specifically, the decision is of limited usefulness in the present context, but two comments ought perhaps to be made, one related to the particular facts, the other of a more general nature.

The particular comment is that the practice in this case was plainly insufficient to provide anything more than a modicum of support to an argument about the interpretation of Article 64 resting on other considerations. Bearing in mind that the government's argument was that clear words in the Convention should be disregarded, only something in the nature of widespread practice could have sufficed to prove its case, since only that would be enough in such circumstances to establish 'the agreement of the parties regarding its interpretation, as the Vienna Convention requires.

The general point is that whatever the extent of practice, the Court is bound to be influenced in cases such as these by the nature of the issue and the consequences of its decision. In *Soering* it was easy for the Court at least to envisage how practice might modify the Convention because a modification of the kind suggested would support its declared policy of evolutive interpretation. In *Cruz Varas*, on the other hand, the Court saw itself as being invited to read a significant new obligation into the Convention, while in *Belilos* the question was whether the article on reservations, which the Court saw as embodying vital safeguards, was to be relaxed. Perhaps therefore it is not surprising that in the former it was disinclined to make much of subsequent practice, while in the latter it found it unnecessary even to discuss the issue of subsequent practice in the judgment.

Implied terms

Treaties, like domestic contracts, cannot cater expressly for everything which may reasonably be regarded as falling within their terms. Foresight is limited, the bounds of acceptable conduct change and even if the future could in some way be anticipated, those responsible for drafting international agreements and securing the necessary consent to their terms can afford neither the time nor the effort to try to provide for every contingency. In treaty law, then, as in the law of contract, it is sometimes necessary to supplement the express provisions of an agreement through recourse to the expedient of an implied term.

Although implied terms are unavoidable if the interpretation of agreements is to produce sensible results, how far the interpreter may go in this direction is always likely to be controversial. Interpreting a treaty is one thing, rewriting it another, and if excessive caution is likely to produce decisions with no regard for the purpose of the agreement, excessive zeal turns the judge into a legislator, abusing his authority as interpreter to impose on the parties an agreement they never made. Thus the issue of implied terms raises in an acute form the question posed in our earlier discussion, namely the limits of legitimate interpretation. In relation to the European Convention, implied terms assume two forms: implied rights and implied limitations.

Implied rights

The leading case on implied rights is *Golder* which arose out of a refusal by the British Home Secretary to allow the applicant, serving a sentence of imprisonment, to consult a solicitor with a view to initiating libel proceedings against a prison officer. In its report the Commission expressed the view that the facts disclosed a breach of Article 6(1) and Article 8, and the Court upheld the Commission's conclusions on both points. The interest of the case lies in the decision on Article 6(1) which, as the Court admitted, does not state a right of access to the courts in express terms, but which, it held, does so by implication.

To reach this conclusion the Court relied on a variety of considerations including the French text, general principles of law and the rules of international law. The key factor, however, was the reference in the Preamble to the rule of law and the references to the same concept in the Statute of the Council of Europe. Finding that if Article 6(1) were concerned exclusively with the conduct of an action, as the government argued, it would be open to a State to abolish its courts altogether, the Court held that it would be inconceivable that the Convention 'should describe in detail the procedural guarantees afforded to parties in a pending lawsuit and should not first protect that which alone makes it in fact possible to benefit from such guarantees, that is, access to a court'.[40] From this, said the Court, it followed that 'the right of access constitutes an element which is inherent in the right stated in Article 6(1)'[41] and which could therefore be properly implied therein.

The Court stated that the above conclusion was 'not an extensive interpretation forcing new obligations on the Contracting States', but one which was 'based on the very terms of the first sentence of Article 6(1) read in its context and having regard to the object and purpose of the Convention'.[42] It is, with respect, difficult to agree. The three judges who dissented on this point certainly saw the decision as a step of major significance and gave a number of reasons for thinking that in reading a right of access into Article 6 the Court had gone too far.

The thrust of their argument was that according to the Preamble the Contracting States had drawn up the Convention to protect 'certain of the Rights stated in the Universal Declaration', those being, according to Article 1, 'the rights and freedoms defined in Section 1 of the Convention'. It followed that the Court's powers were limited to the application of the rights as so defined and could not be extended to other unstated rights by means of what Judge Verdross called 'clues' to their existence derived from other parts of the Convention. It is important to note that this approach did not have the effect of excluding the possibility of implied rights altogether, for, as one judge stated, rights which were necessary inferences could be implied. In the present case, however, the Court had confused 'necessary' with 'desirable' and had therefore, in their view, exceeded the legitimate bounds of interpretation.

Although *Golder* is certainly the most prominent case in which the Court has had to consider the concepts of implied rights, it is by no means the only one. In the *James* case in 1986 the Court was for the first time called upon to decide an important point concerning the scope of Article 1 of Protocol No. 1 which provides that 'No one shall be deprived of his possessions except in the public interest and subject to the conditions provided for by law.' The question was whether the availability and amount of compensation are material considerations when property is expropriated. The Convention is silent on the point and so the question, as in *Golder*, was whether an unstated right could be implied.

The Court decided that it could, explaining that compensation is usually provided under the legal systems of the Contracting States and holding that 'As far as Article 1 is concerned, the protection of the right of property it affords would be largely illusory and ineffective in the absence of any equivalent principle'. As for the standard of compensation required, here the Court held that the effect of the implied right was that 'the taking of property without payment of an amount reasonably related to its value would normally constitute a disproportionate interference which could not be considered justifiable under Article 1'.[43]

In *Golder* and *James* the Court, albeit with some discordant voices,[44] decided that a right claimed by the applicant, though unstated, could be implied. In other cases it has reached the opposite conclusion. A number of cases involving Article 11 illustrate this type of situation.

Article 11(1) lays down that 'Everyone has the right to freedom of peaceful assembly and to freedom of association with others, including the right to form and to join trade unions for the protection of his interests'. In the *National Union of Belgian Police* case, as in many of the cases involving Article 11, the issue concerned trade union rights. The applicant union complained that the Belgian Government had refused to classify it as a 'representative' trade union, with the right to be consulted on such questions as recruitment, promotion and pay. Could it be said that Article 11 implies a right to be consulted? The Court decided unanimously that it could not and rejected the view of a majority of the Commission that the right to be consulted is a necessary condition of effective trade union activity. As the Court noted:

while Article 11(1) presents trade union freedom as one form or a special aspect of freedom of association, the Article does not guarantee any particular treatment of trade unions, or their members, by the State, such as the right to be consulted by it. Not only is this latter right not mentioned in Article 11(1), but neither can it be said that all the Contracting States in general incorporate it in their national law or practice, or that it is indispensable for the effective enjoyment of trade union freedom. It is thus not an element necessarily inherent in a right guaranteed by the Convention, which distinguishes it from the 'right to a court' embodied in Article 6.[45]

In the *Swedish Engine Drivers Union* case[46] the Court employed identical reasoning when it rejected the submission that the State as employer was under an obligation to enter into a collective agreement with the applicant trade union, and in the *Schmidt and Dahlstrom* case,[47] it reached the same conclusion on the issue of the legitimacy of a policy whereby benefits were denied to the non-striking members of unions engaged in industrial action. In all three cases, as we shall see in chapter 9, the Court attached importance to the absence of the right claimed from the European Social Charter and was careful to explain the kind of conduct which might violate Article 11.

The contrast between the cases in which the Court has acceded to the argument that an unstated right should be implied and those in which it has not, demonstrates the extent to which the Court is prepared to use a broad conception of the object and purpose of the Convention as a guiding principle in its interpretation. Where the Court has accepted the argument, it has identified the right concerned as an integral part of the Convention and essential to its effectiveness. Where it has not, it has perceived the right as something extraneous. In both situations the Court has been influenced both by what may be termed the internal logic of the Convention and the status of the asserted right in domestic and international law generally.

The cases also bring out the point that if the Court is prepared to imply a right, it must then define it. Moreover, because the right is implied rather than express, the Court cannot derive much assistance from the text of the Convention. In *Golder* the dissenting judges saw this as a major objection, but here, and in *James*, the Court, having, as it were, accepted the legislator's mantle, was prepared to assume its burdens. In the Article 11 cases, on the other hand, the conclusion that the rights asserted are not an inherent part of the Convention was no doubt fortified by the thought that the opposite decision would require the Court to spell out a whole code of industrial law. This it did not feel called upon to do, in view of the existence of another instrument dealing with these matters expressly.

Implied limitations

The factors which in some cases compel the Court to consider implying certain rights into the Convention, in others require it to contemplate implied limitations. A situation in which this need is particularly apparent is where the Court is concerned to establish the scope of a right which is itself implied. By definition such rights are not explicitly circumscribed by the Convention and so, as we have seen, it is for the Court to determine their limits. Implying a right may therefore involve implying restrictions upon it.

The above point was freely acknowledged in the *Golder* case. For there, having read a right of access to the courts into Article 6, the Court went on to hold that:

the right of access to the courts is not absolute. As this is a right which the Convention sets forth . . . without in the narrower sense of the term, defining, there is room, apart from the bounds delimiting the very content of any right, for limitations permitted by implication.[48]

Similarly, in *Mathieu-Mohin and Clerfayt*, which was the first case to raise an issue under Article 3 of Protocol No. 1, the Court said of the rights implied by the obligation 'to hold free elections' that 'The rights in question are not absolute. Since Article 3 recognises them without setting them forth in express terms, let alone defining them, there is room for implied limitations.'[49]

Implied limitations are not confined to implied rights and may also be required in respect of certain rights which are expressly defined in the Convention. Some rights, such as the right to education, are stated in absolute terms. However, this does not mean that they can be regarded as unqualified. Indeed, it would be absurd to do so. Yet such qualifications being implied, not express, must again come from the interpreter and will reflect his view of the Convention. Thus limitations on express rights, like limitations on implied rights and implied rights themselves, thrust the Court into a legislative role and call for consideration of the object and purpose of the Convention.

The *Belgian Linguistics* case illustrates this aspect of the Court's activity. That case concerned the right to education which is set out in unqualified terms in Article 2 of Protocol No. 1. In its judgment in the case, which raised difficult questions on the Belgian laws governing the use of languages in education, the Court accepted that the right must be qualified and said:

The right to education . . . by its very nature calls for regulation by the States, regulation which may vary in time and place according to the needs and resources of the community and of individuals. It goes without saying that such regulation must never injure the substance of the right to education nor conflict with other rights enshrined in the Convention.[50]

When implied limitations are found to be necessary their effect must be determined. In both the *Belgian Linguistics* case and *Mathieu-Mohin and Clerfayt*, having identified a need for implied limitations, the Court went on to hold that the national authorities had not gone beyond what was permitted by the Convention. These are decisions which reflect the Court's assessment of the latitude available in respect of the rights involved and the facts of the particular cases. Implied limitations are, of course, in no sense a guaranteed defence. Thus in the *Golder* case the Court accepted the idea of implied limitations on the right of access to a court, only to conclude that in the circumstances of the case the applicant's rights under Article 6 had been violated.

Whether there is room for the concept of implied limitations in respect of rights which are both defined and qualified by the Convention is a question on which there has been an important change of view. In a number of early cases involving prisoners' correspondence the Commission held that certain forms of restriction were an 'inherent feature' of imprisonment. As a result, what the Commission termed the 'normal control' of prisoners' correspondence was permitted and did not constitute an interference with the right to respect for correspondence guaranteed in Article 8(1), without there being any need to justify it by reference to the limitations on the right set out in Article 8(2).[51] The doctrine of inherent limitations was the subject of some criticism, but was extended to claims based on Article 9 (freedom of thought) and Article 10 (freedom of speech), despite the fact that here also the Convention contains express qualifications and so inherent limitations were arguably unnecessary.

In the *Vagrancy* cases[52] in 1971 the Court took the first steps along a new path. One of the issues in those cases concerned prisoners' correspondence and instead of considering this matter in terms of inherent limitations, as the Commission had done, the Court relied exclusively on Article 8(2). Although the Court did not reject the concept of inherent limitations in so many words, its judgment prepared the way for this step in the *Golder* case four years later. For when the British Government sought to justify its control of prisoners' correspondence by reference to implied limitations, the Court pointed out that the submission was inconsistent with its treatment of the same issue in the earlier case, and then said:

In addition and more particularly, that submission conflicts with the explicit text of Article 8. The restrictive formulation used at paragraph 2 ('There shall be no interference . . . except such as . . .') leaves no room for the concept of implied limitations. In this regard, the legal status of the right to respect for correspondence, which is defined by Article 8 with some precision, provides a clear contrast to that of the right to a court.[53]

In *Golder* the Court went on to hold unanimously that the interference complained of could not be justified under Article 8(2). It is thus somewhat ironical that in the *Vagrancy* cases the Commission, relying on the vague notion of inherent limitations, found that the Convention had been violated, whereas the Court, applying Article 8(2), decided that it had not. It seems clear, however, that the Court's approach, which is now generally accepted, is the better interpretation of the Convention. The application of Article 8(2) and the other qualifying provisions can often be controversial. But where qualifications are already included in the Convention there is, as the Court has stated, really no justification for implied limitations.

The travaux préparatoires

In its submissions to the Court in the *National Union of Belgian Police* case the Commission suggested that the Vienna Convention on the Law of Treaties places an emphasis on object and purpose which precludes interpretation of a treaty by reference to the parties' intentions. Subsequently, in the *Golder* case it argued that whatever the position under the general law, the special character of the European Convention, and specifically its status as a constitutional instrument, made the Contracting States' intentions irrelevant.

The first view is plainly wrong. Article 32 of the Vienna Convention permits recourse to supplementary means of interpretation, including *travaux préparatoires* to confirm an interpretation arrived at on the basis of the text, or when such an interpretation leaves the meaning ambiguous or obscure. Since the only purpose of referring to the *travaux* is to establish the parties' intentions, it can hardly be said that the Convention treats them as irrelevant to interpretation.

The second view is scarcely more convincing. It may be conceded that the Convention has a special character which calls for the kind of strong emphasis on object and purpose which we have seen is a prominent feature of the Court's jurisprudence. It can also be accepted that the interpretation of the Convention as a living instrument means that some of the ideas which were prevalent in 1950 have no bearing on how it should be interpreted today. But this is very far from saying that the Contracting States' intentions, as revealed in the *travaux*, are completely irrelevant. Apart from the obvious point that reference to the *travaux* is one way of establishing the object and purpose of the treaty, the Convention is the agreement from which the Court's decisions ultimately derive their legitimacy. Unless we are to suppose that the Contracting States gave the Convention institutions absolute legislative autonomy, it is difficult to see how the parties' intentions, any more than the Convention itself, can be simply set aside. If, therefore, the Court recognises the Convention as the source of its authority, one would expect the intentions of the parties, as evidenced by the *travaux préparatoires*, to play some part in its decisions. This indeed is what has happened.

In a number of cases the Court has used the *travaux* to establish the scope of a controversial provision. Thus in the *James* case when called upon to interpret the reference to 'the general principles of international law' in Article 1 of Protocol No. 1, the Court referred to the text and context, then said 'Confronted with a text whose interpretation has given rise to such disagreement, the Court considers it proper to have recourse to the *travaux préparatoires* as a supplementary means of interpretation.' It went on:

Examination of the *travaux préparatoires* reveals that the express reference to a right to compensation contained in earlier drafts of Article 1 was excluded, notably in the face of opposition on the part of the United Kingdom and other States. The mention of the general principles of international law was subsequently included and was the subject of several statements to the effect that they protected only foreigners.

Developing its investigation, the Court added:

Above all, in their Resolution (52)1 of 19 March 1952 approving the text of the Protocol and opening it for signature, the Committee of Ministers expressly stated that, 'as regards Article 1, the general principles of international law in their present connotation entail the obligation to pay compensation *to non-nationals* in cases of expropriation' (emphasis added). Having regard to the negotiating history as a whole, the Court considers that this Resolution must be taken as a clear indication that the reference to the general principles of international law was not intended to extend to nationals.[54]

Accordingly, it concluded that the *travaux préparatoires*, like the other factors it had considered, did not support the interpretation the applicants had put forward.[55]

Sometimes the Court has the same object of demonstrating that a particular view of the scope of a right corresponds to the intention of the parties, but its reference to the *travaux* is less elaborate. In the *Belgian Linguistics* case, for example, the Court was concerned with Article 2 of Protocol No. 1, specifically its opening words 'No person shall be denied the right to education.' And the Court said: 'The negative formulation indicates, as is confirmed by the "preparatory work" . . . that the Contracting Parties do not recognise such a right to education as would require them to establish at their own expense, or to subsidise, education of any particular type or at any particular level.'[56] A particularly striking use of preparatory work is to be found in certain cases in which the Court has decided that it must reject a claim on the ground that it is based on a right which the parties as a matter of policy decided not to include in the Convention. Thus in the *Kosiek* case the Court found that access to the civil service lay at the heart of the applicant's claim and held that it must be rejected on the ground that the preparatory work showed this to be a deliberate omission. Similarly, in the *Johnston* case the Court found that 'the *travaux préparatoires* disclose no intention to include in Article 12 any guarantee of a right to have the ties of marriage dissolved by divorce'[57] and held that this indication of the object and purpose of the Convention precluded the possibility of an evolutive interpretation.

The counter-part to the previous two cases may perhaps be considered to be the *Marckx* case. There, among its other rulings, the Court spelled out a right unstated in the Convention, the 'right to property', on the basis of inferences to be drawn from the text of Article 1 of Protocol 1, saying that 'the *travaux préparatoires*, for their part, confirm this unequivocally'.[58] From the right of property thus identified, the Court proceeded to draw some important (and controversial) conclusions relating to the patrimonial rights in issue in that case.

The Court, then, has made use of *travaux préparatoires* for a variety of purposes and on the evidence considered so far it might be thought that they should be regarded as a major component in the Court's decisions. However, this would be to exaggerate their significance. Preparatory work, it will be recalled, is treated in Article 32 of the Vienna Convention as a supplementary means of interpretation and in all the cases mentioned above the Court employed it in conjunction with other assistance, typically to confirm the ordinary meaning of a term, as in *James*, and to support an interpretation in accordance with the object and purpose of the Convention, as in the *Johnston* case. Thus *travaux* are not, and certainly have not been used as, an independent basis for interpretation.

Moreover, it follows from the supplementary character of preparatory work that reference to it may be dispensed with where the interpreter considers that the text is sufficiently clear. This principle, which international tribunals have frequently recognised, has been used by the Court on several occasions to justify a holding that recourse to preparatory work is unnecessary. Indeed, in its very first case, which raised a question as to the scope of Article 5, it said that 'having ascertained that the text of Article 5 paragraphs 1(c) and 3 is sufficiently clear in itself . . . and . . .

having also found that the meaning of this text is in keeping with the purpose of the Convention, the Court cannot, having regard to a generally recognised principle regarding the interpretation of international treaties, resort to the preparatory work'.[59]

In the above case the Irish Government's attempt to invoke the preparatory work had been met by the Commission with the argument that if recourse to such material was necessary, the preparatory work did not in fact support the government's case. The ruling that recourse to the preparatory work was unnecessary may therefore be a reflection of the limited assistance obtainable from this source. This, of course, will often be the case. If either there is no relevant material, or what exists is itself ambiguous or obscure, then the Court will naturally have to find inspiration elsewhere.

Though the inadequacy or unreliability of preparatory work is no doubt one reason why it is not more prominent in the Court's jurisprudence, there are sometimes other explanations. In the *Golder* case, for example, the Court considered the object and purpose of the Convention and asserting that its interpretation was 'based on the very terms' read in their context, said it had reached, 'the conclusion without needing to resort to "supplementary means of interpretation" as envisaged in Article 32 of the Vienna Convention, that Article 6(1) secures to everyone the right to have any claim relating to his civil rights and obligations brought before a court or tribunal'.[60] The justification for setting aside the preparatory work is unconvincing. For, as the Court recognised, the right in question was not expressed, but had to be implied and whether this was permissible was highly controversial. In such a situation it would seem natural to turn to the preparatory work for guidance.

Two judges who dissented on this point in fact did refer to the preparatory work and their opinions provide the explanation of why the Court did not. For the preparatory work indicates that the right which the Court was prepared to imply into the Convention was considered for inclusion, but deliberately omitted. And as one of them pointed out, 'In the technique of treaty interpretation there can never be a better demonstration of an intention *not* to provide for something than first including, then dropping it'.[61] As we have seen, the Court itself has certainly been influenced by evidence of this kind in other cases. In *Golder*, however, it took the view that an extended reading of Article 6 was called for on compelling grounds of legal policy and so disregarded evidence pointing to a narrower construction.

A variation of the technique used in *Golder* is to refer to the *travaux préparatoires*, but to find that they shed no light on the issue. This achieves the objective, which is to leave the Court free to reach its decision on other grounds, but, like the assertion that no recourse is necessary, may sometimes lack conviction. *Campbell and Cosans* was another case involving Article 2 of Protocol No. 1, the question here being whether the existence of corporal punishment in Scottish schools violated the State's obligation to 'respect the right of parents to ensure such education and teaching in conformity with their own . . . philosophical convictions'. Deciding that it did, the Court based its conclusion on broad grounds of principle and on the key issue of interpretation briefly dismissed the *travaux* with the observation that: 'As regards the adjective "philosophical", it is not capable of exhaustive definition and little assistance as to its precise significance is to be gleaned from the *travaux préparatoires*.'[62]

However, one member of the Court took a different view. In a partly dissenting opinion Sir Vincent Evans pointed out that the *travaux* demonstrate that the reference to 'religious and philosophical convictions' was in fact inserted with the object of prohibiting indoctrination, and not of regulating the organisation or administration of schools which was the issue here. This was indeed the view of Article 2 which the Court itself had earlier adopted in the *Belgian Linguistics* and *Danish Sex Education* cases. In the latter, moreover, as Sir Vincent reminded his colleagues, the Court when considering Article 2(1), had ruled the *travaux préparatoires* to be 'without doubt of particular consequence in the case of a clause that gave rise to such impassioned discussions'.[63] The conclusion is thus inescapable that the Court's unwillingness to employ the *travaux* in *Campbell and Cosans* was not based on the reason given in the judgment, but on the desire to justify a different result.

A third and more subtle technique for side-stepping the preparatory work is to acknowledge its relevance, but to find reasons why the case must nevertheless be decided in the opposite sense. An example of this is to be found in the case of *Young, James and Webster*[64] which raised the question of whether a trade union 'closed shop' may contravene Article 11. The Convention protects freedom to associate and form trade unions, but does not expressly protect the freedom not to associate, which was in issue in this case. The *travaux*, however, indicate that the omission was deliberate because those who drew up the Convention were conscious of the problem posed by the closed shop issue and considered that it was 'undesirable' to try to deal with it.

In these circumstances it would have been possible for the Court to use the kind of argument employed in *Johnston* and, by relying on the *travaux*, to find that the issue of the closed shop fell outside Article 11. A minority of the Court adopted this line of argument, but the majority found an ingenious way of avoiding the apparent implications of the *travaux*.

Referring in some detail to the *travaux*, they agreed that it was possible to argue that the right not to join a trade union was a deliberate omission from the Convention. However, assuming that this was so – and the Court left the point open – the majority held that it would be wrong to conclude that the negative aspect of freedom of association fell completely outside Article 11. In particular, the Court held that compulsion amounting to a threat of dismissal involving loss of livelihood, especially for those engaged before the closed shop agreement came into force, struck at the very substance of freedom of association. Since this was the situation here, the Court concluded that the Convention had been violated.

The reasoning in *Young, James and Webster* enabled the Court to avoid the message of the *travaux* which it plainly found unacceptable. This does not mean that this decision, and the cases considered earlier, should necessarily be regarded as wrong, although in each case there were certainly some members of the Court who thought so. The point is rather that any review must conclude that the Court's use of preparatory work has been highly selective. Thus, while it would be grossly misleading to suggest that the Court has ignored evidence of the intentions of the Contracting Parties altogether, preparatory work has carried variable weight, and not infrequently been displaced by other considerations.

Notes

1 Series A, No. 18 para. 29.
2 Series A, No. 112 para. 51.
3 *Ibid.,* para. 52.
4 Series A, No. 102 para. 114.
5 Series A, No. 29 para. 40.
6 Series A, No. 22 para. 81.
7 *Öztürk* case, Series A, No. 73, dissenting opinion of Judge Matscher, section A, para. 2.
8 *König* case, Series A, No. 27, separate opinion of Judge Matscher, section A.
9 It should be noted that the effect of autonomous interpretation can sometimes be to restrict the protection afforded by the Convention. In the *James* case, for example, the Court was urged to interpret Article 1 of Protocol No. 1, which permits deprivation of possessions 'in the public interest' strictly, on the ground that the corresponding phrase in the French text has a narrow meaning in some systems of domestic law. The Court, however, rejected the argument, holding that in the light of the English text and other factors it should be interpreted autonomously and in the wider sense. See Series A, No. 98 at para. 42.
10 *Golder* case, Series A, No. 18 para. 30.
11 *Abdulaziz* case, Series A, No. 94 para. 60.
12 *Ibid.*
13 Series A, No. 87.
14 Series A, No. 39.
15 Series A, No. 116 para. 78. See also the *Klass* case, Series A, No. 28 para. 68.

16 Series A, No. 112 para. 57.
17 Series A, No. 105 para. 35.
18 *Golder* case, Series A, No. 18, separate opinion of Judge Sir Gerald Fitzmaurice, para. 39.
19 Series A, No. 7 p. 23.
20 See G. G. Fitzmaurice, *The Law and Procedure of the International Court of Justice*, Grotius, Cambridge, 42–9, (1986); and I. Sinclair, *The Vienna Convention on the Law of Treaties,* 2nd ed., Melland Schill Monographs in International Law, Manchester U.P. Manchester, 130–5 and 150–1, (1984). Also F.Ost. 'The original canons of interpretation of the European Court of Human Rights', in M. Delmas-Marty (ed.), *The European Convention for the Protection of Human Rights*. Nijhoff, Dordrecht, 283–318 (1991).
21 Fitzmaurice, *ibid.*, 345.
22 Series A, No. 28 para. 42.
23 Series A, No. 30 para. 65.
24 Series A, No. 98 para. 42.
25 Series A, No. 30 para. 48.
26 For discussion of the distinction between concepts and conceptions as an issue in constitutional interpretation see R. Dworkin, *Taking Rights Seriously*, Duckworth, London, 132–7, (1977).
27 Series A, No. 26 para. 31.
28 Series A, No. 33 para. 37.
29 Series A, No. 31 para. 41.
30 Series A, No. 184, joint dissenting opinion of Judges Palm, Foighel and Pekkanen, para. 2.
31 Series A, No. 106.
32 Series A, No. 184 para. 46.
33 Series A, No. 31 para. 58.
34 Series A, No. 106 para. 47. See also on this point *B v France*, Series A, No. 232C.
35 Series A, No. 161 para. 103.
36 *Ibid.*
37 Series A, No. 201 para. 100.
38 *Ibid.*
39 Series A, No. 132 para. 57
40 Series A, No. 18 para. 35.
41 *Ibid.*, para. 36.
42 *Ibid.*
43 Series A, No. 98 para. 54.
44 The difference of opinion in *Golder* has already been noted. In the *James* case Judge Thór Vilhjálmsson held that if Article 1 had been intended to provide for compensation, it would have done so expressly.
45 Series A, No. 19 para. 38.
46 Series A, No. 20.
47 Series A, No. 21.
48 Series A, No. 18 para. 38.
49 Series A, No. 113 para. 52.
50 Series A, No. 6 p. 32.
51 See F. G. Jacobs, *The European Convention on Human Rights*, Clarendon Press, Oxford, 198–201 (1975).
52 Series A, No. 12.
53 Series A, No. 18 para. 44.

54 Series A, No. 98 para. 64.
55 For a similar close inspection of preparatory work see the Court's demonstration in the *Danish Sex Education* case that Article 2 of Protocol No. 1 was
   intended to cover State as well as private schools, Series A, No. 23 para. 50,
   noted in the first edition of this book at p. 83.
56 Series A, No. 6 p. 31.
57 Series A, No. 112 para. 52.
58 Series A, No. 31 para. 63.
59 *Lawless* case, Series A, No. 3 pp. 52, 53.
60 Series A, No. 18 para. 36.
61 *Ibid.*, separate opinion of Judge Sir Gerald Fitzmaurice, para. 45.
62 Series A, No. 48 para. 36.
63 Series A, No. 23 para. 50.
64 Series A, No. 44.

CHAPTER 5

The effectiveness principle

In the discussion of the object and purpose of the Convention in the previous chapter the point was made that the principle of effectiveness is a means of giving the provisions of a treaty the fullest weight and effect consistent with the language used and with the rest of the text and in such a way that every part of it can be given meaning. It was also suggested that this principle, the value of which is recognised by all schools of interpretation, occupies a very significant place in the Court's judgments. In chapter 3 we saw how the idea of the Convention as an effective instrument, and of the Court as an effective piece of the machinery, have played a major part in the shaping of the Strasbourg system through judicial decisions. In this chapter we shall see how the same considerations of the Convention's effectiveness influence the Court's interpretation of its substantive provisions.

The Convention as a guarantee of rights that are practical and effective

Some of the Court's most striking applications of the effectiveness principle are to be found in cases in which it rejects a government's submission as excessively formal and decides in the applicant's favour on the ground that the Convention is concerned with rights that are practical and effective. Sometimes the question involves the application of the Convention, that is, whether a provision which is clearly relevant has been violated; sometimes, on the other hand, it is the applicability of a provision – whether it has any bearing at all on the matter in hand – which is in issue. In either case, as we shall see, the Court's preference for what it terms a 'practical and effective' interpretation, as against a 'formal' one, has frequently proved an important and creative technique.

Article 6(3)(c) of the Convention provides that everyone charged with a criminal offence has the right 'to defend himself in person or through legal assistance of his own choosing, or if he has not sufficient means to pay for legal assistance, to be given it free when the interests of justice so require'. In the *Artico* case the Italian Court of Cassation had, at the applicant's request, appointed a lawyer to represent him in his appeal. The lawyer, however, pleading other commitments and ill-health which prevented him from undertaking so 'demanding and onerous' a task, had declined to act for him. Despite repeated requests from the applicant, the Italian court refused to appoint a replacement with the result that at the appeal hearing the applicant had to present his case himself.

When the applicant invoked Article 6(3)(c), the Italian Government's reply was that its obligations had been discharged as soon as the applicant was assigned a lawyer and nothing further was required. In particular, there was no duty to provide the applicant with another lawyer when the original appointee failed to act, because this right was not guaranteed in the Convention. This startling assertion, that a government could fulfil its obligations by going through the motions of appointing a defence lawyer without reference to subsequent events, was totally unacceptable to the Court, which repudiated it with a ringing affirmation of the effectiveness principle:

The Court recalls that the Convention is intended to guarantee not rights that are theoretical or illusory but rights that are practical and effective; this is particularly so of the rights of the defence in view of the prominent place held in a democratic society by the right to a fair trial, from which they derive. . . . As the Commission's Delegates correctly emphasised, Article 6(3)(c) speaks of 'assistance' and not of 'nomination'. Again, mere nomination does not ensure effective assistance since the lawyer appointed for legal aid purposes may die, fall seriously ill, be prevented for a protracted period from acting or shirk his duties. If they are notified of the situation, the authorities must either replace him or cause him to fulfil his obligations. Adoption of the Government's restrictive interpretation would lead to results that are unreasonable and incompatible with both the wording of sub-paragraph (c) and the structure of Article 6 taken as a whole; in many instances free legal assistance might prove to be worthless.[1]

Since it was clear that in the present case the applicant never had the benefit of the appointed lawyer's services, the Court had no difficulty in concluding that he had not received effective legal assistance.

A further illustration of the Court's concern for the reality of the individual's position is provided by a number of cases involving the scope and significance of the presumption of innocence. This, plainly one of the key elements in the concept of a fair trial, is guaranteed by Article 6(2) of the Convention, which provides 'Everyone charged with a criminal offence shall be presumed innocent until proved guilty according to law'.

In the *Adolf* case the Court had to decide the meaning of the phrase 'charged with a criminal offence'. It held that the expression has an autonomous meaning and must be interpreted in the context of the Convention and not on the basis of its meaning in domestic law. It went on:

The prominent place held in a democratic society by the right to a fair trial favours a 'substantive', rather than a 'formal', conception of the 'charge' referred to by Article 6; it impels the Court to look behind the appearances and examine the realities of the procedure in question in order to determine whether there has been a 'charge' within the meaning of Article 6.[2]

To seek a substantive rather than a formal conception is, of course, another way of saying that the aim is an effective interpretation, as the Court confirmed when it added that 'the applicant's situation under the domestic legal rules in force has to be examined in the light of the object and purpose of Article 6, namely the protection of the rights of the defence'.[3]

The Court's concern for the effectiveness of Article 6(2) can also be seen in the way in which it has responded to various attempts to limit its scope. The applicant in the *Minelli* case was a journalist who published an article in a daily newspaper making accusations of fraud against a company and its director. In 1972 the company and its director instituted a prosecution for defamation through the press against the applicant. In 1974 the proceedings were adjourned, pending the outcome of a case against another journalist, Mr Fust, who had written a similar article. In 1976 the Chamber of the Canton of Zürich Assize Court decided that it could not hear the complaint against the applicant because the limitation period had expired. However, in view of the fact that Mr Fust had been convicted, the Court concluded that without the time-bar Mr Minelli would 'in all probability' have been convicted. It therefore directed him to pay two-thirds of the investigation and trial costs and to compensate the private prosecutors for their expenses.

Having held that Article 6(2) was applicable,[4] the Court went on to consider whether it had been complied with, and here its decision provides a clear example of the Court's favouring an effective over a restrictive interpretation. The government submitted that the Chamber of the Assize Court had taken the applicant's conduct into account only as a hypothesis for the purpose of apportioning costs, which was different, so it was argued, from a finding of guilt. The Court, however, agreed with the Commission that this distinction was not important. The test was not what the Swiss Court found, but the opinion reflected in its judgment. In the Court's words:

> the presumption of innocence will be violated if, without the accused's having previously been proved guilty according to law and, notably, without his having had the opportunity of exercising his rights of defence, a judicial decision concerning him reflects an opinion that he is guilty. This may be so even in the absence of any formal finding; it suffices that there is some reasoning suggesting that the court regards the accused as guilty.[5]

In view of the Assize Court's finding that Mr Minelli would 'very probably' have been convicted, the Court concluded that its decision was incompatible with respect for the presumption of innocence.

None of the cases considered so far was particularly controversial. In rejecting a narrow view of the Convention the Court was therefore declining to accept somewhat technical arguments which even the respondent probably believed to have little merit. However, not all cases are so straightforward. In the *Golder*[6] case, as we saw in the previous chapter, the Court held that Article 6(1) contains an implied right of access to the courts. Four years later the Court decided that Ireland had infringed the Convention by not providing the applicant with legal aid in civil proceedings, thereby failing to provide her with effective access to the courts. This, one of the Court's most controversial judgments, exposes the dangers, as well as the possibilities, of seeking a practical and effective interpretation.

The facts of the *Airey* case were simple. The applicant, who claimed that her husband was a violent alcoholic, desired to obtain a decree of judicial separation from the courts, divorce being impossible in Irish law. Having no means, she was unable to find a solicitor to act for her since there was no system of civil legal aid in Ireland. The Commission unanimously considered that this constituted a breach of Article 6(1) and the Court, by a majority, agreed.

The government argued that since Mrs Airey was free to take her case to the High Court in person, or through a lawyer if she could afford one, her right of access to the courts had not been impaired. The Court rejected this submission on the ground that it took no account of the effectiveness principle. Holding that 'the Convention is intended to guarantee not rights that are theoretical or illusory but rights that are practical and effective', the Court added that 'This is particularly so of the right of access to the courts in view of the prominent place held in a democratic society by the right to a fair trial.'[7]

Applying the above principle to the facts, the Court was satisfied that in view of the nature of Mrs Airey's case and the complexity of Irish High Court procedure, it was unlikely that she could have represented herself effectively. This conclusion was confirmed by the fact that in 255 judicial separation cases in recent years the petitioner was represented by a lawyer on each occasion. By not having such representation made available to her by the State, the applicant had therefore been denied effective access to the courts.

The Court made a further reference to the effectiveness principle when it considered another of the government's arguments. This was that the Convention should not be interpreted so as to promote social and economic developments in a Contracting State. The Court rejected this submission, saying that it was:

aware that the further realisation of social and economic rights is largely
dependent on the situation – notably financial – reigning in the State in question.
On the other hand, the Convention must be interpreted in the light of present day
conditions . . . and it is designed to safeguard the individual in a real and practical
way as regards those areas with which it deals. Whilst the Convention sets forth
what are essentially civil and political rights, many of them have implications of a
social or economic nature.

It therefore concluded that 'the mere fact that an interpretation of the
Convention may extend into the sphere of social and economic rights
should not be a decisive factor against such an interpretation; there is no
water-tight division separating that sphere from the field covered by the
Convention.'[8]

The Court was careful to state that it was not deciding that there is a
general right to legal aid in all cases concerned with the determination of a
civil right. However, even with this qualification, the decision in *Airey*
must be regarded as an extreme application of the effectiveness principle.
It is therefore not surprising that two members of the Court expressed
strong disagreement with this aspect of the judgment. Judge
O'Donoghue agreed that the Convention's guarantees must be effective,
but held that there is a fundamental difference between actively impeding
access to the courts, as in *Golder*, and not taking steps to facilitate it, as
here. Judge Vilhjálmsson developed this point. Placing particular
emphasis on the fact that the Convention contains no provision on legal
aid in civil cases, he pointed out that an individual's inability to claim his
rights may stem from many factors including his financial position. States
were taking economic and social measures to correct this situation and
where the Convention saw the financial position as an integral part of the
right, as with criminal legal aid, it was expressly mentioned. However,
where there was no such provision, it was not the Court's task to supply
one by interpretation.

Although the *Airey* case is not typical of the Court's application of the
principle of effectiveness with regard to Article 6, it is an instructive
example of the problems which can arise when that principle is pushed
beyond a certain point. The view that there is no water-tight division
separating social and economic rights from civil and political rights is
certainly valid. Yet, to see this as a way of justifying ever-more extensive
readings of the Convention with the aid of the effectiveness principle is to
go beyond anything which can be regarded as interpretation.

Positive obligations

Several articles of the Convention expressly provide for the Contracting
States to do something. Thus Article 6(3)(c), as we have just seen,

requires the State to provide free legal assistance in criminal cases and the other parts of Article 6(3) create analogous obligations. Articles in this form are exceptional, however. Most of the Convention's provisions contain a statement of the right or freedom which must be guaranteed, followed by a description of the circumstances, if any, in which it may be subject to limitation. It follows that the Convention is mainly concerned not with what a State must do, but with what it must not do; that is, with its obligation to refrain from interfering with the individual's rights. Nevertheless, utilising the principle of effectiveness, the Court has held that even in respect of provisions which do not expressly create a positive obligation, there may sometimes be a duty to act in a particular way.

The circumstances in which the Court has employed the principle of effectiveness to place States under a positive obligation can be illustrated by a number of cases involving Article 8. According to Article 8(1) 'Everyone has the right to respect for his private and family life, his home and his correspondence.' In the *Marckx* case the Court had to decide what bearing this provision had on the treatment of illegitimacy in domestic law and specifically whether the fact that in Belgian law a mother and her daughter were placed under certain legal disadvantages as a consequence of the latter's illegitimacy, amounted to a violation of the Convention. The Court decided that it did, relying in part on the positive obligations which it held were inherent in an effective respect for family life.

In the particular context of illegitimacy the Court held that the effect of these obligations was that:

when the State determines in its domestic legal system the regime applicable to certain family ties such as those between an unmarried mother and her child, it must act in a manner calculated to allow those concerned to lead a normal family life. As envisaged by Article 8, respect for family life implies in particular, in the Court's view, the existence in domestic law of legal safeguards that render possible as from the moment of birth the child's integration in his family. In this connection, the State has a choice of various means, but a law that fails to satisfy this requirement violates paragraph 1 of Article 8.[9]

Since the Court found that Belgian law failed to make adequate provision for this integration, it followed that there had been a violation of the Convention.

This was a controversial decision and several members of the Court dissented, some arguing that Article 8 had no bearing on the matter in hand, others that the issue lay within Belgium's margin of appreciation.[10] As regards positive obligations Judge Matscher's opinion is particularly instructive. For while he said that he considered it 'as generally accepted that the implementation of many fundamental rights – and notably family rights – calls for positive action by the State in the shape of the enactment of the substantive, organisational and procedural rules necessary for this purpose', he stressed that 'this positive obligation, flowing from Article 8 of the Convention, is limited to what is necessary for the creation of and development of family life according to the ideas which contemporary European societies have of this concept'.[11] Needless to say, judges' versions of these ideas are likely to vary. Identifying a positive obligation is therefore merely a first step; deciding what the Convention requires in the way of positive action may be far more difficult.

The problems which can arise in establishing the scope of positive obligations can be seen from the *Gaskin* case.[12] The applicant, who had been taken into care when his mother died, wished to obtain details of the foster homes in which he had been brought up, but was refused access to some of the local authority's records on the ground that the information in question was private and confidential. Having decided that this was a case in which an effective respect for the applicant's private and family life imposed a positive obligation, the Court was divided as to its scope. A minority considered that the local authority had gone as far as it reasonably could by writing to each contributor to the case file, asking for permission to release the relevant part of the record. The majority, on the other hand, acknowledged that a system which made access depend on the contributors' consent was not objectionable in principle, but ruled that the interests of those in the applicant's position could only be secured if there was an independent authority to decide on the issue of access when a contributor was not available or refused consent improperly. As no such system was available to Mr Gaskin, they concluded that there had been a violation of Article 8.

The above cases show that the State may be under a duty to take positive measures to ensure that a person is not disadvantaged by official action. Does it follow from this that there may also be a positive obligation to prevent disadvantage stemming from the actions of private individuals? This question, which is one aspect of the more general issue of the extent to which the Convention governs relations between individuals,[13] was crucial in the case of *X and Y v. Netherlands*.

The facts of this case were unusual. The applicant, Miss Y, was a mentally handicapped person whose complaint was that under the law of the Netherlands she was not competent to initiate criminal proceedings against Mr B, who had sexually assaulted her. Since the relevant article of the Criminal Code could only be invoked by a victim, if, as here, such a person lacked competence, there was a gap in the law, and, as a result, Miss Y's assailant escaped prosecution.

Miss Y alleged that the failure of the local law to provide for B's prosecution amounted to a failure to secure respect for her private life, as required by Article 8. The Court agreed. Recalling that 'although the object of Article 8 is essentially that of protecting the individual against arbitrary interference by the public authorities, it does not merely compel the State to abstain from such interference: in addition to this primarily negative undertaking, there may be positive obligations inherent in an effective respect for private or family life', the Court added that 'These obligations may involve the adoption of measures designed to secure respect for private life even in the sphere of the relations of individuals between themselves.'[14] In the circumstances, the Court was satisfied that only the criminal law is an adequate deterrent to protect what it rightly regarded as a crucial area of private life. Since it was evident that the present case was not covered by the criminal law of the Netherlands, the Court held that there had been a violation of Article 8.

The decision in this case is a good illustration of the positive obligations entailed by the notion of respect for private life, as well as the limits of what is normally a wide margin of appreciation. The Court's finding that the Convention had been violated was almost inevitable given that the lack of a criminal sanction was a lacuna in the law rather than a matter of deliberate policy. The case is nevertheless important for the Court's deduction, which was not unexpected, that positive obligations may extend to the regulation of relations between individuals, a principle with implications which are not confined to Article 8.

In the *Plattform 'Ärzte für das Leben'* case,[15] for example, the Court had to consider the extent to which the above principle was relevant to Article 11 which protects freedom of association and assembly. The applicant was an organisation which had had two demonstrations disrupted by opponents of its activities. *Plattform* complained that the Austrian authorities had disregarded the true meaning of freedom of assembly by failing to take more effective measures to discourage the counter-demonstrators. The government's response was to submit that Article 11 does not impose any positive obligation to protect demonstrations.

Not surprisingly, the Court, like the Commission, took a very different view. Without attempting to develop what it called 'a general theory of positive obligations', it made it clear that it regarded the State's responsibilities under Article 11 much more widely than the government did. Thus it pointed out that demonstrations on controversial issues are always likely to provoke a response from those who disagree and while the latter are also entitled to make their views known, they may not do so in such a way as to intimidate their opponents. From this it followed that:

Genuine, effective freedom of peaceful assembly cannot, therefore, be reduced to a mere duty on the part of the State not to interfere: a purely negative conception would not be compatible with the object and purpose of Article 11.

Like Article 8, Article 11 sometimes requires positive measures to be taken, even in the sphere of relations between individuals, if need be . . . .[16]

Having ruled that Article 11 imposes a duty on States to take reasonable and appropriate measures to enable lawful demonstrations to proceed peacefully, the Court decided that no arguable claim of a violation of Article 11 had been made out because the right to demonstrate cannot be guaranteed absolutely and in the Court's view the authorities had not acted unreasonably. This, of course, was a conclusion on the particular facts.[17] The importance of the case in the present context lies in the way the Court interpreted Article 11 in the light of its underlying purpose, leading it to conclude that for freedom of assembly to be fully effective it must entail positive obligations.

Few are likely to disagree with the proposition that the State has a responsibility to provide protection for peaceful demonstrators, and, as in *X and Y v Netherlands*, to protect a mentally handicapped person from rape. It must be pointed out, however, that most decisions on positive obligations are not so straightforward and cases like *Marckx* and *Gaskin* are a reminder that from a general perspective the distinction between refraining from an interference with individual rights and being required to take active steps to promote them touches a sensitive area of legal policy.

Every government is aware that by subscribing to the Convention, it places itself in a position in which domestic laws and practices may have to be modified to avoid impinging on the various liberties the Convention was brought into being to protect. What a government may not bargain for is to find itself put to considerable trouble and expense as a result of an obligation to advance particular social or economic policies which it may not wholly support. While this is not a conclusive objection to the Court's employing the principle of effectiveness to develop the law and identify positive obligations in the Convention, it unquestionably argues for caution in so doing.

The interpretation of particular terms

A further example of the Court's application of the principle of effectiveness is to be found in numerous cases in which it has been required to ascribe a meaning to particular terms. Here, though the Court may not always refer to that principle in so many words, it is clear that its decisions are informed by the desire we have already noted: to interpret the Convention in a way which gives its provisions a maximum of effectiveness, having regard to its language and its object and purpose.

Thus in the *Golder* case the Court had no hesitation in deciding that by preventing the applicant from writing to a solicitor the authorities had 'interfered' with his 'correspondence', even though no letter had actually been written. For, as one judge said 'it would be placing an undue and formalistic restriction on the concept of interference with correspondence not to regard it as covering the case of correspondence that has not taken place only because the competent authority, with power to enforce its ruling, has ruled that it will not be allowed.'[18] Likewise, in the *Klass* case the Court ruled that although telephone conversations are not expressly mentioned in Article 8, they are 'covered by the notions "private life" and "correspondence" referred to by this provision'.[19] And in a further extension of this interpretation in the *Malone* case the Court held that although the practice of 'metering' does not involve the interception of conversations, this also falls within Article 8.[20]

The Court's concern for the effectiveness of the Convention may be further illustrated by its interpretation of the reference to 'family life' in Article 8. In the *Abdulaziz* case, which concerned restrictions on the right of foreign husbands to join their wives in the United Kingdom, one of the government's arguments was that the applicants had not at the time when permission was refused, established any 'family life' with the legitimate expectation of the enjoyment of it in the U.K. The Court rejected the argument. While it was willing to acknowledge that Article 8 'presupposes the existence of a family', the Court observed:

However, this does not mean that all intended family life falls entirely outside its ambit. Whatever else the word 'family' may mean, it must at any rate include the relationship that arises from a lawful and genuine marriage, such as that contracted by Mr and Mrs Abdulaziz and Mr and Mrs Balkandali, even if a family life of the kind referred to by the Government has not yet been fully established. Those marriages must be considered sufficient to attract such respect as may be due under Article 8.[21]

This interpretation of family life, itself a striking application of the effectiveness principle, was taken further when the Court considered the position of the third applicant, Mrs Cabales, the validity of whose marriage had been questioned. For here the Court held that this was no objection because:

Mr and Mrs Cabales had gone through a ceremony of marriage . . . and the evidence before the Court confirms that they believed themselves to be married and that they genuinely wished to cohabit and lead a normal family life. And indeed they subsequently did so. In the circumstances, the committed relationship thus established was sufficient to attract the application of Article 8.[22]

There could be no clearer example of the use of the principle of effectiveness.

The tendency of the Court to look beyond the words of the Convention to its underlying purpose can also be seen in the cases involving the right to legal assistance which is guaranteed by Article 6(3)(c). That article, as we have seen, provides that everyone charged with a criminal offence has the right 'to defend himself in person or through legal assistance of his own choosing or, if he has not sufficient means to pay for legal assistance, to be given it free when the interests of justice so require.'

In the *Pakelli* case the question was the relation between the right to defend oneself and the right to be defended. The applicant, a Turkish citizen resident in the Federal Republic of Germany, was convicted of the illegal importation of cannabis and tax evasion and sentenced to a term of imprisonment. After various proceedings which need not be described, the case came before the Federal Court which received a memorial prepared by the applicant's lawyer R., setting out the grounds of appeal, and decided to hold an oral hearing. An application by R. to be officially appointed as the applicant's lawyer for the oral proceedings was refused on the grounds *inter alia* that neither the facts of the case, nor the legal issues it raised, justified such an appointment. After a hearing in the presence of a Federal public prosecutor at which neither the applicant nor R. was present, the applicant's appeal was dismissed. An attempt to take a further appeal to the Federal Constitutional Court was unsuccessful.

In his application against the Federal Republic Mr Pakelli argued that the Federal Court's refusal to appoint an official defence counsel had violated Article 6(3)(c). The government's reply amongst other matters raised an important point of interpretation. Under German law Mr Pakelli would have been allowed to argue his case in person before the Federal Court. The government, relying on the fact that in the English text the three rights set out in Article 6(3)(c) are linked by the disjunctive 'or', suggested that where a right of audience exists, there is never a right to free legal assistance. This interpretation was rejected. Pointing out that in the French text the second and third rights are linked by 'et' not 'ou', the Court held that:

Having regard to the object and purpose of this paragraph, which is designed to ensure effective protection of the rights of defence . . . the French text here provides the more reliable guidance. . . . Accordingly, a 'person charged with a criminal offence' who does not wish to defend himself in person must be able to have recourse to legal assistance of his own choosing; if he does not have sufficient means to pay for such assistance, he is entitled under the Convention to be given it free when the interests of justice so require.[23]

The Court was saying, then, that for the right of defence to be effective, the accused must have the option of being represented. The government's interpretation, which would obviously limit the right to legal assistance severely, therefore had to be rejected as incompatible with the object of the Convention.

It will be noticed that Article 6(3)(c) gives a person the right to free legal assistance 'if he has not sufficient means to pay' for it, and when 'the interests of justice so require'. The Court's interpretation of these phrases, which, incidentally, are to be found in almost identical form in Article 14(3)(d) of the Covenant on Civil and Political Rights, provides further illustration of its concern for the effectiveness principle.

Thus in the *Artico* case the Italian Government argued that although the applicant was indigent, there was no obligation to provide him with legal assistance because his case was so straightforward that it was unnecessary. This was, of course, hard to reconcile with the fact that counsel had actually been assigned to the case, and with the latter's failure to act on the ground that his task was 'onerous and difficult'. The Court accordingly rejected the government's argument. In concluding that legal representation was necessary, the Court was particularly critical of the government's argument that for Article 6(3)(c) to be violated, the lack of assistance must actually have prejudiced the person charged. Pointing out that here the government were 'asking for the impossible' since it could never be proved that an effective counsel would have made the appropriate plea and been successful, the Court held that there was nothing in Article 6(3)(c) to suggest that such proof was necessary, while 'an interpretation that introduced this requirement into the sub-paragraph would deprive it in large measure of its substance'.[24]

State responsibility

The kinds of issues considered so far do not exhaust the situations in which the Court's judgments may be influenced by the effectiveness principle. For as well as deciding the construction to be put upon the various substantive provisions of the Convention, the Court is frequently faced with the problem of deciding whether conduct of which the applicant complains can be regarded as attributable to the respondent State. This issue, the scope of State responsibility, is, of course, prominent in general international law.[25] In the context of human rights, however, it is particularly important because the law is wholly concerned with the State's obligations towards the individual. Wide though their guarantees are, instruments like the Convention are not intended to make States liable for everyone's behaviour within their territory. On the other hand, too narrow a view of responsibility is likely to deprive such guarantees of much of their force. It would therefore be natural to expect the Court's treatment of responsibility to reflect the view of the Strasbourg system which was outlined in chapter 3 and a concern for the effectiveness of the Convention identical to that just described.

In two of its earliest cases involving Article 11, *Schmidt and Dahlström*[26] and the *Swedish Engine Drivers Union* case,[27] the Swedish

Government argued that the primary purpose of the Convention is to protect the individual against the State as holder of public power and that it does not oblige the State to ensure compliance with its provisions in private law relations between individuals. Since the applicants' claims in these cases were not directed against legislative, executive or judicial acts, but against the National Collective Bargaining Office, that is, the State as employer, the government maintained that Article 11 had no application.

The Court rejected the argument and neatly reversed the government's point. Whereas the government argued that in the sphere of work and employment the Convention cannot impose obligations on the State which are not incumbent on private employers, the Court pointed out that:

The Convention nowhere makes an express distinction between the functions of a Contracting State as holder of public power and its responsibilities as employer. In this respect, Article 11 is no exception . . . Article 11 is accordingly binding upon the 'State as employer', whether the latter's relations with its employees are governed by public or private law.[28]

Although the Court arrived at its conclusion without referring to the effectiveness principle expressly, reversing the burden of proof so that the State is assumed to have obligations under Article 11, unless it can be proved that it has not, is a typical forensic device for extending the scope of a provision. The Court was obviously aware that in Sweden, as in other countries, the State is a major employer and that to adopt the government's interpretation would reduce the impact of the Convention very considerably. Here, therefore, and subsequently in *Young, James and Webster*,[29] it was unanimous in taking the wider view.

A rather different aspect of responsibility has arisen in cases in which the State has, in effect, sought to delegate its duties under the Convention. Here too, in deciding the legal consequences the Court can clearly be seen to have regard to the effectiveness of the Convention. In the *Van der Mussele* case,[30] for example, the applicant, who was a lawyer in pupillage, complained that the system under which he was required to represent poor people in court without any payment violated Article 4(2), which prohibits forced or compulsory labour. The Belgian Government disputed this claim on the merits, but, as a preliminary point, sought to persuade the Court that it had no responsibility for the arrangements which the applicant objected to because the system in question was run by the legal profession, not by the State.

The Court had no hesitation in rejecting this argument. Under the Convention there is, as we have seen, an obligation to provide free legal assistance in criminal cases, while in civil matters such assistance may constitute one of the means of securing access to the courts and ensuring a fair trial, as required by Article 6(1). Belgium, said the Court, chose to delegate its obligations in this matter to the legal profession, which was required by law to set up Legal Advice and Defence Offices for the purpose. Legislation thus compelled the profession to compel its members to defend indigent persons. In these circumstances the responsibility of the State must be the same as if it had chosen to operate the system itself.

The Court reached the same conclusion in the *Goddi* case, where the issue was not responsibility for lack of remuneration, but responsibility for deficient representation. The applicant, a shepherd, was convicted by an Italian court of various criminal offences, fined and sentenced to eighteen months' imprisonment. The prosecutor and the applicant both appealed and after several adjournments the Bologna Court of Appeal increased the sentence. The hearing of the appeal took place without the applicant who, unknown to the court, had been arrested for other offences and imprisoned elsewhere, and without the applicant's counsel because notice of the hearing had been sent to a lawyer who was no longer acting for him. When Mr Goddi's attempt to challenge the appeal proceedings in the Court of Cassation was unsuccessful, he lodged an application with the Commission.

There was no doubt that on the facts the applicant did not have the benefit of the 'practical and effective' defence which we have seen Article 6(3)(c) of the Convention requires. However, the question, and the point which makes the case one of particular interest in the context of the effectiveness principle, was whether the situation in which the applicant found himself was one for which the government was responsible.

With regard to the applicant's absence from the hearing in the Court of Appeal, the European Court decided that the public prosecutor's office had taken the necessary steps to serve the summons on the applicant and that there was insufficient evidence to blame the prison authorities for his non-appearance. As regards the absence of the applicant's lawyer, however, the Court was satisfied that the judicial authorities ought to have realised that only his new lawyer could provide the applicant with an effective defence and should therefore have ensured that he was notified.

At the hearing in the Court of Appeal the applicant was represented by an officially appointed lawyer who was unfamiliar with his case. The government argued that even if this meant that Mr Goddi lacked an effective defence, the State was not responsible because the court could not supervise the way in which counsel carried out his duties. The European Court did not agree. Pointing out that its duty was 'to determine whether the Bologna Court of Appeal took steps to ensure that the accused had the benefit of a fair trial, including the opportunity for an effective defence',[31] it held that the Italian court could have adjourned the hearing (as the public prosecutor's office had requested), or directed that the hearing be suspended to give counsel an opportunity to study the case file, prepare his pleadings and, if necessary, consult his client. The failure to do this, together with the failure to notify Mr Goddi's lawyer, meant that at the hearing in the Court of Appeal there had been a violation of Article 6(3)(c).

The decision is clearly correct and, like the *Van der Mussele* case, shows the Court refusing to allow its attention to be diverted from the central issue. If, despite the handicap of unfamiliarity with the case, the applicant's counsel in the Court of Appeal had succeeded in presenting an effective defence, there would have been no violation, and the absence of counsel would not have mattered. By the same token, however, since the applicant was entitled to an effective defence, it was not open to the government to evade responsibility when he had not.

A further aspect of State responsibility had to be considered by the Court in the *Soering* case. The question there was whether the United Kingdom would violate Article 3 by extraditing the applicant to the United States if doing so would expose him to the risk of inhuman or degrading treatment. The government pointed out, correctly, that the Convention creates obligations only for the Contracting States and that the latter, in turn, are not responsible for acts which occur outside their jurisdiction. According to the government, it followed from these basic principles that extradition to a non-Contracting State could not involve responsibility under Article 3, but the Court, which was considering the point for the first time in this case, disagreed.

In the Court's view the key to the case was the effectiveness principle. Recalling that the object and purpose of the Convention 'require that its provisions be interpreted and applied so as to make its safeguards practical and effective',[32] the Court observed that Article 3 contains an absolute prohibition and enshrines a fundamental value. Although it is not usual for the Convention institutions to pronounce on the existence or otherwise of potential violations of the Convention, a departure from this rule was necessary in order to ensure the effectiveness of the safeguard provided in Article 3. The Court therefore concluded that:

. . . the decision by a Contracting State to extradite a fugitive may give rise to an issue under Article 3, and hence engage the responsibility of that State under the Convention, where substantial grounds have been shown for believing that the person concerned, if extradited, faces a real risk of being subjected to torture or to inhuman or degrading treatment or punishment in the requesting country.[33]

The decision in this case, which it is worth noting was unanimous, has far-reaching implications. The ruling that extradition can give rise to an action under Article 3 has been extended in subsequent cases to other forms of removal[34] and the Court has hinted that the underlying principle could also be relevant to the right to a fair trial under Article 6, which raises the possibility of further extensions. Where responsibility is based upon the risks an applicant faces in a non-Contracting State the Court must, of course, assess conditions in the country concerned against the standards of the Convention.[35] Nevertheless, as the Court emphasised in *Soering*, it is not the responsibility of that country which is at issue, whether under the Convention or otherwise. Rather, 'it is liability incurred by the . . . Contracting State by reason of its having taken action which has as a direct consequence the exposure of an individual to proscribed ill-treatment',[36] a liability which the Court has decided is necessary to ensure the effectiveness of the Convention.

Our last example of effectiveness in the context of State responsibility goes back to a point mentioned earlier. In *X and Y v Netherlands*, it will be recalled, the Court held that the positive obligations inherent in effective respect for family life may require the State to take positive measures even as regards the relations of individuals between themselves. This decision relates directly to an issue raised, but left open, in the Article 11 cases and is a further illustration of the bearing of effectiveness on the scope of State responsibility. Moreover, another aspect of this case demonstrates the same tendency. When the Court, having established the respondent's liability, turned to the issue of compensating Miss Y, the government submitted that the consequences, which the applicant was still suffering seven years after her rape, should be attributed to her assailant rather than to the respondent's failure to provide a criminal sanction for the assault. The Court, however, dismissed this submission and holding that the Netherlands authorities had 'a degree of responsibility'[37] for Miss Y's situation, awarded a sum of 3,000 Dutch guilders as just satisfaction.

It is not difficult to see the connection between this conclusion and the effectiveness of the Convention. Acceptance of the government's argument would have meant that no compensation was called for and largely undermined the decision on the merits. The justification for making the State pay was therefore essentially the same as the basis for the Court's decision on the main issue. Because a criminal sanction should have been available and was not, the State had failed to perform its obligations and must therefore take responsibility for the consequences.

Limitations and reservations

The cases considered so far are, it is hoped, sufficient to demonstrate that the principle of effectiveness has played a central role in the Court's interpretation and application of the substantive provisions of the Convention. In addition, as we saw earlier, the same principle has exercised a major influence on the Court's conception of the nature of the Strasbourg system and of its own place within it. The Convention, however, contains more than provisions laying down rights and setting up arrangements for their enforcement. It also includes articles limiting the scope of the rights protected in various ways, or, which in practice amounts to the same thing, creating exceptions to them. In addition, by virtue of Article 64, States may, when signing or ratifying the Convention, make a reservation to a particular provision 'to the extent that any law then in force in its territory is not in conformity with the provision'. Naturally, reservations and exceptions or limitations contained in the Convention itself may need interpretation. The question which must now be considered, therefore, is the relevance of the principle of effectiveness when one of these derogating texts is in issue.

When discussing the significance of the object and purpose of the Convention in the previous chapter, we saw that the Court regards articles which limit or qualify the rights protected as provisions which must be construed strictly. It follows, as was explained, that in interpreting Article 8(2) in the *Klass* case and Article 10(2) in the *Sunday Times* case[38] the Court was concerned to give these exceptions a minimum, rather than a maximum, effect. This is true generally and, as many other cases confirm, there is a striking contrast to be found between the Court's lack of receptiveness to arguments based on the presumption of maximum effect in these limitation cases and its treatment of that presumption when considering positive obligations, the scope of particular terms and the other issues considered earlier.

The Court's refusal to accept a broad interpretation of the conditions authorising arrest or detention illustrate the point. Article 5 protects liberty and security of person and includes a list of the conditions authorising detention, which includes in Article 5(1)(b) 'the lawful arrest or detention of a person . . . in order to secure the fulfilment of any obligation prescribed by law'. In the *Engel* case the Netherlands Government sought to justify the 'provisional arrest' of one of the applicants on a broad reading of this provision, but the argument was rejected in the following words:

The Court considers that the words 'secure the fulfilment of any obligation prescribed by law' concern only cases where the law permits the detention of a person to compel him to fulfil a specific and concrete obligation which he has until then failed to satisfy. A wide interpretation would entail consequences incompatible with the notion of the rule of law from which the whole Convention draws its inspiration. . . . It would justify, for example, administrative internment meant to compel a citizen to discharge, in relation to any point whatever, his general duty of obedience to the law.[39]

Similarly, Article 5(1)(c) permits the lawful arrest or detention of a person 'for the purpose of bringing him before the competent legal authority on reasonable suspicion of having committed an offence' and in the case of *Fox, Campbell and Hartley* the Court rejected an argument from the British Government that 'reasonable suspicion' should be interpreted to mean no more than 'genuine suspicion'. The applicants in this case had been arrested as suspected terrorists and the Court conceded that on account of the problems posed by terrorism, in particular the need to protect sources of information, the reasonableness of the suspicion justifying such arrests 'cannot always be judged according to the same standards as are applied in conventional crime'. However, it went on to say that these exigencies 'cannot justify stretching the notion of "reasonableness" to the point where the essence of the safeguard secured by Article 5(1)(c) is impaired'.[40]

The same provision also authorises the lawful arrest or detention of a person 'when it is reasonably considered necessary to prevent his committing an offence', but when the Italian Government sought to rely on this provision in the *Guzzardi* case, which involved the detention of a member of the Mafia, the Court said that Article 5(1)(c) does not permit:

a policy of general prevention directed against an individual or a category of individuals who, like Mafiosi, present a danger on account of their continuing propensity to crime; it does no more than afford the Contracting States a means of preventing a concrete and specific offence.[41]

The Court adopted an equally strict approach when the Irish Government tried to invoke Article 17 in the *Lawless* case.[42] Article 17 provides:

Nothing in this Convention may be interpreted as implying for any State, group or person any right to engage in any activity or perform any act aimed at the destruction of any of the rights and freedoms set forth herein or at their limitation to a greater extent than is provided for in the Convention.

In *Lawless*, which concerned the arrest and detention without trial of a member of the IRA, the government argued that since the applicant's activities clearly fell within Article 17, he was not entitled to invoke Article 5, or any other article of the Convention. However, the Court rejected the argument. Article 17 does not, as a broad reading might suggest, have the effect of depriving those engaged in subversive activities of all their rights, but the narrower purpose of preventing a right being used to subvert free democratic institutions. Thus, while Article 17 permits the punishment of, for example, treason, those charged with the offence are still protected from arbitrary arrest and entitled to a fair trial.

These examples of the Court's treatment of limitations, which could be multiplied many times, are not so much instances of the effectiveness principle being ignored, as a demonstration of the obvious, but crucial, point that, as between rules and their exceptions, the application of the effectiveness principle depends on the overall context and the relative priority accorded to each by the interpreter. The principle, it will be recalled, requires a provision to be interpreted so as to give it the fullest effect consistent with the ordinary meaning *and with other parts of the text*. What the Court was doing in the cases referred to was giving a restricted effect to limiting provisions on the justifiable supposition that, looking at the Convention as a whole, the articles concerned with protecting rights should be treated as central and those authorising their restriction as marginal. This does not make limitations meaningless, but does remove any tendency to give such provisions their maximum effect. As a result, the application of the principle of effectiveness can, when limitations are considered, appear to be a highly selective process.

An equally selective approach is to be found in the Court's treatment of reservations. States have made relatively few reservations to the Convention and those which have been made are for the most part not of major significance. Cases involving reservations are correspondingly few and those which pass the barrier of the Commission to reach the Court even fewer. However, in a number of cases the Court has been required to examine arguments prompted by a State's reservation, but, in accordance with its policy in interpreting and applying the limitations set out in the Convention itself, has not used the principle of effectiveness to magnify their significance.

As part of its argument in the *Airey* case the Irish Government pointed out that the only provision dealing expressly with legal aid is Article 6(3)(c) of the Convention, which is confined to criminal cases. It also drew attention to the fact that Ireland had made a reservation in respect of this article and argued that in the circumstances it would be wrong to impose an obligation to provide civil legal aid through a broad interpretation of Article 6(1). This point was made as part of the government's more general argument that the Convention should not be interpreted so as to achieve social and economic developments and, as already noted, the Court rejected it. On the specific issue of the Irish reservation to Article 6(3)(c) the Court simply said that this could not 'be interpreted as affecting the obligations under Article 6(1); accordingly it is not relevant in the present context'.[43]

Since the issue in *Airey* involved civil and not criminal legal aid, the Irish reservation was not directly concerned with the question the Court had to decide. Moreover, as we have seen, the Court was anxious to explain that its decision did not mean that there is a general right to legal aid in civil cases. Even so, there is much to be said for the argument that a State which makes an express reservation as regards criminal legal aid *a fortiori* can scarcely be presumed to have accepted an implicit obligation to provide civil legal aid. The Court's unwillingness to see the Irish reservation as having any bearing on the scope of obligations under Article 6(1) thus demonstrates the circumscribed scope of the effectiveness principle.[44]

The limited significance of reservations is also demonstrated by the case of *Campbell and Cosans* in which a British reservation to Article 2 of Protocol No. 1 was directly in issue. That article, which guarantees the right to education, provides also that 'In the exercise of any functions which it assumes in relation to education and to teaching, the State shall respect the right of parents to ensure such education and teaching in conformity with their own religious and philosophical convictions.' When the United Kingdom signed the protocol in 1952 it made a reservation in which it declared that:

in view of certain provisions of the Education Acts in force in the United Kingdom, the principle affirmed in the second sentence of Article 2 is accepted by the United Kingdom only so far as it is compatible with the provisions of efficient instruction and training, and the avoidance of unreasonable public expenditure.

One of the issues in *Campbell and Cosans* was whether, if the existence of corporal punishment as a disciplinary measure in Scottish schools failed to respect the 'philosophical convictions' of parents, the reservation entitled the government to adopt a policy of eliminating corporal punishment gradually (which it claimed to be doing), and thereby provided an answer to the applicants' claim.

The Court rejected the argument based on the reservation and again did so very briefly. While it was prepared to accept that some of the ways of accommodating parents' wishes which had been suggested were impractical – such as establishing separate schools for the children of parents who objected to corporal punishment(!) – the Court said that it did not 'regard it as established that other means of respecting the applicants' convictions, such as a system of exemption for individual pupils in a particular school, would necessarily be incompatible with "the provision of efficient instruction and training, and the avoidance of unreasonable public expenditure" '.[45] Since the reservation was not applicable, and the Court held that the claim fell within Article 2, the United Kingdom was found to have violated the Convention.

The Court's vagueness as to how compliance with Article 2 might be achieved was seen by Sir Vincent Evans as a basic flaw in the judgment. In his partly dissenting opinion he pointed out that of the three methods of complying with the decision which had been suggested, none could be regarded as compatible with the British reservation. Separate schools had already been rejected by the Court; separate classes in the same school 'would surely involve unreasonable expense and hardly be compatible with efficient instruction and training'; while a third solution, different treatment of children in the same class, was irreconcilable with the fair administration of discipline, since children were 'likely to regard it as arbitrary and unjust if Johnny is exempted simply because his Mum or Dad says so'.[46]

Following the Court's judgment, the United Kingdom decided to abolish all corporal punishment in State schools, which suggests that Sir Vincent's appreciation of practicalities was not wide of the mark. It is, however, unnecessary to form a final view on this issue in order to appreciate that if the Court had interpreted the British reservation by reference to the canons of effectiveness considered earlier, the result would have been different. For then any doubts on the score of practicality would have been resolved in favour of, rather than against the government.[47]

A demonstration of what the Court regards as the role of the effectiveness principle in this area may be seen in cases where the issue has been not the interpretation of a reservation, but its validity. Reservations are governed by Article 64 of the Convention which provides:

1. Any State may, when signing this Convention or when depositing its instrument of ratification, make a reservation in respect of any particular provision of the Convention to the extent that any law then in force in its territory is not in conformity with the provision. Reservations of a general character shall not be permitted under this Article.
2. Any reservation made under this Article shall contain a brief statement of the law concerned.

In the *Belilos* case the Court had to decide whether an 'interpretative declaration' by which Switzerland had sought to restrict the scope of its obligations under Article 6(1), satisfied these requirements. The Court decided that it did not and gave two reasons. The first was that the declaration was 'of a general character' because it sought to qualify Switzerland's obligations in a way that was insufficiently specific. The second was that the declaration contained no reference to national law and so failed to satisfy Article 64(2). The Court therefore concluded that the declaration was invalid and could not be relied on.

This decision, which was subsequently followed in the *Weber* case,[48] is of particular interest in the present context because the Court not only denied effect to a government's attempt to restrict its obligations, as in the cases mentioned earlier, but did so by repudiating arguments which would have limited the significance of Article 64 in favour of considerations supporting that provision's effectiveness. Thus in relation to Article 64(1) the Court rejected the government's submission that the scope of the declaration could be ascertained by taking account of its purpose and circumstances of conclusion and instead chose to emphasise its wording and the illegitimacy of reservations 'couched in terms that are too vague or broad for it to be possible to determine their exact meaning and scope'.[49] It was similarly unimpressed with the argument that holding governments to Article 64(2) would present difficulties for federal States and that compliance should accordingly be treated as a mere technicality. Explaining that this provision applies to all States, whether unitary or federal, it held that the 'brief statement of the law concerned' is both an evidential factor and a contribution to legal certainty. Consequently, whatever the practical problems, the omission of such a statement could not be justified and must render a reservation void.

To avoid misunderstanding it should be explained that the reason for referring to these cases is not to show that reservations are bound to be ineffective. On the contrary, in the rare event of a case reaching the Court and raising a matter falling squarely within a valid reservation, the latter will certainly be applied. In the *Ringeisen* case,[50] for example, the Court had no hesitation in applying an Austrian reservation to Article 6(1) and subsequently did so again in the *Ettl* case.[51] The issue therefore is not whether reservations will be given meaning, for undoubtedly they will. With reservations, however, as with other limitations, the Court does not seek an interpretation with the same enthusiasm for effectiveness as it shows when interpreting provisions of the Convention protecting individual rights.

The limits of the principle of effectiveness

From what has been said so far, it should be clear that considerations of effectiveness play a major part in the Court's jurisprudence. Although, as we have just seen, the Court does not tend to interpret reservations or provisions which limit the rights protected with the aim of maximising their effect, in relation to the rights themselves its use of the principle of effectiveness has been very conspicuous indeed in furnishing the justification for its development of the law of the Convention. It would be easy to conclude from all this that the principle of effectiveness provides the Court, or indeed any judicial tribunal, with a tool of almost limitless potential; that any decision which can plausibly be said to promote human rights, or other object which can be identified, can be justified by reference to the principle of effectiveness; that it is, in short, a *carte blanche* for unlimited judicial legislation. In its more extreme manifestations the principle can certainly seem to have this effect. This is not, however, a consequence of the doctrine of effectiveness, but rather the result of using it in a way which ignores its limitations.

The first limitation is to be found in the words of the text. The effectiveness principle is, after all, a principle of *interpretation*. It requires, it will be recalled, that provisions shall be interpreted 'so as to give them their fullest weight and effect consistent with the normal sense of the words and with other parts of the text'. It follows that the terms of any treaty are the primary reference point and no interpretation which is inconsistent with the text, whatever its other merits, can be regarded as legally correct.

The Court's use of the principle of ordinary meaning – 'the normal sense of the words' – has already been noted and need not be described again. As an example of the way in which attention to the text can restrain the temptation to interpretative excess we may take the Court's treatment of the argument that the presumption of innocence had been violated in the *Engel* case. As we have seen, the Court has made full use of the principle of effectiveness in relation to both the applicability and the application of Article 6(2). However, when the applicants in the *Engel* case sought to argue that it had been violated because a military court took into account in its sentencing their participation in publications for which they had not been prosecuted, the Court decided that the clause had no application. Explaining that 'As its wording shows, it deals only with the proof of guilt and not with the kind or level of punishment', the Court held that Article 6(2) 'does not prevent the national judge, when deciding upon the penalty to impose on an accused lawfully convicted of the offence submitted to his adjudication, from having regard to factors relating to the individual's personality'.[52]

The decision is clearly correct. A domestic court must not, of course, do anything to suggest that a defendant may be guilty of crimes for which he has not been convicted. However, an interpretation of the presumption of innocence which went beyond this, and sought to limit the considerations which can be taken into account in sentencing, would lie outside anything which could be justified by reference to the effectiveness principle.

A second limitation involves consideration of the object and purpose of the agreement. Even if, as the teleological school maintain, it is legitimate to seek the object and purpose of a treaty outside the text itself, no one could argue with any semblance of plausibility either that the European Convention is intended to protect all individual rights, or that in relation to what it does include, the protection of the said rights is its only purpose. The first proposition is disproved by the Preamble with its reference to the States' resolution 'to take the *first* steps for the collective enforcement of *certain of the Rights* stated in the Universal Declaration' and by the text itself and the subsequent protocols. The second proposition is inconsistent with the inclusion of the numerous limitations and qualifications to the rights protected, which however broadly or narrowly they may be interpreted, are clearly relevant evidence of the Convention's purpose.

All this places very significant limitations on the extent to which the principle of effectiveness (or for that matter any other principle) can be used to extend the scope of the Convention. Because the Convention protects some rights but not others, in cases involving rights which were deliberately omitted the Court has usually refused to use the principle of effectiveness to fill the gap. Thus in *Kosiek*,[53] having decided that the applicant was really claiming a right of access to the civil service, the Court rejected his attempt to invoke Article 10; while in *Johnston*,[54] having decided that the right to a divorce was deliberately excluded from Article 12, the Court decided that, considerations of effectiveness notwithstanding, it could not be read into Article 8. Conversely, while the Court has been reluctant to read the various limitations and qualifications in the Convention widely, their presence means that they must be given at least some effect. Thus, as we have seen in chapter 4, in cases such as *Leander*[55] the Court has held that where measures are justified under a provision such as Article 8(2), it will not interpret another article in a way which renders the first provision nugatory.

The point just made is, of course, subject to the qualification that it is for the Court to decide how a given case is to be approached and the importance to be attached to various considerations. What some judges see in one way, others will see in another. Thus in *Kosiek* one member of the Court considered that in the interests of protecting a limited right of access to the civil service, the applicant's case could be brought within Article 10, while in *Johnston* one judge was prepared to hold that the respondent had failed to provide effective respect for the applicants' family life. There is therefore always likely to be scope for argument, just as on the issue of textuality considered earlier. The point which is being made is not that these decisions are necessarily uncontroversial or easy, but that serious reflection on the object and purpose of the Convention indicates that the effectiveness principle can never be simply a device for an unlimited extension of its scope.

A third limitation on the effectiveness principle arises from the relation between the Court and the Contracting States. Suppose the Court is invited to interpret a particular provision in a way which is consistent with the language of the Convention, though not compelled by it. Suppose further that the interpretation in question would clearly have the effect of promoting individual rights in conformity with the object and purpose of this part of the Convention. In other words, suppose that neither of the limitations considered so far is an obstacle. The third consideration which constitutes a major constraint on the utilisation of the principle of effectiveness is whether it is appropriate for the Court, in view of its position, to do so.

Cases in which the Court is required to consider the issue of positive obligations are a good illustration of this point. In the *Abdulaziz* case, for example, the applicants argued that respect for family life encompassed the right to establish a home in the State of one's nationality or lawful residence, and that the dilemma of either moving abroad or being separated from one's spouse was inconsistent with this principle. The Court, however, acknowledged the relevance of positive obligations to 'effective' respect for family life, but held that in relation to such obligations the State enjoys a wide 'margin of appreciation'. It then decided that in the circumstances of the case no obligation of the type invoked had been violated. In the *Rees* case, similarly, when the Court was considering the measures required by Article 8 to provide effective respect for the private life of transsexuals, the Court described its observations in *Abdulaziz* as 'particularly relevant',[56] and again decided that there was no violation.

The point the Court was making in these cases is that not every interpretation which might be justified as securing a more effective protection of individual rights can be regarded as appropriate. In deciding not to adopt an extended interpretation in these cases the Court was really saying that in present circumstances some matters are best left to national regulation. In other words, and to put the issue in terms of effectiveness, although the Court could have found a justification by reference to the principle of effectiveness, it did not consider that in the particular circumstances such a decision was required. Why the Court came to this conclusion in *Abdulaziz* and *Rees* and not in *Marckx* and *Airey* is a question best left until we have considered the margin of appreciation in chapter 7. The immediately relevant point is that the Court's appreciation of its role in relation to the Contracting States, like the constraints imposed by the obligation to interpret a text, and its conception of the object and purpose of the Convention, must always be borne in mind to understand the application of the effectiveness principle in its jurisprudence.

Notes

1 Series A, No. 37 para. 33. See also the *Kamasinski* case, Series A, No. 168.
2 Series A, No. 49 para. 30.
3 *Ibid.*
4 This was because Article 6(2) 'governs criminal proceedings in their entirety, irrespective of the outcome of the prosecution, and not solely the examination of the merits of the charge', Series A, No. 62 para. 30.
5 It should be noted, however, that in the *Lutz*, *Englert* and *Nölkenbockoff* cases, Series A, No. 123, the principle laid down in *Minelli* was given a restricted application. On the other hand, in the subsequent *Salabiaku* case, Series A, No. 141A, the Court held that Article 6(2) has a bearing on the substantive rules of criminal law, as well as on criminal procedure, thus widening the scope of the presumption of innocence quite significantly.

6 Series A, No. 18.
7 Series A, No. 32.
8 *Ibid.*, para. 26.
9 Series A, No. 31 para. 31.
10 For discussion of the role of the margin of appreciation in the *Marckx* case and more generally, see chapter 7.
11 *Ibid.*, partly dissenting opinion of Judge Matscher, section I.
12 Series A, No. 160.
13 Sometimes termed *'drittwirkung'*. See P. van Dijk and G. J. H. van Hoof, *Theory and Practice of the European Convention on Human Rights* (2nd ed.), Kluwer, Deventer, 15–20 (1990); and M. Forde, 'Non-governmental interferences with human rights', *British Year Book of International Law*, LVI, 253 (1985).
14 Series A, No. 91 para. 23.
15 Series A, No. 139.
16 *Ibid.*, para. 32.
17 The significance of the Court's ruling on the facts for the scope of freedom of assembly is discussed in chapter 6.
18 Series A, No. 18, separate opinion of Judge Sir Gerald Fitzmaurice, para. 5.
19 Series A, No. 28 para. 41.
20 Series A, No. 82 paras. 83–7.
21 Series A, No. 94 para. 62.
22 *Ibid.*, para. 63. For subsequent decisions adopting a broad conception of family life see the *Berrehab* case, Series A, No. 138, and the *Gaskin* case, Series A, No. 160.
23 Series A, No. 64 para. 31.
24 Series A, No. 37 para. 35. See also the *Granger* case, Series A, No. 174, and the *Quaranta* case, Series A, No. 205.
25 For an excellent survey see I. Brownlie, *System of the Law of Nations. State Responsibility, Part I*, Clarendon Press, Oxford (1983).
26 Series A, No. 21.
27 Series A, No. 20.
28 *Ibid.*, para. 33.
29 Series A, No. 44.
30 Series A, No. 70. See also the *Martins Moreira* case, Series A, No. 143, and the *Moreira de Azevedo* case, Series A, No. 189, which confirm that the State is responsible for all its authorities and not merely its judicial organs.
31 Series A, No. 76 para. 31.
32 Series A, No. 161 para. 87.
33 *Ibid.*, para. 91.
34 See the *Cruz Varas* case, Series A, No. 201, and the *Vilvarajah* case, Series A, No. 215.
35 In the *Soering* case the Court went on to find that if the applicant was returned to the United States he would run a real risk of a death sentence and consequently exposure to the 'death row phenomenon' which, in the Court's view, would go beyond the threshold of Article 3. It therefore concluded that the decision to extradite the applicant, if implemented, would give rise to a violation of the Convention.
36 Series A, No. 161 para. 91.
37 Series A, No. 91 para. 40. Contrast the *Nielsen* case, Series A, No. 144.
38 Series A, No. 30.
39 Series A, No. 22 para. 69.

40 Series A, No. 182 para. 32.
41 Series A, No. 39 para. 102.
42 Series A, No. 3.
43 Series A, No. 32 para. 26.
44 The Irish Government's argument on this point was, however, weakened by the fact that it had accepted that, in principle, civil legal aid was desirable in cases of this type; see the dissenting opinion of Judge O'Donoghue, *ibid.*, section A.
45 Series A, No. 48 para. 37.
46 *Ibid.*, partly dissenting opinion of Judge Sir Vincent Evans, para. 7.
47 The main issue in *Campbell and Cosans* was whether the institution of corporal punishment in State schools failed to respect the 'philosophical convictions' of parents who objected to it. The Court decided that it did, giving the term 'philosophical convictions' a broad interpretation, which, as we noted in chapter 4, ignored the *travaux préparatoires* and the Court's own more limited interpretation in its previous jurisprudence. The reader cannot help but be struck by the way the Court bent every effort to secure the maximum effect for Article 2, then went out of its way to minimise the effect of the reservation.
48 Series A, No. 177.
49 Series A, No. 132 para. 55.
50 Series A, No. 13.
51 Series A. No. 117.
52 Series A, No. 22 para. 90.
53 Series A, No. 105.
54 Series A, No. 112.
55 Series A, No. 116.
56 Series A, No. 106 para. 37.

CHAPTER 6

Human rights
and democratic values

In the Preamble to the Statute of the Council of Europe the Contracting States declared that they were 'Reaffirming their devotion to the spiritual and moral values which are the common heritage of their peoples and the true source of individual freedom, political liberty and the rule of law, principles which form the basis of all genuine democracy.'

The connection between human rights and democracy indicated here is further emphasised in the Preamble to the European Convention where the Parties not only referred to their 'common heritage of political traditions, ideals, freedom and the rule of law', but also reaffirmed '. . . their profound belief in those Fundamental Freedoms which are the foundations of justice and peace in the world and are best maintained on the one hand by an effective political democracy and on the other by a common understanding and observance of the Human Rights upon which they depend.'

Now the interpretation and application of a human rights convention is not a mechanical process and the Court, as noted earlier, has consistently sought to give the European Convention an effective interpretation. Since the latter's obligations and machinery have the primary purpose of preserving the rule of law and democracy, it is instructive to consider how these conceptions, the spiritual bedrock of the Convention, have influenced the Court's development of the law.

Free elections

Article 3 of Protocol No. 1 provides that 'The High Contracting Parties undertake to hold free elections at reasonable intervals by secret ballot, under conditions which will ensure the free expression of the people in the choice of the legislature.' The Convention, as we shall see shortly, employs the rule of law as a central value and requires its rights and freedoms to be protected by law and any limitations to such rights and

freedoms to be defined by law. Article 3, in turn, requires laws to be made
by a legislature responsible to the people and therefore without exagger-
ation can be said to underpin the whole structure of the Convention.[1] As
the Court has put it, 'According to the Preamble to the Convention,
fundamental human rights and freedoms are best maintained by "an
effective political democracy". Since it enshrines a characteristic principle of democracy, Article 3 of Protocol No. 1 is accordingly of prime
importance in the Convention system.'[2]

The Court considered the scope and significance of Article 3 in the case
of *Mathieu-Mohin and Clerfayt* which concerned a dispute over the
electoral arrangements applicable to voters in the Flemish region of
Belgium. Under the legislation then in force the Flemish region was
under the authority of the Flemish Council, a body with legislative
powers in regional and community matters. The Council consisted of the
members of the Dutch language groups in the Belgian House of Representatives and Senate. In order to belong to one of these groups a
Representative or Senator elected in Brussels must have taken his parliamentary oath in Dutch. It followed that French-speaking voters in
Brussels could elect only Dutch-speakers to the Flemish Council, or
French-speakers who agreed to join the Dutch language group, an action
with constitutional implications. The applicants in the case had been
elected in Brussels and taken their oaths in French. They were thus not
entitled to sit on the Flemish Council and claimed that this discrimination
violated the Convention.

The interest of this case is to be found in the way the Court dealt with
the substance of the claim[3] and, since Article 3 corresponds to provisions
contained in other human rights treaties,[4] with its elucidation of the scope
of the obligation to hold free elections in particular. We have already seen
that in much of its case-law the Court is able to adopt or develop legal
ideas which have evolved through the work of the Commission. This is
certainly the case as regards Article 3 where the Court noted that 'From
the idea of an "institutional" right to the holding of free elections . . . the
Commission has moved to the concept of "universal suffrage" . . . and
then, as a consequence, to the concept of subjective rights of participation – "the right to vote" and the "right to stand for election to the
legislature" . . .'.[5] The Court then stated that it approved the latter
concept.

Although the right to participate in government is fundamental, it is no
part of democratic theory that it should be regarded as absolute. The
Court recognised this when it stated that there is room here for implied
limitations and drew attention to the fact that constitutional arrangements in the Contracting States make the right to vote and to stand for
elections subject to various conditions which are not in principle

prohibited by Article 3. It added, however, that while there is a wide margin of appreciation, it is for the Court 'to satisfy itself that the conditions do not curtail the rights in question to such an extent as to impair their very essence and deprive them of their effectiveness'.[6] Any conditions must also, of course, have a legitimate aim and the means employed must be proportionate. Thus while the Court recognised the scope for national variations, it made it clear that the democratic ideal of 'the free expression of the opinion of the people in the choice of the legislature' remains the core concept.

No less important than the conditions of participation is the question: participation in what? Article 3 refers to 'the legislature' which clearly rules out a citizen's entitlement to elect every body with powers over him, but leaves considerable scope for interpretation. The Court dealt with this point by holding that 'the word "legislature" does not necessarily mean only the national parliament', and adding that the term 'has to be interpreted in the light of the constitutional structure of the State in question'.[7] This was an important ruling because it enabled the Court to conclude that the Flemish Council was a part of the Belgian legislature, so bringing it within Article 3 and, more generally, because while respecting the language of the Convention, it allows the underlying principle of democratic participation to be given its maximum effect.

The central question in any system of democratic government is the method of appointing the legislature. As with the issues already considered, this is a matter on which the Convention supplies only general guidance, providing simply that elections shall be 'free', 'at reasonable intervals', 'by secret ballot' and under conditions which will ensure a free expression of opinion. In the light of this the Court concluded that there is no obligation on the Contracting States to introduce a specific system such as proportional representation and that they enjoy a wide margin of appreciation. However, as in its treatment of the conditions of participation, the Court proceeded to identify what it saw as the guiding principles.

Explaining that 'Electoral systems seek to fulfil objectives which are sometimes scarcely compatible with each other: on the one hand, to reflect fairly faithfully the opinions of the people, and on the other, to channel currents of thought so as to promote the emergence of a sufficiently clear and coherent political will', the Court held that the reference in Article 3 to the free expression of opinion implies two things: freedom of expression, which is already protected by Article 10, and 'the principle of equality of treatment of all citizens in the exercise of their right to vote and their right to stand for election'. The Court added, however, that the principle of equal treatment does not mean 'that all votes must necessarily have equal weight as regards the outcome of the election or that all candidates must have equal chances of victory. Thus no electoral system can eliminate "wasted votes" '.[8]

A final consideration was the particular cultural and constitutional context. For 'any electoral system must be assessed in the light of the political evolution of the country concerned'. As a result, 'features that would be unacceptable in the context of one system may accordingly be justified in the context of another',[9] always provided the chosen system conforms to the Convention's requirements.

Since our concern is with the Court's conception of democratic values and their bearing on the development of the law, it is unnecessary to describe how the Court applied the above principles to decide the particular issues in *Mathieu-Mohin and Clerfayt*. However, one point of general significance should be noted. In accordance with the last consideration mentioned, when the Court upheld the arrangements for French-speaking electors in the district concerned, it attached great importance to the regional and linguistic diversity of Belgium. But five members of the Court found this reasoning unpersuasive. As we shall see in the next chapter, cases involving the margin of appreciation are particularly difficult when, as here, a practice is sought to be justified by conditions peculiar to the respondent State.

The rule of law

The rule of law has been defined in various ways but for present purposes may be taken as the principle that the individual's dealings with the State and his fellow citizens should be regulated by a framework of legal rules, whose interpretation and application are in the hands of independent courts. So understood, it is clear that the concept of the rule of law underlies not only the obvious provisions of the Convention: Article 5 (the right to liberty), Article 6 (the right to a fair trial) and Article 7 (no retrospective criminal laws), but all the other provisions as well. However, the main situations in which the Court has employed the rule of law fall into three distinct, but related, categories.

The right of access to the courts

The first is a group of cases beginning with the celebrated decision in *Golder*, which concerns the right of access to the courts under Article 6(1). Mr Golder, it will be recalled, while in prison, was prevented from consulting a solicitor with a view to initiating libel proceedings against a prison officer. It was explained in chapter 4 that in finding that the authorities had violated the Convention the Court held that Article 6(1), though ostensibly concerned only with the conduct of legal proceedings once they have begun, goes further and contains an implied right to initiate such proceedings. The interest of the case in the present context is that the Court based its conclusion on the object and purpose of the Convention and in developing this interpretation placed considerable weight on the reference to the rule of law in the Preamble.

Thus when confronted with the government's argument that the Convention is not a general, but a selective protection of rights, the Court said:

The 'selective' nature of the Convention cannot be put in question. It may also be accepted, as the Government have submitted, that the Preamble does not include the rule of law in the object and purpose of the Convention, but points to it as being one of the features of the common spiritual heritage of the member States of the Council of Europe. The Court however considers, like the Commission, that it would be a mistake to see in this reference a merely 'more or less rhetorical reference', devoid of relevance for those interpreting the Convention. One reason why the signatory Governments decided to 'take the first steps for the collective enforcement of certain of the Rights stated in the Universal Declaration' was their profound belief in the rule of law. It seems both natural and in conformity with the principle of good faith to bear in mind this widely proclaimed consideration when interpreting the terms of Article 6(1) according to their context and in the light of the object and purpose of the Convention.[10]

The rule of law was not the sole basis for the Court's conclusion in *Golder*. As might be expected in a decision which on account of its far-reaching implications was bound to be controversial, the Court sought to justify its conclusion in a variety of other ways, referring to the French text, general principles of law and international law. It is fair to say, however, that the rule of law is a most prominent element in the judgment and the supreme importance of that principle supplies its central theme.

For the student of the judicial process *Golder* is informative in two ways. As an illustration of judicial technique, it demonstrates how a persuasive judgment can be built on a doctrinal foundation which the members of a court know that they share with their audience. This, it will be recalled, was a point made earlier in chapter 2. Of more immediate relevance, however, is a second point: such values are not simply an effective way of winning support for decisions, they are the source of the decisions themselves. Just as the Court declined to see in the Preamble a 'more or less rhetorical reference' to the rule of law, so it would be wrong to dismiss the Court's invocation of the concept in the same superficial way. It is certainly unwise to take everything said by a court at face value, but when an interpretation of a human rights instrument is justified in terms of a basic cultural precept, it is cynicism, not sophistication, to assume that the real explanation for the decision lies elsewhere.

The legality principle
Another aspect of the rule of law which has influenced the Court's jurisprudence may be termed the legality principle, or the principle that

before something can be regarded as a law, it must meet certain fundamental requirements which distinguish government on the basis of law
from administration resting on discretion and arbitrariness. The
opportunty to emphasise this aspect of the rule of law has arisen because a
number of articles of the Convention authorise limitation of the rights
and freedoms protected therein, provided such limitation is necessary for
the achievement of a specified aim and is 'prescribed by law', 'in accordance with the law', or 'provided for by law'.

In its judgment in the *Sunday Times* case the Court held that the
expression 'prescribed by law' in Article 10(2) must be interpreted as
involving at least two requirements:

Firstly, the law must be adequately accessible: the citizen must be able to have an
indication that is adequate in the circumstances of the legal rules applicable to a
given case. Secondly, a norm cannot be regarded as a 'law' unless it is formulated
with sufficient precision to enable the citizen to regulate his conduct: he must be
able – if need be with appropriate advice – to foresee, to a degree that is
reasonable in the circumstances, the consequences which a given action may
entail.[11]

A commentator has observed that this 'might well be mistaken for a
passage from Dicey's discussion of the Rule of Law'[12] and the point is well
taken. Had the Court accepted the argument put forward by the British
Government and decided that it is sufficient for a law to qualify as such
within the particular national system, many of the Convention's
safeguards would have proved illusory. By rejecting this view in favour of
an autonomous interpretation, the Court was again demonstrating how
the idea of the rule of law can be used to elucidate and consolidate the
protection of the Convention.

Although the principle of legality requires conduct to be regulated by
rules that are clear, there is obviously a limit to what may be demanded in
this regard. The need to approach the legality principle with an awareness
of its practical limitations was recognised in the *Sunday Times* case when
the Court observed that while an individual should in principle be able to
foresee the consequences of his actions:

Those consequences need not be foreseeable with absolute certainty: experience
shows this to be unattainable. Again, whilst certainty is highly desirable, it may
bring in its train excessive rigidity and the law must be able to keep pace with
changing circumstances. Accordingly, many laws are inevitably couched in terms
which, to a greater or lesser extent, are vague and whose interpretation and
application are questions of practice.[13]

Using this principle, the Court was able to conclude that the law in issue
in that case – the common law rules relating to contempt of court – were
formulated with sufficient precision to satisfy the requirements of the

Convention. Subsequently, however, in *Silver*[14], another case involving the United Kingdom, the Court reached the opposite conclusion as regards the authorities' stopping of certain correspondence from the applicants who were serving sentences of imprisonment. In that case, which concerned the right to respect for correspondence guaranteed by Article 8, the Court recognised that the screening of about ten million items of prisoners' correspondence each year is the sort of task for which a significant element of discretion is unavoidable, but was not satisfied that in all the situations complained of an adequately foreseeable basis of interference had been shown to exist.

The requirement of foreseeability gives rise to special problems in cases concerned with security or intelligence issues. Indeed, in the *Malone* case, which concerned interception of communications by the police, the British Government argued that where the law is not concerned with creating obligations for the individual, the paramount consideration should be not certainty, but the lawfulness of the action under domestic law. The Court accepted that the requirements of the Convention cannot be exactly the same in a case of secret surveillance as when the restriction of individuals' conduct is in issue. 'In particular,' said the Court 'the requirement of foreseeability cannot mean that an individual should be enabled to foresee when the authorities are likely to intercept his communications so that he can adapt his conduct accordingly.' However, the Court also observed that the phrase 'in accordance with the law' in Article 8(2) 'does not merely refer back to domestic law but also relates to the quality of the law, requiring it to be compatible with the rule of law, which is expressly mentioned in the preamble to the Convention'.[15] Consequently, the law must still be both accessible and clear enough to provide an adequate indication of when and how this potentially dangerous interference with civil liberty can be used.

Judged by the above criteria, the Court found the law relating to the interception of communications in England and Wales to be conspicuously wanting. Review of the relevant provisions indicated that domestic law was obscure and open to differing interpretations. It could not be said with any certainty how far the power to intercept was regulated by legal rules and how far it was a matter of executive discretion. Agreeing, therefore, with the Commission, the Court concluded that 'the law of England and Wales does not indicate with reasonable clarity the scope and manner of exercise of the relevant discretion conferred on the public authorities. To that extent, the minimum degree of legal protection to which citizens are entitled under the rule of law in a democratic society is lacking'.[16]

The principles elaborated in *Malone* were subsequently applied by the Court in the *Leander* case,[17] which concerned the related issue of security checks on prospective State employees. In that case, however, the Court decided that the Swedish law in question, which closely defined the relevant security procedure, was sufficiently precise to satisfy the Convention's requirements. Like the general question of how certain it is reasonable to demand the law to be, the question of the precision attainable in laws governing security matters is always likely to be difficult. What the Court has done is to recognise that this is so, while preserving the concept of the rule of law as its guiding principle.

Judicial safeguards

Closely related to both the right of access to the courts and the legality principle is a third aspect of the rule of law: the value of judicial safeguards when the authorities seek to justify an interference with the individual's rights under a provision such as Article 8(2). It is not enough for a given limitation to be 'in accordance with the law'; the Convention also requires that the limitation in question should be 'necessary in a democratic society' for achieving a prescribed aim. This involves a number of considerations, one of which – the question of procedural safeguards – the Court has identified as resting on the rule of law.

The *Klass* case, like the *Malone* case, raised the issue of when arrangements for telephone tapping and secret surveillance can be considered compatible with Article 8. However, the West German arrangements in issue in *Klass*, unlike their British counterpart, were based on legislation laying down strict conditions and procedures. There was therefore no doubt that the disputed measures were in accordance with the law. Were they also necessary in a democratic society 'in the interests of national security', or for one of the other aims set out in Article 8(2)?

To answer this question the Court made a detailed review of the disputed legislation and placed particular emphasis on the issue of safeguards. Pointing out that when surveillance is initiated, and subsequently when it is being carried out, the individual will normally be unaware of what is happening, the Court held that it is consequently essential that the relevant procedures should provide adequate guarantees for his rights. It then went on:

In addition, the values of a democratic society must be followed as faithfully as possible in the supervisory procedures if the bounds of necessity, within the meaning of Article 8(2), are not to be exceeded. One of the fundamental principles of a democratic society is the rule of law, which is expressly referred to in the Preamble to the Convention. . . . The rule of law implies, *inter alia*, that an interference by the executive authorities with an individual's rights should be subject to an effective control which should normally be assured by the judiciary, at least in the last resort, judicial control offering the best guarantees of independence, impartiality and a proper procedure.[18]

Here, then, the Court was making the point that in relation to limitations on the individual's rights the rule of law has a double impact, not only demanding satisfaction of the principle of legality, but also requiring the provision of safeguards against abuse. Subsequently, in the *Silver* case it was argued that the relevant safeguards must be incorporated in the law authorising the measures complained of, and that failure to do this meant that the measures concerned were not in accordance with the law. This would not have mattered in *Klass*, since the safeguards were incorporated in the law authorising surveillance, but would be significant in situations such as *Silver* where such safeguards as were available were provided elsewhere. However, this argument, which would in effect have subsumed the safeguards question under the legality principle, rather than as part of the necessity issue (where it is surely more appropriate) was rejected.

Having made the point that in principle judicial control of surveillance is desirable, the Court in *Klass* went on to approve the German system though the supervisory control was vested not in the courts, but in a Parliamentary Board and a body called the G10 Commission which the Board appointed. This was because the Court was satisfied that both bodies were independent of the authorities carrying out the surveillance and were vested with sufficient powers to exercise an effective and continuous control. The Court's decision here is consistent with its treatment of the question of supervision in analogous cases, for example its interpretation of the phrase 'officer authorised by law to exercise judicial power' in Article 5(3)[19] and its ruling that in cases where the Convention requires the intervention of a court 'In order to determine whether a proceeding provides adequate guarantees regard must be had to the particular nature of the circumstances in which such proceeding takes place.'[20]

Finally it should be pointed out that in evaluating the German legislation in *Klass* the Court treated the issue of safeguards in a relative rather than an absolute way and as part of the 'compromise between the requirements for defending democratic society and individual rights . . . inherent in the system of the Convention.'[21] The Court was alive to the danger of secret surveillance 'undermining or even destroying democracy on the ground of defending it'.[22] On the other hand, it was fully aware that 'Democratic societies nowadays find themselves threatened by highly sophisticated forms of espionage and terrorism, with the result that the State must be able, in order effectively to counter such threats, to undertake secret surveillance of subversive elements operating within its jurisdiction.'[23]

The *Klass* case thus brings out a fundamental point about the relationship between human rights, the rule of law and democracy. If, as the

Preamble to the Convention states, and the Court has accepted, democracy is the best guarantee of human rights, then in cases like *Klass*, the values represented by the rule of law, important though they are, are no more than one factor in the balance which must be sought between, on the one hand, the individual's exercise of his rights and, on the other, the necessity for restrictive measures to protect democratic society as a whole.

Freedom of expression

Freedom of expression, which is protected by Article 10 of the Convention, is regarded as a fundamental guarantee in all human rights instruments. It is both an end in the sense that open communication is a condition of self-realisation and a means because it enables claims to be articulated and thereby permits other rights to be protected. Since democracy is based on the idea of consent to and participation in government, freedom of expression, which is essential to both, is one of its preconditions.

The link between freedom of expression and democracy was recognised by the Court in the *Handyside* case where it said:

The Court's supervisory functions oblige it to pay the utmost attention to the principles characterising a 'democratic society'. Freedom of expression constitutes one of the essential foundations of such a society, one of the basic conditions for its progress and for the development of every man. Subject to paragraph 2 of Article 10, it is applicable not only to 'information' or 'ideas' that are favourably received or regarded as inoffensive or as a matter of indifference, but also to those that offend, shock or disturb the State or any sector of the population. Such are the demands of that pluralism, tolerance and broadmindedness without which there is no 'democratic society'. This means, amongst other things, that every 'formality', 'condition', 'restriction' or 'penalty' imposed in this sphere must be proportionate to the legitimate aim pursued.[24]

The reference to 'pluralism, tolerance and broadmindedness' was particularly apt in *Handyside* because the case concerned a publication intended for schoolchildren which contained a variety of controversial material, including a substantial chapter on sex. When the book was banned in England the publisher claimed that his rights under Article 10 had been infringed. The Court, however, decided that in view of the State's margin of appreciation the interference with his freedom of expression could be justified under Article 10(2) as being 'prescribed by law and . . . necessary in a democratic society . . . for the protection of morals'. This may seem paradoxical in the light of the quotation, but it is not. Once it is recognised that freedom of expression is not the only value, there will always be cases where restrictions can be justified as necessary in a democratic society and the Court regarded this as one of them.

The purpose of freedom of expression, as the Court explained in the *Handyside* case, is to allow the exchange of information and opinions. Although, therefore, it is a right precious to everyone in a free society, it is especially valuable to the press which can promote public debate and provide a sounding-board for new ideas. The role of the press was the key issue in the *Sunday Times* case which raised the question of the weight to be attached to freedom of expression in comparison with 'the authority of the judiciary' and generated an unusually detailed discussion of the issues involved.

This case, one of the best-known, as well as one of the most controversial decisions of the European Court, arose out of the preparation by the *Sunday Times* of an article concerning litigation between the representatives of the victims of thalidomide and Distillers, the British manufacturers of the drug. The article, which reviewed evidence on the question of Distillers' liability, was the subject of an injunction, approved by the House of Lords, which restrained its publication on the ground of contempt of court.

The applicants, all of whom were connected with the paper, claimed that the injunction was a breach of Article 10. By a narrow majority the Commission supported this view and referred the case to the Court. By an even narrower margin the Court upheld this conclusion and decided that Article 10 had been infringed because, according to the eleven judges in the majority, the restraint on publication, though 'prescribed by law' and imposed for a legitimate purpose, was not 'necessary in a democratic society' for 'maintaining the authority . . . of the judiciary', as required by Article 10(2).

In its judgment the Court placed great emphasis on the value of press freedom and it is clear that the idea of the press as an essential component of a democratic society played an important part in its reasoning. Thus, after quoting its remarks on freedom of expression in the *Handyside* case, the Court went on:

These principles are of particular importance as far as the press is concerned. They are equally applicable to the field of the administration of justice, which serves the interests of the community at large and requires the co-operation of an enlightened public. There is general recognition of the fact that the courts cannot operate in a vacuum. Whilst they are the forum for the settlement of disputes, this does not mean that there can be no prior discussion of disputes elsewhere, be it in specialised journals, in the general press or amongst the public at large. Furthermore, whilst the mass media must not overstep the bounds imposed in the interests of the proper administration of justice, it is incumbent on them to impart information and ideas concerning matters that come before the courts just as in other areas of public interest. Not only do the media have the task of imparting such information and ideas: the public also has a right to receive them.[25]

The Court also relied on the principle that restrictions on the Convention's rights and freedoms are to be strictly construed. This clearly has the effect of reinforcing the case for freedom of publication. For if freedom of expression is the primary principle and the administration of justice a limited exception, restriction requires a very strong justification. To the minority judges, on the other hand, though freedom of expression was important, the Court's task was to balance competing and correlative objectives. Finding that the disputed injunction was restricted in both its subject matter and its duration, they concluded that as a justly proportionate response, it met the requirements of the Convention.

The principles laid down in the *Sunday Times* case were discussed further in the recent *Observer and Guardian* case.[26] This case concerned temporary injunctions imposed by courts in the United Kingdom relating to the book *Spycatcher* which were in operation between July 1986 and October 1988, pending the decision in a breach of confidence action. *Spycatcher* contained the memoirs of a retired member of the British Security Service and included an account of allegedly illegal activities, as well as other sensitive material. As in the *Sunday Times* case, the Court was prepared to recognise that the restraint on publication was 'prescribed by law'. Thus, like the earlier case, the main issue was whether what was plainly an interference with the applicant's freedom of expression could be justified under Article 10(2).

The Court held unanimously that there was a violation of Article 10 during the period from July 1987 to October 1988, but decided by 14 votes to 10 that there was no violation for the earlier period from July 1986 to July 1987. The reason why, in the view of the majority, a distinction could be drawn between the two periods was that in July 1987 *Spycatcher* was published in the United States. For the period before that publication the Court was prepared to accept that the interference with the applicants' freedom of expression was 'necessary in a democratic society' for maintaining the authority of the judiciary and in the interests of national security. Once the book had been published in the United States, however, and thus become freely available, the Court considered that it was impossible to maintain that such a prohibition was still essential and so ruled that in this period the Convention had been violated.

The Court's unanimous decision in relation to the second period confirms the majority view in the *Sunday Times* case that the role of the press in a democracy is so important that a strong justification, going beyond mere official convenience, is needed to justify interference with the publication of material of legitimate public concern. On the other hand, the division of opinion over the first period indicates that decisions as to when such prohibitions are necessary are still liable to be controversial. A number of the dissenting judges went so far as to argue that prior restraints on publication can never be justified under Article 10(2).[27] This plainly is a radical conception of the scope of freedom of expression which was expressly rejected by the majority. Accepting, however, that prior restraint is legitimate in certain circumstances, it remains to determine what these are in a democratic society, and, as the *Observer and Guardian* case demonstrates, in complex cases that will often be a matter of disagreement.

The contribution of the press to the discussion of current issues is, of course, particularly important in the field of politics. This aspect of freedom of expression, and specifically the role of the press in criticising politicians was reviewed in some detail in the *Lingens* case.

The applicant, who was a journalist and editor of a Vienna magazine, published two articles strongly criticising Mr Bruno Kreisky, the Austrian Chancellor. The criticisms were of the latter's accommodating attitude towards P, the President of the Austrian Liberal Party, who had served in an SS infantry brigade during the war, and for his attacks on Mr Simon Wiesenthal, President of the Jewish Documentation Centre, who had publicly denounced P. Publication of the articles prompted Mr Kreisky to bring a private prosecution against the applicant for defamation in the press as a result of which he was sentenced to a fine. In the European Court the main issue was whether the applicant's conviction could be justified under Article 10(2) and in particular whether it was 'necessary in a democratic society . . . for the protection of the reputation . . . of others'.

In dealing with this issue the Court reviewed the principles relating to freedom of expression laid down in the cases already considered, then said:

Whilst the press must not overstep the bounds set, *inter alia*, for the 'protection of the reputation of others', it is nevertheless incumbent on it to impart information and ideas on political issues just as on those in other areas of public interest. Not only does the press have the task of imparting such information and ideas: the public also has a right to receive them . . . . In this connection, the Court cannot accept the opinion, expressed in the judgment of the Vienna Court of Appeal, to the effect that the task of the press was to impart information, the interpretation of which had to be left primarily to the reader.[28]

Comment and criticism of politicians the Court saw as a matter directly related to the role of the press in a free society. As the Court put it:

Freedom of the press furthermore affords the public one of the best means of discovering and forming an opinion of the ideas and attitudes of political leaders. More generally, freedom of political debate is at the very core of the concept of a democratic society which prevails throughout the Convention.[29]

From this premise it drew the following important conclusion:

The limits of acceptable criticism are accordingly wider as regards a politician as such than as regards a private individual. Unlike the latter, the former inevitably and knowingly lays himself open to close scrutiny of his every word and deed by both journalists and the public at large, and he must consequently display a greater degree of tolerance. No doubt Article 10 para 2 enables the reputation of others – that is to say, of all individuals – to be protected, and this protection extends to politicians too, even when they are not acting in their private capacity; but in such cases the requirements of such protection have to be weighed in relation to the interests of open discussion of political issues.[30]

The primary importance of this case in which the Convention was found to have been violated, lies in the Court's clear statement of the role of the press in politics and uncompromising view that individuals who wish to avoid criticism should not become politicians. In wider perspective, however, the judgment is important for the Court's firm repudiation of the view that press freedom exists only to convey information and that opinion as such is not protected. Such a view, as the Court recognised, would restrict freedom of expression in a quite artificial way and be incompatible with its rationale.

Freedom of assembly and association

Article 11(1) of the Convention lays down that: 'Everyone has the right to freedom of peaceful assembly and to freedom of association with others, including the right to form and join trade unions for the protection of his interests.'

It is easy to see how these freedoms and the idea of democratic government are related. If democracy is concerned with respecting individuals and giving attention to their claims, then permitting people to articulate their concerns by demonstrating or forming interest groups are means to a democratic end. Moreover, the opportunity to act with like-minded people in pursuit of goals which are socially acceptable contributes to the self-realisation of the individual. Thus, as in the comparable case of freedom of expression, the freedoms protected by Article 11 can be regarded as important in their own right.

Freedom of peaceful assembly
In the *Plattform 'Ärzte für das Leben'* case the Court had to consider the scope of freedom of peaceful assembly in a situation in which rival groups of demonstrators had come into conflict. The applicant was an association of Austrian doctors opposed to the legalisation of abortion and their claim was that two demonstrations which had been disrupted by persons opposed to *Plattform*'s activities had not been given proper police protection. The claim was considered by the Court only in the context of the right to an effective domestic remedy under Article 13; however, in order

to decide that issue it was necessary for the Court to determine whether the applicant had ever had an arguable claim under Article 11 and it was this which required the Court to examine the scope of freedom of assembly.

As noted in chapter 5, the Court began by making the vital point that if the concept of freedom of assembly is to perform its functions, Article 11 cannot be regarded as being concerned only with the State's obligation to refrain from interfering with demonstrations, but must include certain positive obligations. The Court justified this conclusion by referring explicitly to the needs and values of a democratic society, saying:

A demonstration may annoy or give offence to persons opposed to the ideas or claims that it is seeking to promote. The participants must, however, be able to hold the demonstration without having to fear that they will be subjected to physical violence by their opponents; such a fear would be liable to deter associations or other groups supporting common ideas or interests from openly expressing their opinions on highly controversial issues affecting the community. In a democracy the right to counter-demonstrate cannot extend to inhibiting the exercise of the right to demonstrate.[31]

The Court then had to determine the scope of the respondent's duty. *Plattform*'s argument that its rights had been infringed relied on the fact that their first demonstration, a march, was disrupted by counter-demonstrators who shouted and threw eggs and clumps of grass at those taking part. The police, who were present, intervened only to separate the opposing groups when tempers had risen to the point where physical violence seemed imminent. The second demonstration, in the Cathedral Square at Salzburg, was also disrupted by counter-demonstrators who were dispersed by the police only at the end. Did the lack of more vigorous action constitute a possible interference with the applicant's freedom of assembly?

The Court ruled that there is a duty incumbent on States under Article 11 to take reasonable and appropriate measures to enable lawful demonstrations to proceed peacefully, but went on to say this cannot be guaranteed absolutely and States have a wide discretion in the choice of means. Reviewing the facts and without expressing a view as to the expediency or efficiency of the tactics adopted by the police, the Court found that the Austrian authorities had not failed to take reasonable and appropriate measures. Both demonstrations had been policed, no damage was done, there were no serious clashes and on each occasion the association had been able to conduct a religious service as planned. In these circumstances the Court concluded that no arguable claim that Article 11 had been violated had been made out and so decided that the claim under Article 13 failed.

In a pluralistic society there is, by definition, a variety of social, moral and political opinions, and the adherents to different points of view will often wish to promote their opinions in action as well as in words. The *Plattform* case thus concerned a situation which is always liable to occur in democratic societies, and the Court's treatment of the scope of Article 11 is important because it shows what the right to demonstrate, and the corresponding right to counter-demonstrate, mean in practice. The applicants had a right to hold their demonstrations and were entitled to a degree of protection by the State. On the other hand, because those who opposed the applicants also had a right to make their views known, the authorities' responsibilities did not extend to suppressing the counter-demonstrations, or ensuring an atmosphere in which the applicant's demonstration could proceed unmolested.

The *Ezelin* case raised a different aspect of the right to demonstrate and was more controversial. The applicant was a French lawyer who practised in Guadeloupe. In 1983 he participated in a demonstration against a law dealing with subversion and its application in a number of recent trials. The demonstration got out of hand and public buildings in the town of Basse-Terre were defaced with insulting and offensive graffiti. Although there was no evidence that the applicant had daubed any of the slogans, the local courts found him guilty of an offence against professional discipline for failing to dissociate himself from these offences and sentenced him to a reprimand. The question for the European Court was whether on these facts there had been a breach of Article 11.

The main issue in the case was whether the sanction could be justified under Article 11(2) which authorises limitations on freedom of peaceful assembly in certain circumstances. The Court decided that it could not. Although it was 'prescribed by law' and aimed at 'the prevention of disorder', in the Court's view the sanction could not be regarded as 'necessary in a democratic society', because it was disproportionate to the aim pursued. The applicant himself had done nothing reprehensible and although he was, as the Court acknowledged, subject to professional discipline, in its opinion, 'the freedom to take part in a peaceful assembly . . . is of such importance that it cannot be restricted in any way, even for an *avocat*'[32] when the person in question is blameless.

Three judges dissented, essentially on the ground that, as one of them put it, 'Attitudes towards the conduct of members of the Bar differ from country to country'[33] with the result that the decision here could be said to lie within the respondent's margin of appreciation. There is room for this view, but the approach of the majority is surely to be preferred. The authorities can be tempted to use disciplinary measures to inhibit the actions of professional men and women, especially if, as was the case in *Ezelin*, the actions in question are embarrassing and those responsible for actual law-breaking cannot be caught. But the idea of guilt by association is a profoundly unattractive one and, as the Court recognised when it gave Article 11(2) a strict interpretation, an expedient which really has no place in a democratic society.

Freedom of association

Although the Convention protects freedom of association, the reference to trade unions is the only mention of how the right may be exercised. In particular, nothing is said about any obligation on the part of the government to listen or respond to collective representations, or to permit particular forms of action such as strikes. Such counter-part obligations would, however, appear to be necessary if the democratic purpose of freedom of association is to be fulfilled. Consequently, whether Article 11 carries with it any of these as a corollary, is a question the Court has had to consider on several occasions.

In the *National Union of Belgian Police* case[34] the applicant union, whose membership was open to municipal policemen, complained that the Belgian Government had refused to classify it as a 'representative' trade union, when three other unions, which were open to all local government employees, had been so classified. Since only 'representative' unions had the right to be consulted on such questions as recruitment, promotion and pay, the applicant union blamed its decline in membership on its failure to achieve representative status, and claimed that its rights under Article 11 of the Convention had been infringed.

The Court decided unanimously that there had been no breach of Article 11. In doing so it rejected the view of the majority of the Commission that the right to be consulted was a necessary condition of effective trade union activity on behalf of its members. However, the Court was also unwilling to endorse the view of a minority of the Commission that the words 'for the protection of his interests' in Article 11 are devoid of legal significance. Deciding that Article 11 requires that trade unions should be able to protect their members' interests, the Court held that this entails a right to be heard on matters of union concern. There had, however, been no breach of the Convention in the present case, because although the applicant union had no right to be consulted, its freedom to present claims and to make representations to the government were a sufficient acknowledgement of its right to be heard.

The Court reached the same conclusion in the *Swedish Engine Drivers Union* case,[35] where the complaint was that the body which negotiated the terms of service of State employees refused to conclude agreements on terms of employment and conditions of service with the applicant union. Again the Court pointed out that the applicant union could engage in various kinds of activity on behalf of its members and held that this was enough to satisfy Article 11. In both cases the applicants also sought to argue that their treatment was discriminatory and violated Article 11 and Article 14 read in conjunction, but in both cases the argument was rejected on the ground that the difference in treatment was justifiable.

The right to strike, which is frequently regarded as a key element in trade union activity, had to be considered by the Court in the *Schmidt and Dahlström* case.[36] The applicants who were members of a striking union were subsequently denied certain benefits on account of the strike although they themselves had not been involved. They argued that the policy of denying benefits to the members of striking unions violated trade union freedom contrary to Article 11 and was also discriminatory. As in the other cases, the Court rejected these arguments. The Court held that the right to strike was one means of complying with Article 11 but was not unlimited. In the circumstances the applicants' capacity to protect their interests through collective action had not been taken away and there was no discrimination.

The questions with which the Court was presented in these cases underline the significance of freedom of association in a democratic system of government. If a government is doing its job, it cannot be under the control of pressure groups or grant unlimited rights to trade unions. On the other hand, if trade unions and other associations are deliberately denied all influence, much of their *raison d'être* disappears. The Court was therefore right to recognise that the words 'for the protection of his interests' in Article 11 carry with them an obligation to permit trade union activity in various forms. What it was not prepared to do was to read into the Convention a code of industrial relations law. Since this would have been more detailed than that of the European Social Charter and have embroiled the Court in inter-union and other disputes where it has no special claims to competence, it is not surprising that it preferred to emphasise the principle, but leave practice in this matter largely to the Contracting States.

The issues considered so far all concern the right to conduct trade union activity. This may be termed 'positive freedom of association' to distinguish it from the 'negative' freedom of association claimed by an individual who asserts a right not to belong to a particular group. The two aspects of freedom of association are not only conceptually distinct, but have a different basis.[37] Whether this distinction is sufficient to take negative freedom of association outside Article 11 has proved a controversial issue.

The scope of Article 11 was one of the issues raised in the case of *Le Compte, Van Leuven and De Meyere*[38] which concerned the disciplinary procedures applicable to medical practitioners in Belgium. There the Court decided that it is acceptable for a State to create bodies to regulate the professions and to make membership compulsory, provided they are not exclusive, but left open the crucial question of whether Article 11 protects negative freedom of association. This was, however, the central issue in the case of *Young, James and Webster* which concerned the propriety of the closed-shop agreement in the British railway industry. Following the conclusion of an agreement between the management and the rail unions, the three applicants were dismissed for refusing to join a union. They claimed that this infringed their rights under Article 11, whereas the government maintained that what they were asserting – a negative right to freedom of association – fell outside the Convention.

The Court decided that the applicants' claim did fall within Article 11(1) but did not directly address the crucial issue of principle. Instead, the Court held that a threat of dismissal involving loss of livelihood against individuals who were engaged prior to the closed-shop agreement was a form of compulsion which struck 'at the very substance' of the freedom guaranteed by Article 11 and therefore fell within the Convention. Three judges disagreed with this conclusion and held that however desirable it might be, negative freedom of association had been deliberately excluded and was not logically required by Article 11. It should be noted that the Court was careful to state that compulsion to join a union might not always amount to a contravention, but emphasised the close connection between freedom of association and freedom of thought and freedom of expression in Articles 9 and 10. The majority thus saw Article 11 not as a qualification of the rights protected by the earlier articles, but as an extension of them, permitting and indeed encouraging collective action, yet at the same time preserving a measure of choice for the individual.

The need to reconcile collective action and individual choice can also be seen in the Court's treatment of the other issue in the case which concerned Article 11(2). Because associations may exercise considerable power, their actions can affect the liberties of others and may need regulation. This is recognised in the Convention which provides in Article 11(2) that:

No restrictions shall be placed on the exercise of these rights other than such as are prescribed by law and are necessary in a democratic society in the interests of national security or public safety, for the prevention of disorder or crime, for the protection of health or morals or for the protection of the rights and freedoms of others. This Article shall not prevent the imposition of lawful restrictions on the exercise of these rights by members of the armed forces, of the police or of the administration of the State.

In *Young, James and Webster* the Court, which considered the point important enough to examine on its own initiative, decided that the applicants' dismissal could not be regarded as 'necessary in a democratic society' because it could not be regarded as proportionate to the aims being pursued. In drawing this conclusion the Court was again careful to circumscribe its decision, but as with its treatment of the earlier question, saw the vital point as the need to avoid the individual interest becoming submerged by the collectivity. Thus the Court explained that the advantages of a closed shop agreement were not in themselves enough to render the interference with the applicants' rights 'necessary', then said:

pluralism, tolerance and broadmindedness are hall-marks of a 'democratic society'. Although individual interests must on occasion be subordinated to those of a group, democracy does not simply mean that the views of a majority must always prevail: a balance must be achieved which ensures the fair and proper treatment of minorities and avoids any abuse of a dominant position. Accordingly, the mere fact that the applicants' standpoint was adopted by very few of their colleagues is again not conclusive of the issue now before the Court.[39]

Young, James and Webster does not decide that a closed-shop agreement or similar arrangement is compatible with Article 11, or that it is not. For, as the Court stated, the closed-shop system as such was not under review. What it does decide is that the operation of such a system may in certain circumstances constitute a violation. This conclusion was not inevitable, and as the minority demonstrated, given the language and background of the Convention, the contrary view is certainly tenable. Why did the Court choose to take a broader approach? In the cases considered earlier the Court recognised the importance of positive freedom of association, but did not regard the development of a code of industrial relations law as its proper task. In *Young, James and Webster*, on the other hand, the Court regarded negative freedom of association as so much a part of the values of a democratic society as to justify granting it a measure of protection under Article 11. Here, then, as in the earlier cases, the Court's interpretation of the scope of the Convention reflects its conception of both the role of a judicial institution and the place of freedom of association in a democratic society.

Human rights and majority sentiment

Anyone who is content to define democracy as simply 'rule by the majority' has a problem when faced with an instrument guaranteeing individual rights. Such instruments may have as one of their purposes the preservation of democracy, but it is clear that the way in which they seek to achieve this is by removing the right of the majority (or anyone else) to take away the rights of others. In so far as this limits the ability of a minority to tyrannise a majority, no one is likely to complain. When, however, the protected group is a minority, as will frequently be the case, the objection may be raised that what is happening is undemocratic.

It is easy to dismiss the above argument as naive, and not difficult to construct a more sophisticated theory in which the question 'Who makes the laws?' is distinguished from the question 'What laws are to be made?' and democratic theory and individual rights once more reconciled. This done, however, there remains the problem for the judge of deciding what weight, if any, should be given to the majority position on any issue when a question of rights has to be decided. In one sense it could be said that this is an issue in virtually every case in the European Court, since these usually involve a challenge to national law or practice which our naive democrat might consider should be taken to represent the general will. This form of argument, however, which is really about the relation between national sovereignty and the Convention, can safely be left to the next chapter. Of greater moment are cases in which the Court has had to consider arguments expressly based on the relation between majority and minority sentiments and, in effect, develop its own democratic theory.

The scope of the majority's power and the nature of democratic responsibility to a minority was the critical issue in the *Danish Sex Education* cases which involved Article 2 of Protocol No. 1. That article guarantees the right to education and goes on to provide that 'In the exercise of any functions which it assumes in relation to education and teaching, the State shall respect the right of parents to ensure such education and teaching in conformity with their own religious and philosophical convictions.' The case arose because a number of parents objected to their children attending the sex-education classes which are compulsory in Danish schools. The Court was therefore required to decide whether obligatory sex education constituted a failure to respect the parents' rights in this area.

In deciding that it did not, the Court held that by virtue of Article 2 the State is responsible for establishing the curriculum and that this necessarily entitles it 'to impart through teaching or education information or knowledge of a directly or indirectly religious or philosophical kind'. This was, however, subject to an important limitation:

the State, in fulfilling the functions assumed by it in regard to education and teaching, must take care that information or knowledge included in the curriculum is conveyed in an objective, critical and pluralistic manner. The State is forbidden to pursue an aim of indoctrination that might be considered as not respecting parents' religious and philosophical convictions. That is the limit that must not be exceeded.[40]

Observing that this interpretation of Article 2 was in conformity with 'the general spirit of the Convention itself, an instrument designed to maintain and promote the ideas and values of democratic society',[41] the Court went on to find the Danish arrangements unobjectionable. Though unavoidably concerned with considerations of a moral order, the sex-education programme was primarily intended to convey useful information and did not overstep 'the bounds of what a democratic state may regard as the public interest'.[42]

The reasoning and the decision in this case reflect the Court's recognition that in the field of education what the Convention requires is not so much a balance between majority and minority points of view as a demarcation between the sphere of the State and that of the individual. Its categorical ruling that the State is forbidden to pursue the aim of indoctrination is, as the Court recognised, a corollary of the rights protected by Articles 8, 9 and 10, as well as a notable affirmation of the values of liberal democracy. At the same time, the very ideals which forbid indoctrination mean that the individual cannot prevent the national educational system from being used to convey useful information. Whilst parents are entitled to respect for their religious and philosophical convictions, the State, in discharge of its responsibility to guarantee the right of education, may act in what it sees as the general interest.

A point which was emphasised in the case just considered – that the majority has no general right to impose its views on the minority – was also significant in *Young, James and Webster* where, as we saw earlier, the Court explained that the fact that most of the workers concerned may have supported the closed shop was not enough to show that such an arrangement was 'necessary' for the purposes of Article 11(2). In the *Tyrer* case, similarly, the Attorney General for the Isle of Man argued that birching did not violate Article 3 because it did not outrage public opinion on the Island. The Court, however, held that even if, as the populace believed, judicial corporal punishment is a deterrent, it could still be degrading. Moreover, as the Court emphasised, 'it is never permissible to have recourse to punishments which are contrary to Article 3, whatever their deterrent effect may be'.[43] And in *Campbell and Cosans*, which concerned use of the tawse (strap) in Scottish schools, the Court made the same point, saying:

Corporal chastisement is traditional in Scottish schools and, indeed, appears to be favoured by a large majority of parents. . . . Of itself, this is not conclusive of the issue before the Court for the threat of a particular measure is not excluded from the category of 'degrading', within the meaning of Article 3, simply because the measure has been in use for a long time or even meets with general approval.[44]

The relevance of public opinion was examined more closely in the *Tyrer* case when the Court considered an unusual argument based on Article 63. That article permits a Contracting State to extend the Convention to territories for whose international relations it is responsible and provides for its provisions to be applied in such territories 'with due regard . . . to local requirements'. The Attorney General argued that in view of the strong feeling on the Island in favour of retaining judicial corporal punishment, Article 63 had the effect of exonerating the United Kingdom.

The Court, however, rejected the proposition that there were any local requirements of this kind. While it was prepared to recognise that 'The undoubtedly sincere beliefs on the part of members of the local population afford some indication that judicial corporal punishment is considered necessary in the Isle of Man as a deterrent and to maintain law and order', the Court held that 'for the application of Article 63(3), more would be needed: there would have to be positive and conclusive proof of a requirement and the Court could not regard beliefs and local public opinion on their own as constituting such proof'.[45] Since there was no evidence to show that law and order could not be maintained without corporal punishment, the respondent's argument failed.

Tyrer was never a very convincing case for the application of Article 63 because, as the Court pointed out, the Isle of Man is clearly a part of European society, whereas Article 63 was primarily intended for colonial territories where, it was thought, full application of the Convention might not be possible. Moreover, the Court made the important point that even if law and order cannot be maintained without recourse to corporal punishment, Article 3 is an absolute prohibition and no derogation from it under Article 63 is possible. Thus there are three points in the judgment which are relevant to the present discussion: public opinion alone is not enough to establish a local requirement, facts are needed; local requirements will be very difficult to establish where European territories are concerned because there is a presumption that in Europe such qualifications are unnecessary; and finally with specific reference to Article 3 and other absolute prohibitions,[46] even if a local requirement can be demonstrated, nothing which would amount to a derogation from the Convention is possible.

The cases considered so far all underline the point that because one of the functions of human rights guarantees is to protect minorities against persecution, the fact that a majority happens to regard particular conduct as correct or desirable cannot in itself be a reason for regarding it as justifiable. The same, of course, is true where the majority sentiment relates to what is undesirable. In the freedom of expression cases we have already seen how the Court has emphasised that the protection of the Convention extends to information and ideas that 'offend, shock or disturb', and the same point was made in the *Dudgeon* case,[47] where the Court said the need for caution and sensitivity to public opinion in Northern Ireland could not be conclusive in assessing the 'necessity' for Convention purposes of legislation making homosexual conduct criminally punishable.

But if majority sentiment in these cases is not compelling, it should not be thought of as entirely irrelevant. In *Campbell and Cosans*, after making the point that parental support for corporal punishment was in itself not enough to take it outside Article 3, the Court went on to say that particularly in view of the circumstances obtaining in Scotland 'it is not established that pupils at a school where such punishment is used are, solely by reason of the risk of being subjected thereto, humiliated or debased in the eyes of others to the requisite degree or at all'.[48] Thus, popular sentiment and local culture have a bearing on how a punishment is regarded and hence, as one would expect, may be relevant to its status for Convention purposes. Opinion is a double-edged weapon, however. In the *Tyrer* case the Court said that it did not 'regard it as established that judicial corporal punishment is not considered degrading by those members of the Manx population who favour its retention', then added pointedly 'it might well be that one of the reasons why they view the penalty as an effective deterrent is precisely the element of degradation which it involves'.[49]

Rather more important than the possible relevance of popular opinion in relation to Article 3, is its bearing on the question whether an interference with a Convention right or freedom can be regarded as 'necessary' under a provision such as Article 8(2). Here the *Dudgeon* case is particularly instructive. The Court held in that case that the legislation in question had a legitimate aim, namely the protection of morals in Northern Ireland and used as evidence the government's judgment of the strength of feeling against any change in the law and 'in particular the strength of the view that it would be seriously damaging to the moral fabric of Northern Irish society'.[50]

Moreover, although the Court held that the strength of feeling on the subject of homosexuality did not in itself demonstrate that the criminalisation of such conduct was necessary, it recognised that there were in this respect differences between Northern Ireland and the rest of the United Kingdom and agreed that 'in assessing the requirements of the protection of morals in Northern Ireland, the contested measures must be seen in the context of Irish society'.[51] From this it followed that the moral climate in Northern Ireland on sexual matters was a matter which the national authorities could legitimately take into account in exercising their discretion.

The Court eventually concluded that the criminalisation of homosexual conduct could not be considered 'necessary' and so ruled against the United Kingdom. Its reasons for doing so are bound up with the scope of the margin of appreciation in cases of this kind and can more appropriately be discussed in the next chapter. The significance of the case here lies in the Court's recognition that local opinion on homosexuality could be used to establish the aim of the legislation and that 'Whether this point of view be right or wrong, and although it may be out of line with current attitudes in other communities, its existence among an important section of Northern Irish society is certainly relevant for the purposes of Article 8(2).'[52] Democracy, then, is a poor justification for always giving the majority what they want, but it would be a perverse judge who could not accept that local sentiment may at least be relevant when deciding whether a limitation of individual rights can be justified as 'necessary in a democratic society'.

Notes

1 F. G. Jacobs, *The European Convention on Human Rights*, Clarendon Press, Oxford, 178 (1975).
2 *Mathieu-Mohin and Clerfayt* case, Series A, No. 113 para. 47.
3 See also, however, paras. 48–50 in which the Court considered an important point concerning *locus standi*.
4 See the International Covenant on Civil and Political Rights, Article 25(b), the American Convention on Human Rights, Article 23(1)(b) and the African Charter of Human and Peoples' Rights, Article 13(1). Each of these provisions is more elaborate than Article 3 of Protocol No. 1 to the European Convention, but the underlying idea of popular government is common to all four instruments.
5 Series A, No. 113 para. 51.
6 *Ibid.*, para. 52.
7 *Ibid.*, para. 53.
8 *Ibid.*, para. 54.
9 *Ibid.*
10 Series A, No. 18 para. 34. See also the Court's references to the place of the rule of law in the Statute of the Council of Europe, later in the same paragraph.
11 Series A, No. 30 para. 49.
12 D. J. Harris, *British Year Book of International Law*, L, 260 (1979).
13 Series A, No. 30 para. 49.
14 Series A, No. 61.
15 Series A, No. 82 para. 67.
16 *Ibid.*, para. 69. The Court came to the same conclusion as regards the practice of 'metering'.
17 Series A, No. 116. See also the *Kruslin* and *Huvig* cases, Series A, Nos. 176 A and B.
18 Series A, No. 28 para. 55.
19 See, for example, the *Schiesser* case, Series A, No. 34.
20 See the *Vagrancy* cases, Series A, No. 12 para. 78. Where the Convention specifically requires a 'court', judicial safeguards must, of course, be interpreted more strictly.
21 Series A, No. 28 para. 59.
22 *Ibid.*, para. 49.
23 *Ibid.*, para. 48.
24 Series A, No. 24 para. 49. See also the *Müller* case, Series A, No. 133.
25 Series A, No. 30 para. 65.

26 Series A, No. 216. In the *Sunday Times* (No. 2) case, Series A, No. 217, which was decided at the same time, the Court was concerned with the same issue, but in that case the disputed injunction related only to the period from July 1987 to October 1988. For further discussion of this aspect of Article 10(2) see the *Barfod* case, Series A, No. 149 and the *Weber* case, Series A, No. 177.
27 See the partly dissenting opinion of Judge De Meyer, joined by Judges Pettiti, Russo, Foighel and Bigi.
28 Series A, No. 103 para. 41.
29 *Ibid.*, para. 42.
30 *Ibid.* See also on this point the *Oberschlick* case, Series A, No. 204 and the *Castells* case, Series A, No. 236.
31 Series A, No. 139 para. 32.
32 Series A, No. 202 para. 53.
33 *Ibid.*, dissenting opinion of Judge Matscher.
34 Series A, No. 19.
35 Series A, No. 20.
36 Series A, No. 21.
37 See *Young, James and Webster* case, Series A, No. 44, dissenting opinion of Judge Sorensen, joined by Judges Thór Vilhjálmsson and Lagergren, para. 6.
38 Series A, No. 43.
39 Series A, No. 44 para. 63.
40 Series A, No. 23 para. 53.
41 *Ibid.*
42 *Ibid.*, para. 54.
43 Series A, No. 26 para. 31.
44 Series A, No. 48 para. 29.
45 Series A, No. 26 para. 38.
46 Derogation from most articles of the Convention is permitted 'in time of war or other public emergency threatening the life of the nation' under Article 15(1). However Article 15(2) provides that 'No derogation from Article 2, except in respect of deaths resulting from lawful acts of war, or from Articles 3, 4 (paragraph 1) and 7 shall be made under this provision.'
47 Series A, No. 45.
48 Series A, No. 48 para. 29.
49 Series A, No. 26 para. 31.
50 Series A, No. 45 para. 46.
51 *Ibid.*, para. 56.
52 *Ibid.*, para. 57. Contrast, however, the *Inze* case where the convictions of the local population were put forward by the government as a justification for discriminating against illegitimate children, but were dismissed by the Court as 'merely reflecting the traditional outlook', Series A, No. 126 para. 44.

CHAPTER 7

The margin of appreciation

Lord Denning once said, 'when we come to matters with a European element, the Treaty is like an incoming tide. It flows into the estuaries and up the rivers. It cannot be held back'.[1] These words were spoken with reference to the European Economic Community Treaty, but are equally apt to describe the impact of the European Convention. For, as we have seen, the Court constantly deals with all kinds of issues of law and policy which have traditionally been regarded as matters of domestic jurisdiction. This raises an important question. How far is the Court authorised to go in scrutinising the laws and practices of the Contracting States and measuring them against the Convention? The Strasbourg system was not set up to replace governments or destroy their authority, and so clearly many matters must be left to national regulation. No less clearly, unless the Court and the other institutions exercise a degree of control through their decisions, the main object of the Convention – which is to achieve an effective and uniform standard of protection for human rights in Europe – will be frustrated.

To assist it in resolving this problem, which is present in all human rights adjudication, the Court has developed a concept known as the 'margin of appreciation'. The underlying idea is a simple one: that in respect of many matters the Convention leaves the Contracting Parties an area of discretion. However, easy as this is to state, its application in concrete situations is fraught with difficulty. Cases in which the margin of appreciation is pleaded – whether the plea is successful or not – are therefore likely to be controversial.

Moreover, since the Convention itself makes no mention of the concept, the law has been developed on a case-by-case basis and the record indicates that the margin of appreciation has not been applied identically to every article, nor even to different parts of same article. To see whether this denotes inconsistency on the part of the Court, or reflects the complex character of the relation between the Strasbourg institutions and the national authorities, requires a closer look at the variety of situations in which the margin of appreciation is applied.

Emergency powers

Article 15 of the Convention provides for the possibility of derogation 'in time of war or other public emergency threatening the life of the nation'.[2] In these situations a State may take measures derogating from its obligations under the Convention 'to the extent strictly required by the exigencies of the situation', and so long as the measures are not inconsistent with its other obligations under international law. The power of derogation is not unlimited, however. There can be no derogation from Articles 3, 4(1) and 7 and only a limited derogation from Article 2. In addition, a State which desires to make use of Article 15 must keep the Secretary General of the Council of Europe fully informed of the measures which it has taken and their justification.

The need for Article 15 is plain enough. Just as most of the individual rights contained in the Convention cannot be absolute, but need qualifying in various ways in order that other interests may be protected, so in relation to the guarantees as a whole, a government must be permitted to reduce the scope of its obligations when faced with an emergency requiring individual rights to be restricted for the greater good. Here, however, Article 15 presents the Strasbourg institutions with a problem. On the one hand the exercise of a general power to derogate from the Convention appears to call for the most careful monitoring if it is not to become a way of enabling governments to make their obligations meaningless; on the other, deciding that an emergency exists and the measures which should be taken is a political responsibility which judges are neither equipped, nor authorised, to discharge. Since the issue here is the relation between the Convention institutions and the Contracting States in its most dramatic form, it is not surprising that when the Court has been called upon to consider Article 15, the margin of appreciation has played a prominent part in its deliberations.

The decision as to whether an emergency exists is, of course, in the first instance a matter for the government concerned. But is it conclusive? In the *Lawless* case, which concerned measures to counter the IRA in the Republic of Ireland, the government argued that its decision could not be challenged because the Convention provided no machinery to do so and because it was 'inconceivable that a Government acting in good faith should be held to be in breach of their obligations under the Convention merely because their appreciation of the circumstances which constitute an emergency, or of the measures necessary to deal with the emergency, should differ from the views of the Commission or of the Court'.[3]

The Commission disagreed. Following the approach it had adopted in an earlier case, the Commission urged the Court to consider the justification put forward by the government and make its own appraisal. In doing so, however, the Commission indicated that the Court should recognise the limitations of its competence and grant the government a significant margin of appreciation. As the Commission's submission to the Court put it:

The concept behind this doctrine is that Article 15 has to be read in the context of the rather special subject matter with which it deals: the responsibilities of a Government for maintaining law and order in times of war or public emergency threatening the life of the nation. The concept of the margin of appreciation is that a Government's discharge of these responsibilities is essentially a delicate problem of appreciating complex factors and of balancing conflicting considerations of the public interest; and that, once the Commission or the Court is satisfied that the Government's appreciation is at least on the margin of the powers conferred by Article 15, then the interest which the public itself has in effective Government and in the maintenance of order justifies and requires a decision in favour of the legality of the Government's appreciation.[4]

Presented with these conflicting arguments as to its competence, the Court decided that it should review the situation which had led to the government's action. Holding that 'it is for the Court to decide whether the conditions laid down in Article 15 for the exercise of the exceptional right of derogation have been fulfilled',[5] it decided that it must determine whether the facts and circumstances which had prompted the Irish Government's actions brought them within Article 15. In deciding that they did, however, it held that 'the existence at the time of a public emergency threatening the life of the nation was *reasonably deduced* by the Irish Government'.[6] These words suggested that the Court agreed with the Commission that the question was not whether a public emergency existed, but whether the national authorities had sufficient reason to believe that it did, in other words, there was here a margin of appreciation.

The scope of the Court's powers of review in respect of Article 15 were the subject of further attention in the *Irish* case. Here again the measures complained of were prompted by the activities of the IRA, only on this occasion in Northern Ireland, with the result that the United Kingdom was the respondent, and the Irish Government the applicant. As in *Lawless* the respondent relied on Article 15. However, unlike the earlier case, the existence of an emergency was not in dispute and so the crucial issue was whether internment and various other measures which would constitute violations of the Convention in normal circumstances, could be regarded as 'strictly required by the exigencies of the situation'.

The Court prefaced its answer to this question by considering its role in cases of this type. Having observed that the limits of its powers of review are 'particularly apparent' where Article 15 is concerned, it made the following notable comment on the margin of appreciation:

It falls in the first place to each Contracting State, with its responsibility for 'the life of [its] nation', to determine whether that life is threatened by a 'public emergency' and, if so, how far it is necessary to go in attempting to overcome the emergency. By reason of their direct and continuous contact with the pressing needs of the moment, the national authorities are in principle in a better position than the international judge to decide both on the presence of such an emergency and on the nature and scope of derogations necessary to avert it. In this matter Article 15 (1) leaves those authorities a wide margin of appreciation.[7]

It then qualified this by adding:

Nevertheless, the States do not enjoy an unlimited power in this respect. The Court, which, with the Commission, is responsible for ensuring the observance of the States' engagements (Article 19), is empowered to rule on whether the States have gone beyond the 'extent strictly required by the exigencies' of the crisis. . . . The domestic margin of appreciation is thus accompanied by a European super-vision.[8]

The facts of the *Irish* case were complex and it is unnecessary to describe how the Court applied the above principles in detail. An example, however, will serve to illustrate its approach. The Irish Government argued that the policy of extrajudicial deprivation of liberty introduced in August 1971 was ineffectual and therefore could not be shown to have been necessary. The Court rejected the argument with the comment that:

It is certainly not the Court's function to substitute for the British Government's assessment any other assessment of what might be the most prudent or most expedient policy to combat terrorism. The Court must do no more than review the lawfulness, under the Convention, of the measures adopted by that Government from 9 August 1971 onwards. For this purpose the Court must arrive at its decision in the light, not of a purely retrospective examination of the efficacy of those measures, but of the conditions and circumstances reigning when they were originally taken and subsequently applied.
     Adopting, as it must, this approach, the Court accepts that the limits of the margin of appreciation left to the Contracting States by Article 15(1) were not overstepped by the United Kingdom when it formed the opinion that extra-judicial deprivation of liberty was necessary from August 1971 to March 1975.[9]

Thus, as in the *Lawless* case, the Court made an independent examination of the evidence but in respect of the question of necessity took the margin of appreciation point further, by upholding the respondent's view wherever it was reasonable.

The development of the margin of appreciation to deal with the emergency issue and the necessity issue in relation to Article 15 is an ingenious solution to a unique problem. To have decided that these questions were outside the Court's competence altogether would have been an abrogation of judicial responsibility, as well as an unconvincing reading of the Convention. As the decision of the International Court in the *Nicaragua* case[10] demonstrates, the argument that treaty provisions cannot be applied by international judges is never a very attractive one. Equally, however, some limitations on the judicial role have to be acknowledged and to require the European Court to decide whether a government's decisions under Article 15 were correct – an argument put forward by the applicant in *Lawless* – would be grotesque.

Once the case for a margin of appreciation is accepted, the question of how broad it should be arises. On the limited evidence available it appears that the Court is prepared to grant the respondent considerable latitude as regards both the emergency and the necessity issues. While the Court has conscientiously examined the evidence and in both cases supported its decision with persuasive reasoning, the requirement that the respondent should merely have acted reasonably does not seem unduly difficult to satisfy. Certainly the respondent has more latitude here than in respect of some of the issues to be considered later.

The justification for this approach is to be found in the words of the Commission quoted above. The view has been expressed that the Court and the Commission are not in fact the most appropriate organs for dealing with cases under Article 15[11] and confirmation of this may be found in a point made earlier, that cases with significant political content tend to be referred to the Committee of Ministers, rather than the Court. Nevertheless it is clear that the Court is bound to have cases under Article 15 referred to it from time to time and must have a legal technique to deal with them. The adoption of a broad margin of appreciation in such cases is a way of acknowledging the fact that courts are not the best places to investigate difficult matters of political judgment, and ensuring that at the same time the law of the Convention is respected and applied.

Restrictions 'in the public interest'

Article 1 of Protocol No. 1 protects the peaceful enjoyment of possessions and lays down that 'no one shall be deprived of his possessions except in the public interest'. This clearly gives rise to the kind of question which has just been considered in relation to Article 15. By whom is the 'public interest' to be determined? Or, more accurately, when a State has decided that a deprivation of possessions is justified, how far is it open to the Court to review its decision?

In the *James* case the question was whether the compulsory transfer of the applicant's property under the Leasehold Reform Act 1967, as amended, constituted a deprivation of possessions contrary to the Convention. When the British Government pleaded that the measures in question were 'in the public interest', the Court's starting point in evaluating the argument was, as might be expected, the margin of appreciation:

Because of their direct knowledge of their society and its needs, the national authorities are in principle better placed than the international judge to appreciate what is 'in the public interest'. Under the system of protection established by the Convention, it is thus for the national authorities to make the initial assessment both of the existence of a problem of public concern warranting measures of deprivation of property and of the remedial action to be taken. . . . Here, as in other fields to which the safeguards of the Convention extend, the national authorities accordingly enjoy a certain margin of appreciation.[12]

The Court then proceeded to explain why in the particular context of property rights it regarded the margin of appreciation as a wide one:

. . . the decision to enact laws expropriating property will commonly involve consideration of political, economic and social issues on which opinions within a democratic society may reasonably differ widely. The Court, finding it natural that the margin of appreciation available to the legislature in implementing social and economic policies should be a wide one, will respect the legislature's judgment as to what is 'in the public interest' unless that judgment be manifestly without reasonable foundation. In other words, although the Court cannot substitute its own assessment for that of the national authorities, it is bound to review the contested measure under Article 1 of Protocol No. 1 and, in so doing, to make an inquiry into the facts with reference to which the national authorities acted.[13]

Thus the Court was here prepared to grant the national authorities a wide discretion and when it came to examine the facts concluded that both the aim of the legislation and the means adopted were within the margin of appreciation. As regards Article 1 of Protocol No. 1, there had therefore been no breach of the Convention.

In the *Lithgow* case,[14] which was decided in the same year and also involved the United Kingdom, the Court had to consider the public interest exception in a dispute over nationalisation. The applicants claimed not that the nationalisation of the aircraft and shipbuilding industries was unjustified, but that the compensation provided was inadequate. The Court decided that in principle compensation is required for a taking of property and that normally such compensation must be reasonably related to the value of the property. It emphasised, however, that the national authorities have a wide margin of appreciation as regards both the decision to nationalise and the compensation terms. Following its reasoning in the *James* case, the Court held that it would respect the judgment of Parliament in the latter connection, unless it was manifestly without reasonable foundation. A detailed review of the facts led the Court to conclude that it was not. Consequently there was again no violation of the Convention.

If the reference to the 'public interest' in the first part of Article 1 grants States a wide discretion in relation to the control of property, the second part of the article is in even wider terms. It lays down that the provision concerning the peaceful enjoyment of possessions 'shall not, however, in any way impair the right of a State to enforce such laws as it deems necessary to control the use of property in accordance with the general interest or to secure the payment of taxes or other contributions or penalties'. As the Court pointed out in the *Handyside* case, 'this paragraph sets the Contracting States up as sole judges of the "necessity" for an interference. Consequently, the Court must restrict itself to supervising the lawfulness and the purpose of the restriction in question'.[15] It is clear, therefore, that as regards the control of the use of property, the margin of appreciation, though not unlimited, is even wider than under the first paragraph.

In the *Mellacher* case, for example, the Court had to decide whether Austrian legislation which drastically restricted the rents which could be charged for apartments violated the rights of the landlords under Article 1. It held that the legislation could be justified as 'in accordance with the general interest' on the ground that to implement its social and economic policies in the field of housing 'the legislature must have a wide margin of appreciation both with regard to the existence of a problem of public concern warranting measures of control and as to the choice of the detailed rules for the implementation of such measures'.[16] Accordingly, only a measure which was 'manifestly without reasonable foundation' could be overturned at Strasbourg and, provided the legislature remained within its margin of appreciation, it was 'not for the Court to say whether the legislation represented the best solution for dealing with the problem or whether the legislative discretion should have been exercised in another way'.[17]

Can there be an interference with property rights falling outside those which may be justified by reference to the public or the general interest? If so, what is the scope of the margin of appreciation in relation to such an interference? These questions were considered by the Court in the case of *Sporrong and Lönnroth* which concerned expropriation permits and prohibitions on construction imposed by the Swedish authorities in respect of the applicants' properties in Stockholm. The expropriation was never carried out and so it was agreed that there had been no 'deprivation of possessions' requiring justification under the first paragraph. On the other hand, a majority of the Court took the view that since the expropriation permits were intended to deprive the applicants of their property, rather than to control its use, the case did not fall under the second paragraph either. This did not, however, mean that the situation fell outside the Convention. For although there was no deprivation of property, there was an interference with the peaceful enjoyment of possessions. In the Court's view this could be justified if it could be shown that 'a fair balance was struck between the demands of the general interest of the community and the requirements of the protection of the individual's fundamental rights'.[18] Here there was room for a margin of appreciation because, as the Court observed, it was 'natural that, in an area as complex and difficult as that of the development of large cities, the Contracting States should enjoy a wide margin of appreciation in order to implement their town planning policy'.[19] However, in view of the inflexibility of the law concerned, the Court found that it failed to strike the appropriate balance and accordingly decided that there had been a breach of the Convention.

In a joint dissenting opinion eight judges challenged this line of reasoning. In their view the case should properly have been considered under the second paragraph. Although expropriation had been intended, pending its completion there was an interference with the applicants' use of their property. The justification for the respondent's action was therefore to be found in the wide 'general interest' test laid down in the Convention. In their view this test was satisfied because the duration of the permits did not exceed the periods which the authorities could reasonably deem to be in the public interest. The majority were well aware of the need for flexibility, but by deciding that the case should be considered under paragraph one, then devising the balancing of interests test, succeeded in reducing the margin of appreciation very significantly. This is a questionable reading of the Convention. Although the legislation in question left a good deal to be desired, until the expropriation was carried out, the situation seems to fall naturally under paragraph two.

Looking at the Court's jurisprudence as a whole, it is not difficult to see why, whatever the result, the point has invariably been made that there is a wide margin of appreciation in these cases. The view that 'the right to the enjoyment of one's possessions . . . does not belong (any longer) to fundamental rights',[20] would have astonished John Locke, but is clearly reflected in the qualifications to be found in the Convention. In applying those qualifications in a way which confines it to a marginal review, the Court is therefore following the intentions of those who drew up the Convention. It is, of course, also avoiding the controversy which might be caused both within and outside the Court, if it were to pronounce upon the merits of nationalisation as a policy, or to try to regulate the details of rent control or leasehold reform. The disagreement in *Sporrong and Lönnroth* is perhaps a warning here. Thus in relation to Article 1 of Protocol No. 1, as in relation to Article 15, the width of the margin of appreciation reflects a narrow conception of justiciability and a correspondingly limited scope for judicial review.

Restrictions 'necessary in a democratic society'

In previous chapters we have seen that the authorisation of restrictions on rights, provided they are 'necessary in a democratic society', occurs in a number of articles of the Convention. From earlier discussion it may also be recalled that when it is established that an interference with the relevant right or freedom has occurred, the Court will consider whether the infringement can be justified by reference to the limiting provision. This requires it to consider whether the infringement is 'prescribed by law' or 'in accordance with the law', and then whether the infringement is justified by one of the prescribed aims and is 'necessary in a democratic society'. The first requirement has already been considered. The remaining two are relevant here because as regards both, the Court will grant the authorities a certain margin of appreciation.

The width of the margin of appreciation varies a good deal. Since the Court is dealing with different rights, different claims in respect of the same right, by applicants in different situations, and with different justifications advanced by States at different times, such variation is inevitable. Though this sometimes makes it hard to predict a decision accurately, the factors which may influence the Court to adopt a broad or narrow approach are not too difficult to identify.

The margin of appreciation is generally a broad one if the applicant's position is such that some restriction of his rights would normally be expected. Thus 'the Convention does not in principle prohibit the Contracting States from regulating the entry and length of stay of aliens'[21] and so restrictions on aliens are permissible under Article 8(2), which would constitute an interference with the right to respect for family life if they were applied to nationals.[22] Similarly, in the *Engel* case, two of the applicants complained that military punishments imposed for having collaborated in the publication and distribution of an allegedly subversive periodical, infringed their rights under Article 10. The Court, however, held that the authorities' action was justified under Article 10(2).

Observing that 'the proper functioning of an army is hardly imaginable without legal rules designed to prevent servicemen from undermining military discipline', the Court recognised that servicemen are entitled to freedom of expression, but added that it could not disregard 'either the particular characteristics of military life . . . the specific "duties" and "responsibilities" incumbent on members of the armed forces, or the margin of appreciation'.[23] Having regard to the circumstances and content of the publication, the Court concluded that there had been no infringement of the Convention in the present case because 'the Supreme Military Court may have had well-founded reasons for considering that they had attempted to undermine military discipline and that it was necessary for the prevention of disorder to impose the penalty inflicted'.[24]

The treatment of Article 10 here echoes the Court's earlier comment in relation to claims under Article 5 that 'Each State is competent to organise its own system of military discipline and enjoys in the matter a certain margin of appreciation'.[25] Later, as we shall see, the Court dealt with the applicant's claims under Article 14 in the same spirit.

Of course, the margin of appreciation in cases such as this is not unlimited. In *Engel* the Court made the familiar point that it has jurisdiction to supervise the way in which domestic law is applied, while in *Golder* the British Government's argument that a limitation on a prisoner's correspondence could be justified on various grounds under Article 8(2) was rejected with the observation that 'Even having regard to the power of appreciation left to the Contracting States, the Court cannot discern how these considerations, as they are understood "in a democratic society", could oblige the Home Secretary to prevent Golder from corresponding with a solicitor.'[26] This also demonstrates an advantage of using a broad margin of appreciation rather than the concept of 'inherent limitations' on an applicant's rights which was developed in the early jurisprudence of the Commission, but rejected by the Court in the *Vagrancy* cases.[27] Whereas the idea of inherent limitations put interference with prisoners' correspondence, for example, completely outside Article 8(1), the margin of appreciation approach requires the Court to examine the matter under Article 8(2). Although the effect in both instances is to restrict the applicant's rights, the Court's approach ensures that the limitation is 'in accordance with the law', has an acceptable aim and is no more extensive than is 'necessary in a democratic society'.

Another situation in which the margin of appreciation is likely to be broad is where the Court is presented with a case involving a complex or controversial political, economic or social issue. We have already seen how such considerations affect the margin of appreciation in relation to security issues under Article 15 and property rights under Protocol No. 1 and the same is true in the present context. In the *Powell and Rayner* case, for example, one of the questions was whether the noise from Heathrow Airport had arguably resulted in a violation of the applicants' right to respect for their private life and home under Article 8. The Court, when dealing with this point in the judgment, noted the various steps which had been taken by the authorities, and said:

it is certainly not for the Commission or the Court to substitute for the assessment of the national authorities any other assessment of what might be the best policy in this difficult and technical sphere. This is an area where the Contracting States are to be recognised as enjoying a wide margin of appreciation.[28]

On the basis of this premise it was then able to conclude that in deciding its policy and determining the scope of the relevant noise abatement measures, 'the United Kingdom Government cannot arguably be said to have exceeded the margin of appreciation afforded to them or upset the fair balance required to be struck under Article 8'.[29]

The control of obscene publications, which the Court had to deal with in the *Handyside* case is another good example. This case concerned a publication entitled *The Little Red Schoolbook* by two Danish authors. The book, which was intended for schoolchildren, contained a good deal of radical material, including a controversial chapter on sex. When it was published in England, a successful prosecution under the Obscene Publications Acts 1959 and 1964 was brought against the applicant, as the English publisher, and over a thousand copies of the book were seized by the authorities. The applicant's claim that these actions constituted a violation of his rights under Article 10 was decisively rejected. Although it was clear that for the purposes of Article 10(1) the applicant's freedom of expression had been curtailed, the Court held that the interference could be justified under Article 10(2) as being 'prescribed by law and . . . necessary in a democratic society . . . for the protection of morals.'

The corner-stone of the judgment was the margin of appreciation available to the national authorities. Emphasising that 'the machinery of protection established by the Convention is subsidiary to the national systems safeguarding human rights', the Court explained that this was especially important in the present situation because:

it is not possible to find in the domestic law of the various Contracting States a uniform European conception of morals. The view taken by their respective laws of the requirements of morals varies from time to time and from place to place, especially in our era which is characterised by a rapid and far-reaching evolution of opinions on the subject. By reason of their direct and continuous contact with the vital forces of their countries, State authorities are in principle in a better position than the international judge to give an opinion on the exact content of these requirements as well as on the 'necessity' of a 'restriction' or 'penalty' intended to meet them.[30]

The Court went on to say that the domestic margin of appreciation is not unlimited, but subject to the supervision of the Court. In exercising that power, it stated that the Court must recognise the fundamental importance of freedom of expression, but also the duties and responsibilities of those who sought to utilise it. On the particular facts the Court took note of the book's intended readership and was satisfied that competent authorities were entitled to regard it as morally pernicious.

As far as the 'necessity' for the interference was concerned, the Court attached little significance to the fact that in other parts of the United

Kingdom and elsewhere in Europe the authorities had not prosecuted the book. Referring again to the margin of appreciation the Court reasoned that:

The Contracting States have each fashioned their approach in the light of the situation obtaining in their respective territories; they have had regard, *inter alia*, to the different views prevailing there about the demands of the protection of morals in a democratic society. The fact that most of them decided to allow the work to be distributed does not mean that the contrary decision of the Inner London Quarter Sessions was a breach of Article 10.[31]

Since the requirement of proportionality was also satisfied, the Court concluded that there had been no breach of the Convention.

In the *Müller* case, which involved Switzerland, the Court applied the reasoning in *Handyside* to the graphic arts and decided that neither the applicants' conviction and fine for exhibiting obscene paintings, nor the confiscation of the offending works, violated Article 10. The Court acknowledged that 'Those who create, perform, distribute or exhibit works of art contribute to the exchange of ideas and opinions which is essential for a democratic society'.[32] Consequently, freedom of artistic expression is important and the State has an obligation not to encroach on it unduly. However, having itself viewed the paintings, which crudely depicted sexual activity between people and animals, the Court found that the Swiss courts had not acted unreasonably in finding them grossly offensive. While the Court noted that conceptions of morality had changed in recent years, it also took into account the fact that Mr Müller's paintings were displayed in a way which gave the public free access to them, the organisers of the exhibition having imposed no charge or age-limit for admission. Having regard to the respondent's margin of appreciation, the Court concluded that, as in the *Handyside* case, the authorities' interference with the applicant's freedom of expression could be justified as necessary in a democratic society for the protection of morals. Accordingly, it decided that there was no violation of the Convention.

It is clear that the latitude which the Court was prepared to grant to the authorities in these cases stemmed from its view that in the absence of a 'uniform European conception of morals' only a limited review of national decision-making was appropriate. A critic of the decision in *Handyside* has suggested that even if the premise is correct, one is left 'with the question of whether it is then not up to the Court to develop such a "European conception" in its case-law, since the term "morals" is repeatedly mentioned in the Convention'.[33] To this the answer is surely no. The Court's function is not to decree uniformity wherever there are national differences, but to ensure that fundamental values are respected. Whether State actions exceed the permissible limits is, of course, a matter for decision. But the Court cannot pretend that a certain standard exists before there is any evidence and so on a matter where there are clear differences of view there must be room for a significant margin of appreciation.

It should not be assumed that because the Court is prepared to grant the national authorities a broad discretion in relation to some of the Convention's qualifying provisions, it will do so in all. If the Court is satisfied that a precise requirement can be identified, then the margin of appreciation may be very narrow. Deciding how much latitude is appropriate in a particular case may naturally be controversial. What one judge sees as a legitimate exercise of national sovereignty may strike another as outside the boundaries of permissible conduct. The *Sunday Times* case,[34] which we encountered in chapter 6 and which raised another aspect of Article 10, divided the Court in just this way.

In that case the majority took the view that the margin of appreciation was narrower than in *Handyside*, because the authority of the judiciary is the subject of a broad measure of agreement among the parties to the Convention and a more 'objective' notion than that of the protection of morals. The nine dissenting judges disagreed and, referring to considerable variations in national practice, concluded that States must be granted a wide measure of discretion as regards both the method employed to maintain the authority of the judiciary and its results. The contrast between this reasoning and the approach of the majority is clear-cut. Whereas the minority were content to abide by national determinations that were not obviously unreasonable, the Court's detailed appraisal of the merits of the House of Lords' decision has been aptly described as reducing the margin of appreciation doctrine in this type of case 'almost to vanishing point'.[35]

The Court's ability to vary the scope of the margin of appreciation is equally evident in another controversial case. The main issue in the *Dudgeon* case was whether the penalisation of homosexuality in Northern Ireland violated the applicant's right to respect for his private life, guaranteed by Article 8(1). The government argued that the matter fell within Article 8(2) because the disputed legislation had as its object the 'protection of health or morals'. The question for the Court was whether it was 'necessary in a democratic society' for that end and this depended on the margin of appreciation.

The government emphasised that Northern Ireland is a conservative society in moral matters and that a strong body of opinion was opposed to any change in the law. The Court accepted that this was so, observing that:

The fact that similar measures are not considered necessary in other parts of the United Kingdom or in other member States of the Council of Europe does not mean that they cannot be necessary in Northern Ireland. . . . Where there are disparate cultural communities residing within the same State, it may well be that different requirements, both moral and social, will face the governing authorities.[36]

The Court also accepted that the government had acted carefully and in good faith in deciding not to change the law. It pointed out, however, that good faith alone is not enough, because 'Notwithstanding the margin of appreciation left to the national authorities, it is for the Court to make the final evaluation as to whether the reasons it has found to be relevant were sufficient in the circumstances, in particular whether the interference complained of was proportionate to the social need claimed for it.'[37]

In the government's view the *Handyside* judgment indicated that the margin of appreciation is more extensive where the protection of morals is in issue. The Court agreed that the aim is an important consideration, but explained that 'not only the nature of the aim of the restriction but also the nature of the activities involved will affect the scope of the margin of appreciation'. This was a key point in the present case because it concerned 'a most intimate aspect of private life'.[38] Consequently, there must exist 'particularly serious reasons' before interferences could be justified under Article 8(2).

On the particular facts the Court found that the government had failed to justify the legislation. Homosexuality was not subject to criminal penalties in the majority of European States and in Northern Ireland itself the authorities now followed a policy of not enforcing the law against those over the age of twenty-one. In such circumstances it could not be said that there was a 'pressing social need' for the legislation, nor that whatever benefits flowed from the law outweighed the disadvantages, as the principle of proportionality required. Accordingly, the government had not succeeded in demonstrating that the law in question was 'necessary in a democratic society' and was therefore in violation of Article 8(1).

In this case the Court interpreted the margin of appreciation more narrowly than might have been anticipated; however, it did not seek to remove it entirely. The applicant's complaint that the law prevented him from having sexual relations with males under twenty-one was rejected on the ground that a degree of control over homosexual conduct is necessary to prevent exploitation and corruption and that 'it falls in the first instance to the national authorities to decide on the appropriate safeguards of this kind required for the defence of morals in their society and, in particular, to fix the age under which young people should have the protection of the criminal law'.[39] Similarly, the verdict in *Dudgeon* does not mean that the Court would necessarily condone advertising by homosexuals, or other behaviour which the authorities might wish to control.

In the *Sunday Times* case, as we saw in the previous chapter, the Court was influenced in its attitude to the margin of appreciation by its view of freedom of the press as a fundamental value. The counter-part in *Dudgeon* was the Convention's protection of sexual behaviour, which the Court termed 'an essentially private manifestation of the human personality'.[40] This way of looking at the matter did not go unchallenged, however. And, as in the earlier case, the dissenting judges' point of departure was the role of the margin of appreciation. For Judge Zekia the guiding principles were to be found in the *Handyside* case and on a moral issue as sensitive as homosexuality the national authorities were entitled to a substantial, though not unlimited, margin of appreciation. Likewise, in the view of Judge Walsh the Court was in no position to challenge the national authorities' assessment because 'The law has a role in influencing moral attitudes and if the respondent Government is of the opinion that the change sought in the legislation would have a damaging effect on moral attitudes then . . . it is entitled to maintain the legislation it has.'[41]

The approach adopted by the majority in the *Dudgeon* case was subsequently endorsed in the *Norris* case[42] which concerned similar legislation in the Republic of Ireland. The government put forward an argument very much like that of the dissenting judges in *Dudgeon* and maintained that the moral fibre of a democratic nation is a matter for its own institutions and could justify a margin of appreciation wide enough to support the disputed law. The Court disagreed. Although it acknowledged that the national authorities enjoy a wide margin of appreciation in matters of morals, it was not prepared to grant the virtually unlimited discretion which the government's argument appeared to demand. Emphasising that it is the Court's duty to review a State's observance of its obligations, even in matters of morals, the Court found that the government had adduced no convincing evidence to support retaining the legislation. On the contrary, as in *Dudgeon*, the authorities had refrained from enforcing the law without apparent injury to moral standards or provoking a demand for stricter enforcement. In these circumstances it could not be maintained that there was a pressing need for the legislation, from which it followed that there had been a breach of Article 8.

What the provisions we have been considering have in common is a recognition that in any democratic society there are situations in which the rights set out in the Convention may be limited. The question which then arises is how and by whom the need for a disputed limitation is to be judged. No one, of course, would wish to argue that the matter should be wholly in the hands of the respondent State. The difficulty, however, is that the limitations are permitted for reasons which on the face of it only the State can properly assess.

In a number of cases, as we have seen, the Court has accepted this view and while satisfying itself that the national decision was appropriate within certain limits, has granted the State a broad power of appreciation. Where it has taken a different approach, it was because a majority of the Court considered the respondent's argument to be contrary to the Convention's basic values. The result is not so much an inconsistency in the Court's jurisprudence, as a demonstration of a point which has been made already, that decisions about human rights are not a technical exercise in interpreting texts, but judgments about political morality.

The scope of rights

Although many of the most prominent cases on the margin of appreciation have concerned restrictions on the rights guaranteed, the Court has often used the concept as an aid in establishing the scope of the rights themselves. In the *Engel* case, for example, the Court had to decide whether various punishments which had been imposed on the applicants as measures of military discipline constituted deprivations of liberty falling within Article 5. The Court recognised that punishments imposed in the course of military discipline may in principle engage Article 5, but added that 'the bounds that Article 5 requires the State not to exceed are not identical for servicemen and civilians'. In respect of the former, States are allowed a certain margin of appreciation:

A disciplinary penalty or measure which on analysis would unquestionably be deemed a deprivation of liberty were it to be applied to a civilian may not possess this characteristic when imposed upon a serviceman. Nevertheless, such penalty or measure does not escape the terms of Article 5 when it takes the form of restrictions that clearly deviate from the normal conditions of life within the armed forces of the Contracting States. In order to establish whether this is so, account should be taken of a whole range of factors such as the nature, duration, effects and manner of execution of the penalty or measure in question.[43]

Applying this principle to the Dutch military punishments which were in issue, the Court decided that 'light' and 'aggravated' arrest were not deprivations of liberty for the purposes of Article 5, whereas 'strict' arrest and committal to a disciplinary unit were. In the Court's view the crucial consideration was that light and aggravated arrest limited a soldier's movements by confining him to barracks, whereas strict arrest and committal to a disciplinary unit involved locking him up.

In a number of cases involving the detention of mental patients the Court has explained that in deciding whether an individual should be detained as a 'person of unsound mind' in accordance with Article 5(1)(e) 'the national authorities are to be recognised as having a certain margin of appreciation since it is in the first place for the national authorities to evaluate the evidence adduced before them in a particular case'. However, this does not mean that the Court is displaced. Its task 'is to review under the Convention the decisions of those authorities'. Specifically, the following minimum conditions must be satisfied: 'he must be reliably shown to be of unsound mind; the mental disorder must be of a kind or degree warranting compulsory confinement; and the validity of continued confinement depends upon the persistence of such a disorder'.[44]

The margin of appreciation, then, is here simply an acknowledgement that the Court is not engaged in rehearing the detention proceedings, a task for which it is not equipped, but in ensuring that the national authorities' decision was at all times supported by cogent evidence. Likewise, in cases under Article 5(3) the Court has recognised that the preservation of public order is a factor which the authorities may take into account when deciding whether a suspect should be released, but has stressed that 'this ground can be regarded as relevant and sufficient only provided that it is based on facts capable of showing that the accused's release would actually disturb public order'.[45] It is therefore not possible for a State to argue that such decisions fall within a broad margin of appreciation and must be taken on trust. Although it is for the national authorities to make the initial decision, the Court must be satisfied that if an accused person has not been released, this is because there is evidence of a genuine threat to public order and not just because the crime in question is serious.

In the *Abdulaziz* case one of the applicants' arguments was that British immigration law failed to recognise the right to establish one's home in the State of one's nationality or lawful residence and consequently violated the right to respect for family life as guaranteed by Article 8. The Court, while acknowledging that effective respect for family life can impose positive obligations, observed that in this regard: 'the notion of respect is not clear-cut: having regard to the diversity of practices followed and the situations obtaining in the Contracting States, the notion's requirements will vary considerably from case to case. Accordingly, this is an area in which the Contracting States enjoy a wide margin of appreciation in determining the steps to be taken to ensure compliance with the Convention with due regard to the needs and resources of the community and of individuals'.[46]

In the specific context of immigration the Court held that 'the extent of a State's obligation to admit to its territory relatives of settled immigrants will vary according to the particular circumstances of the persons involved'.[47] And reviewing the applicants' cases in the light of these observations, the Court held that in the circumstances there had been no lack of respect for family life and accordingly no breach of Article 8.

In the *Rees* case, which concerned the requirements of Article 8 as regards effective respect for the private life of transsexuals, the Court used similar reasoning and came to the same conclusion. In that case, as in *Abdulaziz*, the Court emphasised the diversity of national practice, then added that, 'In determining whether or not a positive obligation exists, regard must be had to the fair balance that has to be struck between the general interest of the community and the interests of the individual, the search for which balance is inherent in the whole of the Convention.'[48] In the *Cossey* case, which was decided five years after *Rees* and presented the same issue, the Court was invited to reconsider the earlier decision, but declined to do so. Instead, it reaffirmed its approach to the question of positive obligations and finding that national approaches to the issue of transsexualism still showed considerable variation, concluded that 'this is still, having regard to the existence of little common ground between the Contracting States, an area in which they enjoy a wide margin of appreciation'.[49]

The introduction of the notion of a 'fair balance' underlines the point that especially when positive obligations are in issue, the scope of the margin of appreciation is likely to be controversial. Three members of the Court dissented on this issue in *Rees* and no less than eight disagreed with the Court's treatment of Article 8 in *Cossey*. Most of the dissenting judges relied on recent improvements in the position of transsexuals in national law, but Judge Martens made a more fundamental point. In his view transsexuals have a right to have their new identity recognised which stems from everyone's right to self-realisation. It follows that while there is some discretion as regards the requirements and form of such recognition, there is no room at all for a margin of appreciation on the central question.[50] This, it should be noted, is the type of argument which the Court has accepted in relation to homosexuality, where, as we have seen, consideration of the value of what is at stake has largely displaced the margin of appreciation. The fact that the *Rees* case was decided by 12 votes to 3 while the *Cossey* case was decided by a majority of only 10 votes to 8 suggests that views on transsexualism may be undergoing a similar transformation.[51]

Controversy over the scope of the margin of appreciation is also to be found on other matters. In the *Airey* case, several judges dissented on the issue of positive obligations and one referred to the Court's 'far-fetched' interpretation of Article 8. In the *Abdulaziz* case Judge Bernhardt held that the Court's treatment of Article 8(1) had the effect of placing 'inherent limitations' upon the rights guaranteed, while in a stinging dissent in the *Marckx* case, which concerned the same article, Sir Gerald Fitzmaurice took the opposite point of view and maintained that even if the Convention was applicable – which he denied – the Court's decision that Article 8(1) had been violated gave insufficient scope to the margin of appreciation.

In addition to those already mentioned, the margin of appreciation has also been treated as relevant to the right of access to the courts under Article 6(1), the right to education in Article 2 of Protocol No. 1 and, as we saw in the previous chapter, the issue of free elections in Article 3. Even this does not exhaust the situations in which it is relevant. There are, for example, certain cases which appear to have turned on what is effectively an argument about the scope of the margin of appreciation, although the concept has not been specifically referred to.[52] Leaving these aside, however, some particularly interesting questions concerning the concept arise in relation to the protection from discrimination in Article 14, which must now be considered.

Non-discrimination

Article 14 of the Convention provides: 'The enjoyment of the rights and freedoms set forth in this Convention shall be secured without discrimination on any ground such as sex, race, colour, language, religion, political or other opinion, national or social origin, association with a national minority, property, birth or other status.'

Article 14 is complementary to the other substantive provisions in the sense that it can be applied only where the facts fall within the ambit of one or more of the other articles. On the other hand, Article 14 is autonomous in the sense that it can be applied in situations in which there has been no breach of another provision. For the purposes of Article 14 a difference of treatment is discriminatory if it has no objective and reasonable justification, that is, if it does not pursue a legitimate aim, or if there is not a reasonable relationship of proportionality between the means employed and the aim sought to be realised. In relation both to the issue of aim and that of proportionality, the concept of the margin of appreciation has had a significant role to play.

Cases in which the only issue before the Court is that of discrimination are rare. Usually applicants claim that they have been victims of a violation of specific substantive articles and in addition that discrimination contrary to Article 14 has occurred. Because so many claims are in this form it is frequently the case that where the Court has considered the margin of appreciation in relation to the substantive claim, the same or similar factors come into play in relation to Article 14.

In the *James* case, for example, as well as arguing that there had been a violation of Article 1 of Protocol No. 1, the applicants submitted that they were the victims of discrimination on grounds of property contrary to Article 14. This was because the leasehold reform legislation was a redistributive measure applying to only a restricted class of property, that is, long leasehold houses occupied by leaseholders, and also because under the legislation the lower the value of his property, the more harshly the landlord was treated. The Court rejected both arguments. As regards the first, it pointed out that 'it was inevitable that the contested legislation, being designed to remedy a perceived imbalance in the relations between landlords and occupying tenants under the long leasehold system of tenure, should affect landlords coming within that restricted category rather than all or other property owners'.[53] The objection that the legislation took no account of the respective resources and needs of landlord and tenant was regarded by the Court as simply another way of making the point that had earlier been rejected when it had considered Article 1 of Protocol No. 1 alone. The Court therefore concluded 'having regard to the margin of appreciation', that there had been no transgression of the principle of proportionality.

The Court's treatment of the second argument was essentially similar. Referring again to its earlier finding that Parliament was entitled to consider the scheme of the legislation as reasonable and appropriate, it held that 'in view of the legitimate objectives being pursued in the public interest and having regard to the respondent State's margin of appreciation, that policy of different treatment cannot be considered as unreasonable or as imposing a disproportionate burden on the applicants'.[54] It was therefore again able to conclude that the difference of treatment complained of must be deemed to have a reasonable and objective justification and consequently should not be regarded as discriminatory.

A similar approach may be discerned in the Court's treatment of Article 14 in the very different circumstances of the *Irish* case. The Court, as we have seen, held that since the requirements of Article 15 were met, various derogations from Article 5 which had occurred were not a violation of the Convention. The Irish Government, however, pointed out that for a substantial period the extrajudicial powers in question were employed only against IRA suspects, and that even when later this policy was abandoned, they were employed only to a limited extent against suspected 'Loyalist' terrorists. On these grounds it was argued that the United Kingdom was guilty of discrimination contrary to Article 14.

In considering whether this difference of treatment lacked an 'objective and reasonable justification' the Court found that initially there were profound differences between Loyalist and Republican terrorism as regards both the scale and organisation of their activities. Although these differences disappeared, the Court held that it would be 'unrealistic to carve into clear-cut phases a situation that was inherently changing and constantly evolving'. Observing that it could 'understand the authorities' hesitating about the course to take, feeling their way and needing a certain time to try to adapt themselves to the successive demands of an ugly crisis', it concluded that: 'on the basis of the data before it, and bearing in mind the limits on its powers of review, the Court cannot affirm that, during the period under consideration, the United Kingdom violated Article 14, taken together with Article 5, by employing the emergency powers against the IRA alone'.[55]

The resonance of the Court's earlier comments on Article 15 and in particular the scope of the respondent's margin of appreciation are clearly audible here. Just as in the *James* case the Court decided that there had been no discrimination on grounds of property by reference to considerations which had also governed its application of Article 1 of Protocol No. 1, so in the *Irish* case the margin of appreciation arising from the national emergency which the Court had read into Article 5, exercised a similar influence over its approach to Article 14.

In some cases, then, the Court resolves the issue of discrimination by applying very much the same criteria as regards the margin of appreciation as it will already have applied when considering the substantive article alone. In other situations, however, the effect of Article 14 is to introduce a quite new element. In the *Abdulaziz* case, for instance, the margin of appreciation appeared in a very different light when the Court turned to the issue of sex discrimination. For although, as we have seen, the Court decided that Article 8 had not been violated, the facts of the case fell within its ambit. As a result Article 14 was applicable and the Court had to decide whether, as the applicants alleged, their right to respect for family life had been secured in a way that was discriminatory and contrary to the Convention.

It was not disputed that under the relevant immigration rules it was easier for a man settled in the UK to obtain permission for his non-national spouse to enter for settlement than for a woman to do so. Unless this difference of treatment had an objective and reasonable justification, it would amount to discrimination on grounds of sex. The government argued that the aim of the immigration rules was to protect the domestic labour market at a time of high unemployment. The Court accepted this, and that such an aim was legitimate. It pointed out, however, that whether the government could justify treating male and female immigrants differently was a quite separate question. Although the margin of appreciation was relevant, its scope must vary with the circumstances, subject-matter and background. Specifically, 'it can be said that the advancement of the equality of the sexes is today a major goal in the member States of the Council of Europe. This means that very weighty reasons would have to be advanced before a difference of treatment on the ground of sex could be regarded as compatible with the Convention'.[56]

On the evidence before it the Court held that no such reasons had been shown. The statistics supplied by the government failed to convince the

Court that any difference there might be between the impact of men and women on the labour market was sufficiently important to justify treating them differently. Neither was it persuaded that the additional aim of advancing public tranquility by regulating immigration was served by distinguishing between men and women. The Court thus concluded that the three applicants had been victims of discrimination on grounds of sex, contrary to Article 14, in conjunction with Article 8, in securing their right to respect for family life.

Although the Court's reasoning in *Abdulaziz* might lead one to suppose that differences of treatment based on sex can rarely be justified, six months before, just such a situation had been found to exist. The applicant in the *Rasmussen* case had sought leave from the Danish courts to institute proceedings to contest the paternity of a girl borne by his wife some years earlier. This was refused on the ground that he was out of time, men being subject to time-limits in paternity matters, although women were not. The Commission by a narrow majority expressed the opinion that there had been a breach of Article 14, taken in conjunction with Articles 6 and 8. Having decided that the facts were such as to raise an issue under those articles, the Court had to decide whether the difference of treatment between the sexes in Danish law was contrary to the Convention.

The government pleaded that the difference of treatment was justified by the interests of the child and that regard should be had to the margin of appreciation enjoyed by the national authorities in matters of this kind. The Court agreed. Pointing out that in its previous jurisprudence it had often held the latter to be highly relevant in cases involving Article 14, the Court explained that an important factor in determining the scope of the margin of appreciation can be the extent to which the legislation of the Contracting States adopts a uniform approach. The fact that there was no such common ground in the treatment of paternity proceedings supported the government's argument. This was reinforced by the background of the legislation and the purpose of time-limits which was to ensure legal certainty and to protect the interests of the child, whilst: 'The difference of treatment established on this point between husbands and wives was based on the notion that such time-limits were less necessary for wives than for husbands since the mother's interests usually coincided with those of the child, she being awarded custody in most cases of divorce or separation.'[57]

In deciding whether a difference of treatment has an objective and reasonable justification the Court has indicated that it will attach importance to any trends which may be discernible in the practice of the Contracting States. This is, of course, a consequence of the Court's declared intention to regard the Convention as a living instrument to be interpreted in the light of modern conditions. The way in which this has influenced the application of provisions such as Article 8(2) has already been mentioned, and a similar effect can be seen with respect to Article 14. The difficulty, as always, is to decide the point at which such trends should be regarded as bearing upon the margin of appreciation.

It is clear that a change in the respondent's own practice will not in itself carry much weight. While the *Rasmussen* case was pending before the Commission, the Danish Government introduced legislation establishing uniform time-limits for men and women in paternity proceedings. This legislation did not, of course, relieve the Court of the need to consider the application, nor did the Court regard it as an admission that the previous state of the law was incompatible with the Convention. This is obviously a sensible approach. It would be most undesirable for governments to be discouraged from introducing necessary reforms by the thought of their possible impact on claims brought under the Convention. More important, one of the functions of the margin of appreciation is to give States time to adjust to the impact of changes and it would therefore be strange if recognition of the need for change were itself to provide grounds for criticism.

The Court has also indicated that a change in domestic law which forms part of a larger trend will not necessarily be regarded as removing the margin of appreciation either. In the *Engel* case, for example, the applicants complained of a breach of Article 14 in conjunction with Article 5(1) on the ground that the disciplinary penalties in issue were not applied to all ranks equally. The Court acknowledged that a distinction based on rank could infringe Article 14 and stated that it was 'not unaware that the respective legislation of a number of Contracting States seems to be evolving, albeit in various degrees, towards greater equality in the disciplinary sphere between officers, non-commissioned officers and ordinary servicemen'. However, despite the fact that recent Dutch legislation provided further evidence of the tendency, the Court concluded that there had been no violation of Article 14 because:

The hierarchical structure inherent in armies entails differentiation according to rank. Corresponding to the various ranks are differing responsibilities which in their turn justify certain inequalities of treatment in the disciplinary sphere. Such inequalities are traditionally encountered in the Contracting States and are tolerated by international humanitarian law. . . . In this respect, the European Convention allows the competent national authorities a considerable margin of appreciation.[58]

Thus there is room for the application of the margin of appreciation even in circumstances where it is clear that views as to what constitutes appropriate distinctions are changing. It is otherwise, however, when the situation as regards change is judged to have passed beyond a certain point and the respondent's practice can be presented as backward looking or seriously out of line. This is how the Court appears to have viewed the situation in the *Marckx* case.

Responding to the allegation that the distinction between married and unmarried mothers as regards the establishing of maternal affiliation constituted a violation of Article 14 taken in conjunction with Article 8, the Belgian Government argued that the law favoured the traditional family, and consequently was founded on objective and reasonable grounds relating to morals and public order. The Court recognised that support for the traditional family is a worthy objective, but held that measures to promote such an objective must not prejudice the 'illegitimate' family whose members 'enjoy the guarantees of Article 8 on an equal footing with the members of the traditional family'.[59] While it was true that when the Convention was drafted in 1950, it was common to distinguish between the legitimate and the illegitimate family, the Court stated that it was 'struck by the fact that the domestic law of the great majority of the member States of the Council of Europe has evolved and is continuing to evolve, in company with the relevant international instruments, towards full juridical recognition of the maxim *"mater semper certa est"*'.[60] Quoting in this connection two recent international conventions and legislation incorporating the principle which was currently under consideration in Belgium, the Court decided that in the circumstances the distinction complained of lacked objective and reasonable justification. Accordingly, there had been a breach of Article 14 taken in conjunction with Article 8, as regards maternal affiliation. By the same token the Court concluded that there had been unjustifiable discrimination as regards the legal extent of family relationships and the scope of patrimonial rights.

Deciding whether European thought and practice has reached the stage at which conduct which might once have been regarded as unexceptionable should now be condemned is never easy. If the Court is too conservative it will be accused of failing to uphold the objectives of the Convention. If it is too radical it will be accused of improper judicial legislation. The function of the margin of appreciation is not to supply a pat answer to the problem, but to provide part of the conceptual framework necessary for thinking about it.

A critic of the margin of appreciation doctrine once described it as a way of establishing 'a no man's land juxtaposed between compliance and contravention by a Member State in which the Commission and Court are powerless to intervene, despite their statements that the Convention requires them to do so'.[61] The inaccuracy of this view, has, it is hoped, been demonstrated. Far from establishing 'a no man's land', the margin of appreciation is a way of recognising that the international protection of human rights and sovereign freedom of action are not contradictory but complementary. Where the one ends, the other begins. In helping the international judge to decide how and where the boundary is to be located, the concept of the margin of appreciation has a vital part to play.

Notes

1 *Bulmer Ltd v Bollinger SA*, [1974] Ch. p. 401 at p. 418.
2 For a penetrating discussion of the scope of Article 15 see R. Higgins, 'Derogations under human rights treaties', *British Year Book of International Law*, XLVIII, 281 (1976–7); and J. Oraá, *Human Rights in States of Emergency in International Law*, Clarendon Press, Oxford (1992).
3 See A. H. Robertson, *Human Rights in Europe*, 2nd ed., Manchester U.P., Manchester, 112 (1977).
4 *Lawless* case, Series B, p. 408.
5 Series A, No. 3, p. 55.
6 *Ibid.*, p. 56.
7 Series A, No. 25 para. 207.
8 *Ibid.*
9 *Ibid.*, para. 214.
10 *Military and Paramilitary Activities in and against Nicaragua (Nicaragua v United States)* Merits, Judgment, [1986] I.C.J. Rep., 14.
11 See P. Van Dijk and G. J. H. van Hoof, *Theory and Practice of the European Convention on Human Rights*, Kluwer, Deventer, 468–72 (1984).
12 Series A, No. 98 para. 46.
13 *Ibid.*
14 Series A, No. 102.
15 Series A, No. 24 para. 62.
16 Series A, No. 169 para. 45.
17 *Ibid.*, para. 53. Note, however, that five members of the Court dissented on the ground that in two instances the reductions in rent were so drastic as to constitute a disproportionate interference with the applicants' rights. For another case in which national measures were held to satisfy the 'general interest' test see the *Allan Jacobsson* case, Series A, No. 163.
18 Series A, No. 52 para. 69. For discussion of this and other aspects of the *Sporrong and Lönnroth* case see R. Higgins, 'The taking of property by the State: recent developments', 176, *Hague Recueil des Cours*, 259 at 343 and 367 (1982).
19 *Ibid.*
20 Van Dijk and van Hoof, *Theory and Practice*, 340.
21 *Berrehab* case, Series A, No. 138 para. 28.
22 On the role of the margin of appreciation in relation to aliens who are also residents compare the judgment of the Court in *Berrehab* (*ibid.*) with the dissenting opinion of Judge Thór Vilhjálmsson in that case.
23 Series A, No. 22 para. 100.
24 *Ibid.*, para. 101.
25 *Ibid.*, para. 59.
26 Series A, No. 18 para. 45.
27 Series A, No. 12. For discussion of this issue see chapter 4.
28 Series A, No. 172 para. 44.
29 *Ibid.*, para. 45.

30 Series A, No. 24 para. 48.
31 *Ibid.*, para. 57.
32 Series A, No. 133 para. 33.
33 Van Dijk and van Hoof, *Theory and Practice*, 435.
34 Series A, No. 30. For a more recent examination of this issue see the *Observer and Guardian* case, Series A, No. 216..
35 D. J. Harris, *British Year Book of International Law*, L, 258 (1979). But contrast the very wide view of the margin of appreciation taken by a bare majority of the Court in the *Markt Intern* case, Series A, No. 165, which concerned the German law relating to unfair competition and Article 10.
36 Series A, No. 45 para. 56.
37 *Ibid.*, para. 59.
38 *Ibid.*, para. 52.
39 *Ibid.*, para. 62.
40 *Ibid.*, para. 60.
41 *Ibid.*, partially dissenting opinion of Judge Walsh, para. 20.
42 Series A, No. 142.
43 Series A, No. 22 para. 59.
44 See, for example, the *Luberti* case, Series A, No. 75 para. 27.
45 *Letellier* case, Series A, No. 207 para. 51. See also the *Kemmache* case, Series A, No. 218.
46 Series A, No. 94 para. 67.
47 *Ibid.*
48 Series A, No. 106 para. 37.
49 Series A, No. 184 para. 40.
50 *Ibid.*, dissenting opinion of Judge Martens, para. 3.6.5.
51 See on this point the recent decision in *B v France*, Series A, No. 232C, where the judgments in *Rees* and *Cossey* were distinguished and the Court held by 15 votes to 6 that the rights of a transsexual under Article 8 had been violated.
52 For instance, *F v Switzerland*, Series A, No. 128, (scope of the State's right to regulate remarriage). See especially the views expressed in the joint dissenting opinion. Also the *Vilvarajah* case, Series A, No. 215 ('margin of discretion' as regards Article 13).
53 Series A, No. 98 para. 76.
54 *Ibid.*, para. 77.
55 Series A, No. 25 para. 229.
56 Series A, No. 94 para. 78.
57 Series A, No. 87 para. 41.
58 Series A, No. 22 para. 72.
59 Series A, No. 31 para. 40.
60 *Ibid.*, para. 41.
61 C. Feingold, 'The Little Red Schoolbook and the European Convention on Human Rights', *Human Rights Review*, III, 21 at 42 (1978).

CHAPTER 8

General principles of law

The European Convention's only reference to general principles of law is to be found in Article 7(2) which deals with the particular issue of retrospective criminal law.[1] It therefore contains no equivalent to Article 38(1)(c) of the Statute of the International Court, directing that Court to apply 'the general principles of law recognised by civilised nations', along with other source material, to disputes which are submitted to it. The omission of a provision corresponding to Article 38 was quite deliberate, not because those responsible for producing the Convention wished to withhold access to general principles from those entrusted with its interpretation, but, on the contrary, because they saw the use of general principles as inevitable. As the Court put it in the *Golder* case, 'the Legal Committee of the Assembly of the Council of Europe foresaw in August 1950 that "the Commission and the Court must necessarily apply such principles" in the execution of their duties and thus considered it to be "unnecessary" to insert a specific clause to this effect in the Convention.'[2]

There is, of course, a very considerable difference between recognising that recourse to general principles is necessary in principle, and deciding that use of a general principle is appropriate in a particular case. The latter requires a demonstration that the principle in question will promote and not subvert the development of human rights law and, equally important, that in the particular circumstances use of a general principle is a justifiable, not an excessive, act of judicial legislation. The Court's treatment of general principles is thus central to the issues with which this book is concerned.

Waiver

An excellent illustration of the Court's utilising a general principle of law can be found in its treatment of the doctrine of waiver. The Convention, like other human rights instruments, has no provision permitting an individual to waive his rights, or to consent to treatment which would otherwise be impermissible. On the other hand, the possibility of rights being waived is not expressly prohibited and the concept of waiver is a familiar one in domestic law. As noted earlier, however, it is wrong to think of the Convention solely in terms of the interests of individuals. There is also a public interest involving wider considerations. Whether a waiver of rights is possible is therefore a question which may call for a different answer in relation to different parts of the Convention. Such decisions, along with associated rulings as to how, if waiver is possible, it may be exercised, provide significant opportunities for judicial development of the law.

Avoidance of waiver

The issue of waiver was first raised in the *Vagrancy* cases in 1971 where the question was whether the applicants had been deprived of their liberty contrary to Article 5(1). The applicants were detained in vagrancy centres in Belgium following a magistrate's order. They had, however, reported voluntarily to the police and relying on this, the government argued that their detention was in each case the result of a request and as such, could not be a violation of Article 5. The Court had no hesitation in rejecting the government's argument. Pointing out that a person may give himself up to the police out of temporary distress or misery, but that this in no way denotes that he is properly to be regarded as a vagrant, the Court explained that in any event, the detention procedure which formed the subject of the complaint was mandatory rather than contractual. It then said:

Finally and above all, the right to liberty is too important in a 'democratic society' within the meaning of the Convention for a person to lose the benefit of the protection of the Convention for the single reason that he gives himself up to be taken into detention. Detention might violate Article 5 even although the person concerned might have agreed to it. When the matter is one which concerns *ordre public* within the Council of Europe, a scrupulous supervision by the organs of the Convention of all measures capable of violating the rights and freedoms which it guarantees is necessary in every case.[3]

The Court therefore concluded that the fact that the applicants reported voluntarily in no way relieved the Court 'of its duty to see whether there has been a violation of the Convention'.[4]

Three years after this decision on Article 5 the Court was presented with a rather similar question concerning Article 50. At the final stage of the *Neumeister* case the Austrian Government submitted that the applicant, whose claim based on Article 5(3) had been upheld by the Court, had waived all claims for financial compensation in the event of his obtaining a remission of the sentence of imprisonment he was currently serving. Since the remission in question had been granted, the government's view was that there was no longer any basis for a claim under Article 50. Again the Court disagreed. Taking the view that on the facts as stated the case should be treated as analogous to those in which an applicant has indicated his wish to discontinue proceedings, the Court held that in itself the applicant's alleged waiver of his rights could not be conclusive. In a passage reminiscent of the cases on discontinuation considered in chapter 3, as well as of its treatment of waiver in the *Vagrancy* cases, the Court said:

Having regard to its responsibilities in pursuance of Article 19 of the Convention, the Court would not be relieved of its duty by the sole fact that an individual had stated to his Government that he waived rights guaranteed by the Convention. Even if the Court were to reach the conclusion in this case that Neumeister had waived his claims, it could not terminate the proceedings and strike the case out of its list without first being satisfied that the aim of Article 50 has been achieved.[5]

The Court's conclusion that the doctrine of waiver has no bearing on Article 50 is an important one and, like the previous case, shows how there can be no room for a general principle running counter to the fundamental purposes of the Convention. It is worth noting, however, that conduct which may be irrelevant as a waiver may be taken account of in another way. The *Neumeister* case illustrates this point also. For, having dismissed the argument based on waiver, the Court continued:

On the other hand, the fact that an applicant has declared at a particular time that he would settle for the satisfaction obtained or to be obtained from his Government may be an important or even a decisive factor when the Court comes to assess the just character of that satisfaction within the meaning of Article 50.[6]

When the Court turned to examine the facts, it found that the applicant had indicated that remission of the remainder of his sentence would be the best possible form of reparation for the wrong he had suffered. In the light of this and other factors the Court decided that no financial compensation was called for.

In the *Van der Mussele* case in 1983 the Court adopted a similar approach to Article 4. Although this case concerned consent rather than waiver, the Court again decided that the applicant's conduct did not have the consequences asserted by the government, but at the same time held that it could not be altogether disregarded. The question in *Van der Mussele* was whether the Belgian practice of requiring pupil barristers to represent indigent persons without a fee could be regarded as 'compulsory labour' contrary to Article 4(2). To the government and a majority of the Commission the applicant had offered himself voluntarily for the work by deciding to qualify as an *avocat* and could not now complain. He had gone into the profession with his eyes open and must be taken to have accepted its burdens as the price of its benefits. The Court took a rather different view. In its opinion the important point was not that the applicant chose to enter the legal profession voluntarily, but that he had to accept the obligation to render his services free of charge whether he wanted to or not and that 'his consent was determined by the normal conditions of exercise of the profession at the relevant time'.[7] It followed that his prior consent without more, was not sufficient to prevent a finding that he had been required to perform compulsory labour.

Having made this point, the Court went on to say that the scope of Article 4(2) can best be appreciated by considering its underlying objectives. These are indicated by the provisions of Article 4(3) which excludes specified activities from the definition on the ground of what the Court called 'the governing ideas of the general interest, social solidarity and what is the normal or ordinary course of affairs'.[8] At this stage the applicant's situation became highly relevant. The services to be rendered were not something unusual, but fell within the normal activities of an *avocat*. More significantly in the present context, the services in question were part of the applicant's training and he knew this when he entered the profession. For these reasons, and because the work in question was moderate in scale and a means of ensuring that an accused was legally represented, the Court was satisfied that it should not be regarded as 'compulsory labour' for the purposes of Article 4(2).

It is clear that slavery or servitude, which are prohibited by Article 4(1), cannot be rendered lawful by the subject's consent because 'it should not be possible for any person to contract himself into bondage'.[9] The *Van der Mussele* case indicates that the same can now be said of 'forced or compulsory labour' under Article 4(2), with the sensible proviso that while consent alone is certainly insufficient, when taken into account with other factors, it may lead to the conclusion that a given exaction of work does not amount to a contravention.

In the cases examined so far the Court has considered arguments based on waiver, or the related notion of consent, and rejected them, at least in the form they were presented. In other cases, however, the Court has indicated that in relation to certain articles of the Convention there is room for the doctrine of waiver. These cases and the conditions the Court has laid down for its application, reveal another side of the issue.

Utilisation of waiver

In the case of *Albert and Le Compte* the Court considered the possibility of waiver in relation to Article 6(1) and specifically the requirement that in the determination of civil rights or obligations, or of any criminal charge, everyone is entitled to a fair and public hearing. In that case, which concerned disciplinary proceedings against two medical practitioners, the Court was prepared to recognise that as far as the public aspect of proceedings is concerned, the doctrine of waiver can apply. As the Court put it:

The rule requiring a public hearing, as embodied in Article 6 para 1, may also yield in certain circumstances to the will of the person concerned. Admittedly, the nature of some of the rights safeguarded by the Convention is such as to exclude a waiver of the entitlement to exercise them . . . but the same cannot be said of certain other rights. Thus, neither the letter nor the spirit of Article 6 para 1 would prevent a medical practitioner from waiving, of his own free will and in an unequivocal manner . . . the entitlement to have his case heard in public; conducting disciplinary proceedings of this kind in private does not contravene Article 6 para 1 if the domestic law so permits and this is in accordance with the will of the person concerned.[10]

Permitting a waiver in respect of the public aspect of legal proceedings seems an unobjectionable piece of judicial legislation. On the facts of *Albert and Le Compte* it was clear that the applicants had not in fact waived their rights and so the Court found that holding the proceedings in private amounted to a violation. However, it is easy to imagine circumstances in which a private hearing might be very much in the individual's interests. There is therefore no reason why in the absence of express authorisation, the possibility of waiver should not be read into the Convention.

The decision that the right to a public hearing can be waived was confirmed in *H v Belgium*[11] and the *Håkansson and Sturesson* case.[12] In the former, which concerned proceedings by a disbarred barrister who wished to be restored to the roll of *avocats*, the Court found that there was no evidence that the applicant had intended to waive his rights under Article 6(1) and reached the same conclusion as in *Albert and Le Compte*. In *Håkansson and Sturesson*, on the other hand, the Court held that the applicants had tactily but unequivocally waived their right to a public hearing by failing to apply for one and accepting an appeal court's usual procedure. In this case, therefore, there was no violation of Article 6(1) as regards this point.

One member of the Court dissented in *Håkansson and Sturesson* and challenged the idea of tacit waiver. Judge Walsh maintained that the failure to request a public hearing cannot be equated with a waiver of the right, as this would run counter to the object and purpose of the Convention:

The public hearing requirement of Article 6(1) is enshrined in the Convention because the Contracting States thought it was important, not because a party may think that it is important. The administration of justice in public is a matter of paramount importance in every democracy and is one of the cornerstones put in place by the Convention to guarantee the impartial administration of justice and the defence of the rights guaranteed by the Convention. The fact that the public may not manifest any particular interest in a given case is not a consideration. Equally a lack of interest in having a hearing in public on the part of one or both parties to a suit does not alter the matter. *Only where both parties agree to a hearing other than in public can the mandatory provisions of Article 6(1) be waived.*[13]

The Court, it should be noted, was careful to state that waiver, whether tacit or express 'must not run counter to any important public interest'[14] and found that the present case, which concerned a land permit, involved no interest which made a public hearing necessary. This clearly goes some way to meet Judge Walsh's point. Nevertheless, his view that waiver 'must be manifested by clear and unambiguous words or by conduct from which the only reasonable inference to be drawn is that both parties were so agreed'[15] is a reminder that whether waiver is allowed is only one question, and that in some circumstances, as we shall see again below, what actually constitutes waiver may be just as important.

In the *Pfeifer and Plankl* case the first applicant had been tried on various criminal charges before a regional court in Austria and complained that his rights had been violated because the bench included two judges who were involved in the case at an earlier stage, so rendering the domestic court neither 'impartial', as Article 6(1) of the Convention requires, nor, since national law disqualified the judges concerned, 'established by law'. The government's response was to argue that as the applicant had not objected to the composition of the court, even when invited to do so, he must be taken to have waived the rights concerned. Like the earlier cases on the right to a public hearing, the case thus raised two issues: whether this aspect of the protection granted by Article 6(1) can be waived; and, if so, whether it had actually been waived on the present facts.

The Court, aware no doubt of the far-reaching significance of the first question, declined to answer it, but limited itself to the observation that the right to be tried before a properly composed court 'is of essential importance and its exercise cannot depend on the parties alone'.[16] On the second question, which could not be avoided, the Court was more forthcoming. Agreeing with the Commission that to be effective a waiver must not only be unequivocal, but in the case of procedural rights 'requires minimum guarantees commensurate to its importance',[17] it held that the fact that the applicant's lawyer had not been present to advise him when he made his decision, rendered his alleged waiver ineffective. 'Thus', said the Court, 'even supposing that the rights in question can be waived by a defendant, the circumstances surrounding the applicant's decision deprived it of any validity from the point of view of the Convention'.[18] It therefore concluded that there had been a violation of Article 6(1).

It is clear, then, that in principle waiver is possible in relation to the guarantee of the right to a public hearing in Article 6(1) and has not been ruled out in relation to certain other aspects of a trial, although the precise position is unclear. Whether the same reasoning can be applied to the right to a hearing itself is more difficult. It was this aspect of waiver which the Court had to consider in 1980 in the *De Weer* case. The applicant, who ran a butcher's shop, was found by an official to be selling pork at a price higher than the maximum permitted by Belgian law. An administrative order was therefore made requiring him to close his shop pending a hearing of the case. However, the closure could be terminated on payment of a small fine by way of settlement. The applicant, wishing to keep his shop open, paid the fine, but then argued that the combined use of the settlement and closure proceedings violated the right to a fair hearing guaranteed by Article 6(1). One of the arguments raised by the government was that the applicant had waived his rights by paying the fine. The Court was therefore called upon to consider this as an issue of principle.

In what may be regarded as one of its most important pronouncements on the scope of waiver, the Court accepted that in this kind of situation a waiver of the applicant's rights under Article 6(1) is possible. Holding that 'The "right to a court", which is a constituent element of the right to a fair trial is no more absolute in criminal than in civil matters' the Court pointed out that in the Contracting States' legal systems waiver of the right to have one's case dealt with by a tribunal:

is frequently encountered both in civil matters, notably in the shape of arbitration clauses in contracts, and in criminal matters in the shape, *inter alia,* of fines paid by way of composition. The waiver, which has undeniable advantages for the individual concerned as well as for the administration of justice, does not in principle offend against the Convention; on this point the Court shares the view of the Commission.[19]

This is clearly a more profound development than the point made in *Albert and Le Compte.* Not surprisingly, therefore, having committed itself to a bold piece of judicial legislation, the Court sought to allay any anxiety as to the dangers of this approach by emphasising the significance of the right to a court and the corresponding limitations on the scope for waiver. The passage concerned is a good example of the way in which a potentially subversive general principle can be accepted, and at the same time, limited. Dealing with the scope for waiver in this context, the Court said:

Nevertheless, in a democratic society too great an importance attaches to the 'right to a court' . . . for its benefit to be forfeited solely by reason of the fact that an individual is a party to a settlement reached in the course of a procedure ancillary to court proceedings. In an area concerning the public order (*ordre public*) of the member States of the Council of Europe, any measure or decision alleged to be in breach of Article 6 calls for particularly careful review. . . . The Court is not unaware of the firmness with which the Belgian courts have condemned, on the basis of Article 8 of the Constitution and Article 6 of the Convention, failure to respect the 'right to a court' in private legal relationships. . . . At least the same degree of vigilance would appear indispensable when someone formally 'charged with a criminal offence' challenges a settlement that has barred criminal proceedings. Absence of constraint is at all events one of the conditions to be satisfied; this much is dictated by an international instrument founded on freedom and the rule of law. . . . Here again, the Court concurs with the Commission.[20]

The Court's concern that waiver should not become a way of undermining the effectiveness of Article 6(1) is also evident in its treatment of the facts of the case, and specifically the issue of constraint. Here the Court explained that although the prospect of having to appear in court is certainly likely to prompt a willingness to compromise, in itself this cannot amount to constraint – otherwise, of course, there could never be any possibility of a valid waiver. In the present case, however, considerably more pressure than this was evident. The alternative to paying the fine was an indefinite closure of the applicant's business. Moreover, the fine demanded was so small as to create a 'flagrant disproportion' between the alternatives available. In these circumstances the Court was unanimous in concluding that the applicant's waiver of a fair trial was tainted by constraint and therefore ineffective.

The *De Weer* case, then, shows the Court breaking new ground in two ways. First, by establishing the possibility of waiver in a field where it had not been recognised hitherto. Then, having accepted the general principle, by defining and applying the conditions for its exercise. In the next case to be considered, the Court avoided the first issue, but paid particular attention to the question of conditions.

In the *Colozza* case the Court held that Italy had committed a violation of Article 6(1) by trying the applicant in his absence. One of the arguments put forward by the government was that the inability of the authorities to discover the applicant's whereabouts at the material time meant that he must be deemed to have waived his right to appear and defend himself. This novel interpretation of the doctrine of waiver was rejected by the Court, which decided that even if the right to appear at the hearing can be waived – a matter which it left open – no waiver had actually occurred. This was because, as the Court put it, 'waiver of the exercise of a right guaranteed by the Convention must be established in an unequivocal manner',[21] whereas on the facts there was no indication that the applicant was aware that criminal proceedings against him had begun, let alone that he had waived his right to appear. Administrative incompetence had led to his being classified as a fugitive from justice, but this was very different from the true position.

In deciding that waiver, if it is to be effective, must be proved unequivocally, the Court was not making new law since the same point had been made in *Neumeister* and subsequently, as we have seen, in *Albert and Le Compte*. In the present case, however, the point was particularly important because in relation to trial *in absentia* any concept of 'presumed waiver' could seriously undermine the Convention. A similar approach was adopted subsequently in the *Brozicek* case[22] and in *F.C.B. v Italy*.[23] In these cases, which involved trials *in absentia* in slightly different circumstances from those in *Colozza*, the Court again made it clear that it was not prepared to entertain the idea of waiver without clear evidence relating to the applicant's intention. In relation to the right to publicity we have seen that the Court has been prepared to accept the concept of tacit waiver in certain circumstances. It is interesting that as regards trial *in absentia* it appears to have ruled this out. A cogent justification would be that in any hierarchy of rights the right to a 'public' hearing and the right to a hearing itself ought to be treated as occupying different positions. It is worth repeating, however, that waiver of any right under Article 6(1) must be unequivocal. By giving attention not only to the question of when waiver is permissible, but also to the conditions of its exercise, the Court has thus sought to leave room for genuine cases of waiver, while discouraging attempts to use the doctrine in a way which could undermine the Convention.

Equality of arms

Égalité des armes, which translates as 'equality of arms' or, more felicitously, as 'equality of the parties' is another general principle which has played an important part in the work of the Court. Derived from and developed by the early work of the Commission, the principle has been used by the Court in two distinct strands of its jurisprudence. First, as might be expected, the idea that litigation should be ordered in a way which ensures that neither party enjoys an improper advantage has played a significant part in the Court's application of the concept of a 'fair trial' in Article 6. Secondly, as a way of showing that the standards demanded of others are no less pertinent to the Strasbourg system, the principle of equality of arms has inspired a major development of the Court's own procedures. The latter was historically the first use of the principle and is therefore an appropriate place to begin.

The Court's procedures

From the discussion in chapter 3 it will be recalled that in the *Lawless* case[24] the Court considered but rejected a number of arguments which

would have placed an impenetrable barrier between an individual applicant and the Court. Although Article 44 of the Convention provides that
only Contracting States and the Commission have the right to bring a case
before the Court, in *Lawless* the Court decided that the Commission
could make its report available to the applicant and that the transmission
of the applicant's observations on it to the Court was in principle permissible. However, as noted earlier, it reserved its decision as to whether
transmission was justified on the particular facts until it had had an
opportunity to examine the merits.

The Court's treatment of the preliminary issues in the *Lawless* case was
an early and welcome recognition of the fact that while an individual
cannot be a party to proceedings in the Court, with the result that full
equality of arms is impossible, it is nevertheless feasible, by using the
Commission, to move in the direction of the general principle. That this
was the Court's objective is clear from its reasoning in which, it will be
recalled, the 'proper administration of justice' was its primary concern.
However, when the Court turned to the particular facts in *Lawless,* it
appeared to qualify its earlier ruling by indicating that the Commission
should not simply reproduce the applicant's statements, but, if it believed
they could assist the Court. take them into account in its own submissions.[25] The Commission, in other words, is more than a postbox, a
ruling which emphasises the point that, like any other general principle,
equality of arms can only properly be relied on to the extent that it is
consistent with both the aims and structure of the Convention.

The question which has just been raised – how far recourse to the
principle of equality of arms is compatible with the procedural framework
of the Convention – was raised by another matter which was considered in
Lawless. This was whether the Commission could invite an applicant to
nominate a person to assist it during the proceedings before the Court.
This procedure, which was based on Rule 29(1) of the Rules of Court, was
challenged by the Irish Government which maintained that if, as was
likely to happen, the Commission had the assistance of the applicant's
counsel in presenting the case, its impartiality and ability to act as
defender of the public interest would be impaired. The Commission, as
might be expected, took the opposite view and maintained that far from
the proposed procedure prejudicing the Commission's position, it was
part of the latter's duty to ensure that the Court was informed of all
aspects of the case.

Here, as on the earlier point, the Court agreed with the Commission,
and in the *Vagrancy* cases in 1970 the significance of the above ruling was
demonstrated when, for the first time, the Commission indicated that it
was its intention to be assisted by the applicant's lawyer, who would be
asked to supply the Court with details on a number of points on which the

Commission considered itself insufficiently informed. Belgium immediately protested and in preliminary proceedings concerned with this point, argued that the Commission's proposal was contrary both to Article 44, and to 'the whole spirit of the Convention' which, according to the government, prohibited individuals from pleading before the Court.

Again, however, the Court rejected the government's arguments in favour of those of the Commission. Pointing out that Rule 29(1) 'does not place any limit on the freedom of the Delegates in their choice of persons to assist them', and that 'therefore, it does not preclude them, *inter alia,* from having the assistance of the lawyer or former lawyer of an individual applicant',[26] the Court added a reminder that the role of any person so appointed is to assist the Commission's Delegates, while, they, in turn, have the function of assisting the Court. Consequently, 'the person assisting the Delegates must restrict himself in his statements to presenting to the Court explanations on points indicated to him by the Delegates, and this always subject to the control and responsibility of the Delegates'.[27]

This was an important qualification and the lawyer appointed to assist the Commission in the *Vagrancy* cases actually played a relatively minor part in the proceedings. However, with the legitimacy of having the applicant's lawyer present to assist the Commission thus established, full use was made of the opportunities presented by Rule 29(1) in subsequent cases. For example, in the two cases decided in 1975 (*Golder* and the *National Union of Belgian Police*)[28] the applicant's lawyer was present and in four out of the five cases decided in 1976 Rule 29(1) was used. In one of those cases (*Schmidt and Dahlström*)[29] a very unusual situation occurred. Professor F. Schmidt, who was himself one of the applicants, addressed the Court on Swedish labour law on which he was an expert.

In 1982 the final step in enabling an individual to put his case to the Court was taken. The Court's Rules were amended so as to make specific provision for the representation of the applicant. Under Rule 30 the applicant may now present his own case, or have it put for him by his representative, quite separately from the Commission. Other Rules, which need not be described here, deal with the applicant's position in relation to the written and oral proceedings, interim measures, the taking of evidence and the receipt of judgments. In the light of these arrangements it is apparent that everything which can be done to improve the applicant's position, short of amending the Convention,[30] has now been done. Changes in the Court's Rules are not, of course, examples of judicial legislation, at least in the accepted sense. It is clear, however, that the ground was prepared for these developments by the Court's early recognition that if it was to do its job, individual applicants could not be excluded from its proceedings. In ensuring that the principle of equality of arms was a benchmark of its own procedure, the Court therefore demonstrated the role which an imaginative use of general principles can play in the progressive development of the law.

Fair trial

As regards the substantive provisions of the Convention the Court's main application of the principle of equality of arms has been in relation to Article 6(1) which contains the guarantee of a fair trial. Although the obligation here is a wide one and cannot be satisfied merely by showing that the individual has been afforded procedural equality, if he has not, the trial will be unfair. In many cases, moreover, a real or imagined inequality has been the basis of the applicant's complaint. Thus the concept of equality of arms has played an important part in the Court's application of this article.

Equality of arms was, for example, the crucial element in the *Bönisch* case where the applicant, who had been convicted in the Austrian courts on charges of supplying adulterated food, claimed that the handling of the evidence in his case had violated Articles 6(1) and 6(3)(d) of the Convention. His specific complaint was that he had been convicted on the evidence of the Director of the Federal Food Control Institute whom the domestic court had appointed as its expert. In the first set of proceedings against him in 1977 the applicant was allowed to challenge the Director's evidence by calling a witness, though in the second set in 1979 he was not. His complaint was that this deficiency, together with the special position occupied by the Director generally, entailed a breach of his rights under the Convention.

Article 6(3)(d) of the Convention provides that everyone charged with a criminal offence has the right 'to examine or have examined witnesses against him and to obtain the attendance and examination of witnesses on his behalf under the same conditions as witnesses against him'. It is thus clearly an application of the principle of equality of arms to the particular issue of witnesses. In *Bönisch,* however, the Director had been involved as an expert rather than a witness and in the government's submission this meant that Article 6(3)(d) had no bearing on his position. On the other hand, the Court has consistently made the point that the various guarantees of Article 6(3) are themselves constituent elements of a larger whole, namely the concept of a fair trial, contained in Article 6(1). In view of this the Court decided that it should avoid resolving the issue of classification and review the proceedings in the Austrian Court for conformity with the more general obligation.

To assess the role played by the Director of the Institute in the particular circumstances the Court examined his procedural position and the manner in which he performed his function. It noted that he drafted the reports which set the criminal proceedings against Mr Bönisch in motion and then, as expert, had the duty of explaining and supplementing these findings. Pointing out that 'it is easily understandable that doubts should arise, especially in the mind of an accused, as to the neutrality of an expert when it was his report that in fact prompted the bringing of a prosecution',[31] the Court concluded that in appearance the Director was more like a witness against the accused. From this it followed that in accordance with the principle of equality of arms, there must be equal treatment as between the hearing of the Director and the hearing of persons called by the defence.

On the facts the Court found that equal treatment had not been afforded. Because of his appointment as expert the Director's statements must have carried greater weight than those of the witness which Mr Bönisch was allowed to call in the 1977 proceedings. Yet, as already noted, his independence and impartiality were capable of appearing open to doubt. The Court therefore concluded that there had been a violation of the applicant's right to a fair trial, as guaranteed by Article 6(1), and that it was unnecessary to give a separate ruling on Article 6(3)(d).[32]

Equality of arms is not just relevant to the treatment of witnesses and experts, but also has implications for the whole institutional framework within which a trial is conducted. This may be seen strikingly in the *Borgers* case where the Court, in controversial circumstances, overruled a long-standing precedent and gave the concept of equality of arms an extended application. The case concerned a government official, the *avocat général*, and his special role in criminal proceedings in Belgium. The applicant had been convicted of certain offences and his case eventually reached the Court of Cassation. His complaint was that at his appeal an *avocat général* had made submissions to the court which Mr Borgers had no opportunity to reply to, and had then participated in its deliberations. Although this was standard practice in Belgium, the applicant argued that it violated the principle of equality of arms and accordingly his right to a fair trial under Article 6(1).

When an identical question was considered in the *Delcourt* case[33] in 1970 the Court took the view that as the *avocat général* was unquestionably independent and impartial, no objection could be raised to his playing the role of adviser to the domestic court. In the present case, however, although it accepted the premise of the earlier judgment, the Court came to a different conclusion. Observing that the concept of a fair trial had 'undergone a considerable evolution in the Court's case law, notably in respect of the importance attached to appearances and to the increased sensitivity of the public to the fair administration of justice',[34] the Court held that by recommending that the appeal of an accused be allowed or dismissed the *avocat général* 'becomes objectively speaking his ally or his opponent'.[35] It followed that in the latter event the principle of equality of arms must be respected and since the applicant had not been able either to see or reply to the *avocat général*'s submissions, there had been a violation of Article 6(1).

The Court came to a similar conclusion as regards the official's participation in the decision. This too was found to be unobjectionable in *Delcourt*, but the Court in *Borgers* disagreed, saying:

> Further and above all, the inequality was increased even more by the *avocat général*'s participation, in an advisory capacity, in the court's deliberations. Assistance of this nature, given with total objectivity, may be of some use in drafting judgments, ... It is however hard to see how such assistance can remain limited to stylistic considerations, . . . if it is in addition intended, as the Government also affirmed, to contribute towards maintaining the consistency of the case law. Even if such assistance was so limited in the present case, it could reasonably be thought that the deliberations afforded the *avocat général* an additional opportunity to promote, without fear of contradiction by the applicant, his submissions to the effect that the appeal should be dismissed.[36]

On this ground also, therefore, the Court decided that there had been a violation of the principle of equality of arms.

Four judges dissented from this decision and, like the judgment, their separate opinions had as their focal point the principle of equality of arms. Their view, however, was that as the *avocat général* is not a party to a case and had an independent role, neither for the accused nor against him, the principle had no application to the present facts. In their view, therefore, the *Delcourt* case should have been followed, a conclusion which they reinforced by stressing the value of precedent. While they recognised the importance of appearances in cases such as *Bonisch*, they considered that to decide whether the applicant had had a fair trial in the present case, it was necessary to look behind appearances at the realities of the situation. As the reality was that the *avocat général* was impartial and independent, they considered that there had been no violation of Article 6(1).

Although the principle of equality of arms is particularly important in relation to Article 6, this is not its only sphere of application. Since the principle is concerned with procedural fairness, it has been utilised by the Court in cases involving other provisions which require adversarial proceedings either explicitly or implicitly. In the *Lamy* case, for example, the Court used the principle in a case involving Article 5(4).

The applicant in *Lamy* had been arrested in Belgium and charged with fraudulent bankruptcy. However, when he challenged his arrest in the courts he was denied access to the case file which, in accordance with the standard procedure in Belgium, had been opened by the investigating judge. The applicant claimed that this denial infringed Article 5(4) of the Convention, which guarantees the right to take proceedings to challenge the lawfulness of detention. This was because it is well established that Article 5(4) requires adversarial proceedings and in the applicant's submission such proceedings must respect the principle of equality of arms. The government, on the other hand, argued that Mr Lamy had had the benefit of adversarial proceedings and maintained that equality of arms simply had no relevance to applications for provisional release.

The Court rejected the government's arguments. It found that access to the case file was essential for the defence to be able to challenge the lawfulness of the applicant's arrest effectively and, in an important ruling on the scope of equality of arms, held that 'The appraisal of the need for a remand in custody and the subsequent assessment of guilt are too closely linked for access to documents to be refused in the former case when the law requires it in the latter case'.[37] The prosecution in *Lamy* was familiar with the whole file, whereas the applicant had been denied the chance to challenge the reasons relied on to justify a remand in custody. There had been a failure to respect the principle of equality of arms and so the procedure was not truly adversarial. The Court was therefore satisfied that Article 5(4) had been violated.

The relation between equality of arms and the concept of a fair trial was explored further in the *Feldbrugge* case. The applicant had been refused health insurance benefits and claimed that the proceedings before the President of the competent Appeals Board had violated her rights under Article 6(1). In this connection she alleged a two-fold violation of the principle of equality of arms vis-à-vis the Occupational Association which had contested her claim. First, she had been denied an opportunity of appearing either in person or through her lawyer, to argue her case. Secondly, the reports of two permanent medical experts, which provided the basis of the President's decision, had not been made available to her. Thus she had been denied an opportunity to comment on them, or to call evidence in rebuttal.

Although the applicant's points may appear persuasive, the Court, after reviewing the procedure employed in such cases, decided that there had been no breach of the principle of equality of arms. This was because the principle in question is concerned with procedural inequality and on the facts nothing of the kind had occurred. As the Court put it:

The Occupational Association did not enjoy a procedural position any more advantageous than Mrs Feldbrugge's, in that had the experts expressed an opinion unfavourable to its standpoint, the Association would likewise have been unable to present oral or written arguments or to challenge the validity of the unfavourable opinion. No lack of fair balance thus obtained between the parties in this respect.[38]

This, however, was not the end of the matter. Although there was no inequality of arms, there was a violation of Article 6(1) because the procedure followed before the President was 'clearly not such as to allow proper participation of the contending parties, at any rate during the final and decisive stage of that procedure'. This was for the reasons put forward by the applicant and already mentioned. She had been neither heard, nor asked to file pleadings. Nor had she or her representative had any opportunity to consult the evidence in the case file, in particular the two crucial reports. In view of these deficiencies the proceedings conducted before the President 'were not attended, to a sufficient degree, by one of the principal guarantees of a judicial procedure'.[39] Accordingly, there was a violation of the Convention.

From the applicant's point of view it matters little whether the finding of the violation of Article 6 is based on a lack of equality of arms or on some other ground. However, from the perspective of those responsible for ensuring that domestic procedures conform to the Convention, the distinction is important. What *Feldbrugge* confirms is that equality of arms is a necessary, but not a sufficient, condition of a fair trial. While the Court has used the general principle to flesh out the content of Article 6(1), it has not made the mistake of treating it as exhaustive of these obligations. Properly used, general principles are an aid to decision-making, not a substitute for it, so sometimes, as here, the correct judicial response is to recognise their limitations.

Estoppel

Another very clear example of the Court's use of a general principle of law is to be found in its reliance on estoppel in a number of cases concerning its relations with the Commission. In the *Vagrancy* cases, as we have seen in chapter 3, the Court decided that it is competent in certain circumstances to review rulings of the Commission concerned with issues of admissibility. However, having established its competence to review Belgium's submissions as to admissibility, the Court decided that with only one exception they must be rejected. This was because it took the view that, as a general rule, objections to jurisdiction and admissibility must first be raised before the Commission. Because Belgium had failed to comply with this requirement, it was now estopped from raising the issues in the Court.

In rejecting Belgium's submissions on the non-substantive ground of estoppel the Court was making use of a concept which is not only well known in domestic law, but also used from time to time by international tribunals. There is, however, no express reference to it in the European Convention. Thus, as in the cases already considered, we have here a demonstration of judicial legislation, and in the *Vagrancy* cases the Court explained very clearly why it considered this to be necessary. It gave two reasons. The first was procedural economy. The Court noted that 'it is in fact usual practice in international and national courts that objections to admissibility should as a general rule be raised *in limine litis*. This, if not always mandatory, is at least a requirement of the proper administration of justice and of legal stability'. It then went on:

Doubtless, proceedings before the Court are not the same as those which took place before the Commission and usually the parties are not even the same; but they concern the same case and it results clearly from the general economy of the Convention that objections to jurisdiction and admissibility must, in principle, be raised first before the Commission to the extent that their character and circumstances permit.[40]

The second reason was the optional quality of the admissibility requirements, at least as far as the local remedies rule is concerned. As the Court put it:

Furthermore, there is nothing to prevent States from waiving the benefit of the rule of exhaustion of domestic remedies, the essential aim of which is to protect their national legal order. There exists on this subject a long-established international practice from which the Convention has definitely not departed as it refers in Article 26, to 'the generally recognised rules of international law'. If there is such a waiver in the course of proceedings before the Commission, it can scarcely be imagined that the Government concerned is entitled to withdraw the waiver at will after the case has been referred to the Court.[41]

The first of these reasons is a good deal more persuasive than the second. Although, as the Court stated, there is certainly relevant international practice relating to the domestic remedies rule, the same cannot be said of the requirements of Articles 25 and 27, one of which (the six months rule) was in issue here. Moreover, in the present context the Court seems satisfied with much less evidence of 'waiver' than in the cases considered earlier. All this, however, is not very important. The idea of procedural economy, which simply means requiring States to use the Commission for the purpose intended, is the only justification needed. It is certainly this principle, as we shall see, which has governed the Court's approach to the concept of estoppel in subsequent cases.

One of the questions left open in the *Vagrancy* cases was the stage at which objections to admissibility have to be raised before the Commission in order to avoid a government's being barred from raising them in the Court. This question was considered in the *Artico* case, where Italy wished to argue that the application was out of time and also that it was inadmissible *ratione temporis* because the complaint concerned events prior to the period when Italy had accepted the right of individual petition. The government had raised these pleas when the Commission was considering the case on the merits, but had failed to do so earlier when it was considering the issue of admissibility. The Court decided that in these circumstances it was barred from raising them before the Court by the principle of estoppel. Its justification is to be found in the part of the judgment in which it said:

The Court observes that the structure of the machinery of protection established by Sections III and IV of the Convention is designed to ensure that the course of the proceedings is logical and orderly. The function of sifting which Articles 26 and 27 assign to the Commission is the first of its tasks. . . . Admittedly Article 29, which has been in force since 21 September 1970, provides for a subsequent review of admissibility but it makes an *a posteriori* rejection of an application conditional on a unanimous vote by the Commission. The stringency of this condition, which marks a departure from the principle of decision by a majority laid down in Article 34, demonstrates that the spirit of the Convention requires that respondent States should normally raise their preliminary objections at the stage of the initial examination of admissibility, failing which they will be estopped.[42]

This was a useful clarification of the scope of estoppel and is clearly consistent with the underlying justification of the principle. Since the Court's competence to examine issues of admissibility is intended neither to duplicate nor to undermine the functions of the Commission, it is necessary to apply the principle of estoppel in such a way as to encourage governments to raise their objections to admissibility at the earliest possible moment.

Further light was shed on the scope of estoppel by a different aspect of the same case. Another of the government's objections to admissibility was the familiar argument that the applicant had failed to exhaust his domestic remedies. This had been raised before the Commission and at the admissibility stage and so was not open to the same objection as the pleas under Articles 25 and 27. However, the government had raised the plea before the Commission only in relation to the applicant's claim under Article 5, and not in relation to his claim under Article 6(3)(c), which was the only issue when the case reached the Court. It was therefore decided that although there had been some discussion of domestic remedies before the Commission, the government's failure to raise the question in the proper context meant that here too the principle of estoppel prevented the Court from considering the argument.

This ruling, which again appears to be a logical application of the principle, was applied in a rather similar situation in the *Foti* case. In that case the respondent was again Italy which once more invited the Court to consider the issue of domestic remedies. In relation to three of the applicants, however, the government had put the issue to the Commission in a quite different way from the argument it wished the Court to consider, while in relation to the fourth applicant, the government had raised the issue only in the most general way. With respect to the three applicants the Court held that the government was now estopped from raising the issue of domestic remedies for essentially the same reasons as in *Artico*. With respect to the fourth applicant, on the other hand, it held that the plea was insufficiently specific. Here the Court stated that:

when a Contracting State seeks to shelter behind the duty to exhaust remedies, it is for the State to establish the existence of available remedies that have not been utilised by those concerned. However, the short passage cited above from the observations of 10 October 1977 went no further than vague assertions; it did not in any sense identify the means of redress to which according to the Government, Mr Gulli had wrongly neglected to have recourse. It was not for the Commission to ascertain what were the particular remedies alluded to.[43]

Since the government had raised the issue of domestic remedies in a way which made clear what it had in mind only in its memorial to the Court, it had failed to raise the issue in time and was now estopped.

The principle established in the *Vagrancy* cases is that the Court has jurisdiction to consider issues of admissibility in so far as the respondent has raised them before the Commission 'to the extent that their character and circumstances permit'. Having examined various situations in which a plea was not raised in time, it is now necessary to consider several cases in which, exceptionally, estoppel has not operated to bar a plea, despite the fact that the issue was not raised at an early stage before the Commission.

A clear, though not especially common example of such a situation is where the government's plea is prompted by action taken by the applicant in the course of the proceedings. In the *Corigliano* case, for example, the government's pleas under Articles 26 and 27 were barred by estoppel, but its plea under Article 25 was not. This was because after the Commission's decision on admissibility, the applicant wrote a letter indicating that he wished to withdraw his application and stating that in his view the object of the dispute had disappeared. In the government's opinion the letter demonstrated that the applicant's real concern was not to speed the course of the proceedings against him, but to secure an acquittal, with the result that, according to the government, he failed to qualify as a 'victim' for the purposes of Article 25. The government raised this issue for the first time when the Commission was considering the case on its merits. The Court held that although the point had not been raised at the admissibility stage, the letter's timing made this 'easily explicable'[44] and so there was no estoppel.

Limitations on the principle of estoppel are more frequently encountered in cases concerned with the exhaustion of domestic remedies under Article 26. If it is possible to plead domestic remedies before the Commission, a government must do so or lose the right to raise the issue before the Court. Moreover, as we have seen, the plea must be specific as regards both the article of the Convention and the remedy concerned. However, because domestic remedies raise questions of domestic law and the latter may be uncertain and can change in the course of the proceedings, it may not always be possible for a government to maintain a completely consistent line of argument. When this is the case, the Court will not hold a government estopped from raising a domestic remedies point, even if it took a different line of argument before the Commission.

The Court's treatment of the issue of domestic remedies in the case of *Campbell and Fell* is a good illustration of its approach to this aspect of estoppel. In its memorial to the Court the government submitted that by failing to apply for judicial review, seeking an order of *certiorari*, of the adjudication of the Board of Prison Visitors in his case, Mr Campbell had not exhausted his domestic remedies. This point had also been put to the Commission, but at the merits rather than the admissibility stage. The reason for this delay was that in December 1977, shortly before the proceedings on admissibility, a Divisional Court had accepted the government's argument that *certiorari* did not lie in respect of Board of Visitors' proceedings. As the European Court pointed out, it would therefore have been difficult for the government to plead before the Commission that this remedy was available. In 1978, however, the Court of Appeal reversed the Divisional Court's decision and it was this judgment which prompted the government to raise the issue of *certiorari* before the Commission. In the circumstances the Court was satisfied that the government could not 'reasonably have been expected to raise the plea of non-exhaustion at an earlier stage'.[45] Here, then, unlike *Artico*, the delay in raising an issue of admissibility in the Commission was excusable and accordingly there was no estoppel.

It should be noted that in all the cases mentioned the Court, having held that it was entitled to consider the governments' pleas, decided to reject them on the merits. This was also the result in the *Vagrancy* cases as regards the one plea where the Court held there was no estoppel. In practice, therefore, applying the concept of estoppel only to situations in which the government really has no excuse for failing to put its arguments to the Commission is not so much a major inroad into the Court's ability to decide cases on the merits, as a way of ensuring that governments have a reasonable opportunity to put issues of admissibility before the Court. Since this was, of course, the whole point of the Court's broad view of its competence in the *Vagrancy* cases, using estoppel to promote the 'logical and orderly' conduct of proceedings, but not as an absolute bar on the Court's consideration of issues of admissibility which have not been raised earlier, is an entirely sensible use of the principle.

In the cases discussed so far the Court has been concerned with the role of estoppel in the context of admissibility. Whether there is a place for estoppel, or for an approach reflecting the same basic idea, is, as might be expected, a question which the Court has also had to consider in relation to substantive issues. For the Court's purposes the ambit of a case is determined by the Commission's decision on admissibility and this principle, which has been described in chapter 1, places major limitations on the issues which can be raised before the Court, without recourse to considerations of estoppel. There are nevertheless situations falling outside the 'ambit' principle where the scope of the Court's powers of review may be disputed. When these are such as to raise the question of the Court's relationship to the Commission, the situation – at least at first glance – seems similar to that which obtains with regard to admissibility and so there might appear to be scope for estoppel.

In fact, however, in a number of cases where estoppel has been raised as a possible bar to the Court's considering issues of substance, the argument has been rejected. In the *Bönisch* case, for instance, where the principal claim concerned Article 6(1), the applicant also complained of a breach of Article 6(2) which concerns the presumption of innocence. He had not previously raised this point with the Commission and for this reason the government and the Commission were agreed that it should be regarded as inadmissible. The Court, however, held that it was entitled to deal with the issue, notwithstanding its novelty. As the judgment put it:

Even though the complaint in question was not mentioned in the applicant's oral and written arguments before the Commission, it has an evident connection with the complaints he did make. . . . The Court thus has jurisdiction to entertain the matter, subject to taking into consideration possible preliminary objections such as non-exhaustion of domestic remedies.[46]

In the *James* case the Court came to a similar conclusion as regards a new complaint concerning Article 6(1). On this occasion the Court expressed itself a little more fully and explained the basis of its approach to cases of this kind, saying:

The applicants also allege violation of Article 6 para 1 of the Convention. . . . This complaint was new in that it was not pleaded before the Commission. It does have, however, an evident connection with the complaints examined by the Commission. Indeed, it recurs in another form in the arguments advanced under Article 1 of Protocol No 1 and Articles 13 and 14 of the Convention; it concerns the very same facts which were the subject of the application declared admissible by the Commission and no preliminary objection going to the admissibility of this complaint was raised either by the Commission or by the Government. The Court thus considers that it has jurisdiction to entertain the matter.[47]

It is clear that *Bönisch* and *James* both posed the same fundamental

question. Does the way a case is presented to the Commission prevent a
government, or an applicant, from putting it in a rather different way to
the Court? In rejecting an answer to this question in terms of estoppel, or
what would amount to the same thing, a restrictive view of its jurisdiction,
the Court has in effect drawn a quite fundamental distinction between its
role as regards admissibility on the one hand, and substantive issues on
the other. In relation to the former, it recognises that the Commission has
the primary role. Thus, unless there is a good explanation, arguments
must be raised before the Commission prior to being considered by the
Court. As regards substantive matters, however, the position is different.
The Commission deals with the case first and has the very considerable
power to determine the object of the case. Once that has been done,
however, it is open to the Court, as the body responsible for interpreting
the Convention, to consider any substantive issue sufficiently connected
with the facts, whether it has been previously pleaded or not, or even if it
has been conceded.[48] That there is no place here for estoppel, which
would have the effect of narrowing the Court's competence, is therefore
another example of how the Court's conception of the Strasbourg system,
and in particular its own place within it, has governed its approach to
general principles.

The scope for general principles of law

The principles discussed above – estoppel, waiver and equality of arms –
are not the only general principles to be used by the Court, although they
are the most prominent. In the *Marckx* case, for example, the Court
referred to two general principles of law which the Court of Justice of the
European Communities had recently described as follows:

The practical consequences of any judicial decision must be carefully taken into
account, [but] it would be impossible to go so far as to diminish the objectivity of
the law and compromise its future application on the ground of the possible
repercussions which might result, as regards the past, from such a judicial
decision.[49]

The particular problem in the *Marckx* case was that in requiring the
inheritance rights of legitimate and illegitimate children to be assimi-
lated, the Court was aware that it was departing from the position taken
in an earlier case by the Commission and also that it was ruling unlawful
arrangements which until recently had been regarded as normal in a large
number of Contracting States. In view of this and the obvious difficulties
which would be caused if its decision were to be treated as retrospective,
the Court held that 'the principle of legal certainty, which is necessarily
inherent in the law of the Convention, as in Community Law, dispenses

the Belgian State from re-opening legal acts or situations that antedate the delivery of the present judgment'.[50]

In the *Handyside* case the Court referred to a general principle of law to clarify the meaning of part of Article 1 of Protocol No. 1 which, it will be recalled, preserves the right of a State 'to enforce such laws as it deems necessary to control the use of property in accordance with the general interest or to secure the payment of taxes or other contributions or penalties'. The applicant complained that following his conviction under the Obscene Publications Acts, the offending publication had been destroyed by the authorities, an action which in his view constituted an unlawful deprivation of his possessions contrary to Article 1. The Court, however, rejected the argument on the ground that the measures taken by the authorities 'were authorised by the second paragraph of Article 1 of Protocol No. 1, interpreted in the light of the principle of law, common to all the Contracting States, whereunder items whose use has been lawfully adjudged illicit and dangerous to the general interest are forfeited with a view to destruction.'[51]

Another general principle which the Court has applied is the so-called *ultra petita* rule which, it has been said, 'precludes that an international tribunal or equivalent body should deal with matters that are not the subject of the complaint brought before it, and still more that it should give a decision on those matters against the defendant party in the case. If it does this, *proprio motu,* it is acting *ultra vires*'.[52]

The bearing of this principle on the work of the Court has been examined in two cases, both involving Italy. In the first, *Guzzardi,* the respondent maintained that the issue of Article 5 had been introduced on the initiative of the Commission, the applicant's actual complaint being directed to other matters. The Court briefly rejected the argument,[53] but subsequently took the matter further in the *Foti* case. There Italy's complaint was that the Commission had exceeded its jurisdiction by raising the issue of Article 6(1) *ex officio.* Again, however, the Court rejected the argument, on this occasion giving it closer attention.

Acknowledging the place of the *ultra petita* rule the Court said:

The international system of protection established by the Convention functions on the basis of applications, be they governmental or individual, alleging violations (see Articles 24 and 25). It does not enable the Commission and the Court either to take up a matter irrespective of the manner in which it came to their knowledge or even, in the context of pending proceedings, to seize on facts that have not been adduced by the applicant – be it a State or an individual – and to examine those facts for compatibility with the Convention.[54]

Then, having identified the general principle, the Court defined the scope for initiatives of the sort exercised in here and in *Guzzardi* by adding:

The institutions set up under the Convention nonetheless do have jurisdiction to review in the light of the entirety of the Convention's requirements circumstances complained of by the applicant. In the performance of their task, the Convention institutions are notably free to attribute to the facts of the case, as found to be established on the evidence before them, a characterisation in law different from that given by the applicant or, if need be, to view the facts in a different manner; furthermore, they have to take account not only of the original application but also of the additional documents intended to complete the latter by eliminating initial omissions or obscurities.[55]

This is not only an important indication of the place of a general principle in the law and procedure of the European Convention; it is also a pronouncement of obvious relevance to the American human rights system[56] and other schemes of protection which may be established. The *ultra petita* rule is, of course, not unique in this respect. Of the general principles considered earlier, legal certainty and the confiscation of condemned property are in their different ways likely to be equally serviceable in other contexts. The same can be said of estoppel (though its application must clearly depend on the particular institutional arrangements); waiver, which must always raise difficult issues where individual rights are concerned; and equality of arms, which no tribunal concerned with procedural justice can ever ignore. These ideas are found in the work of the European Court because they are part of the fundamental legal fabric, in short because they are general principles of law. For this reason they are no less relevant elsewhere.

In this connection it is perhaps also worth pointing out that neither the list of general principles, nor the use the Court may choose to make of those it has already recognised, are fixed for all time by its current jurisprudence. A general principle which has so far received little attention may suddenly be seen to contain the answer to an apparently insoluble problem and take on a new vitality. A principle which has not yet been recognised at all may burst upon the scene and inspire an entirely new line of development. In examining general principles, then, one is examining not a finished product, but a process in which the resources of legal culture are constantly being scanned by the judicial mind in a search for new solutions. There are, as we have seen, limits beyond which the international judge, constrained as he is by the special responsibilities of his role, cannot safely go. Even so, after reviewing the place of general principles in the work of the International Court, Lauterpacht's conclusion was that 'this aspect of the contribution of the Court provides one of the not least significant features of its activity'.[57] In the light of the evidence considered in this chapter, the same can be said of the work of the European Court.

Notes

1 Article 1 of Protocol No. 1, which refers to 'the general principles of international law', is discussed in chapter 9.
2 Series A, No. 18 para. 35.
3 Series A, No. 12 para. 65.
4 *Ibid.*
5 Series A, No. 17 para. 33.
6 *Ibid.*
7 Series A, No. 70 para. 36.
8 *Ibid.*, para. 38.
9 See J. E. S. Fawcett, *The Application of the European Convention on Human Rights,* 2nd ed., Clarendon Press, Oxford, 63 (1987).
10 Series A, No. 58 para. 35.
11 Series A, No. 127. See also on this point the case of *Barberá, Messegué and Jabardo*, Series A, No. 146.
12 Series A, No. 171.
13 *Ibid.*, dissenting opinion of Judge Walsh, para. 4, emphasis added.
14 *Ibid.*, para. 66.
15 *Ibid.*, dissenting opinion of Judge Walsh, para. 4.
16 Series A, No. 227 para. 38.
17 *Ibid.*, para. 37.
18 *Ibid.*, para. 39.
19 Series A, No. 35 para. 49.
20 *Ibid.*
21 Series A, No. 89 para. 28.
22 Series A, No. 167.
23 Series A, No. 208B.
24 Series A, No. 1.
25 Series A, No. 2.
26 Series A, No. 12 p. 7.
27 *Ibid.,* p. 8.
28 Series A, No. 19.
29 Series A, No. 21.
30 As mentioned in chapter 1, Protocol No. 9, which is not yet in force, will give individuals the right to take cases to the Court and consequently to be a party to its proceedings.
31 Series A, No. 92 para. 32.
32 The bearing of Article 6(3)(d) on expert evidence was examined further in the *Brandstetter* case, Series A, No. 211.
33 Series A, No. 11.
34 Series A, No. 214A para. 24.
35 *Ibid.*, para. 26.
36 *Ibid.*, para. 28
37 Series A, No. 151 para. 29.
38 Series A, No. 99 para. 44.
39 *Ibid.*
40 Series A, No. 12 para. 54.
41 *Ibid.,* para. 55.
42 Series A, No. 37 para. 27.
43 Series A, No. 56 para. 47. See also on this point the *Pine Valley Developments* case, Series A, No. 222.

44 Series A, No. 57 para. 31.
45 Series A, No. 80 para. 59.
46 Series A, No. 92 para. 37.
47 Series A, No. 98 paras. 79–80.
48 See on this point the *Barthold* case, Series A, No. 90, where the Court rejected the argument that the government was estopped from raising the applicability of Article 10 and said, 'For the purposes of the procedure before the Court, the applicability of one of the substantive clauses of the Convention constitutes, by its very nature, an issue going to the merits of the case, to be examined independently of the attitude of the respondent State.' *Ibid.*, para. 41.
49 Series A, No. 31 para. 58.
50 *Ibid.* For the problems encountered in determining the effect of such prospective overruling see the *Vermeire* case, Series A, No. 214C.
51 Series A, No. 24 para. 63.
52 *Guzzardi* case, Series A, No. 39, dissenting opinion of Judge Sir Gerald Fitzmaurice, para. 4.
53 *Ibid.*, paras. 58–63. Fitzmaurice's dissenting opinion dealt with the issue in more detail, however.
54 Series A, No. 56 para. 44.
55 *Ibid.* See also the separate opinion of Judge Pinheiro Farinha.
56 See the discussion of the related principle *iura novit curia* in the decision of the Inter-American Court of Human Rights in the *Velasquez Rodriguez* case, Judgment of 29 July 1988, para. 163, *Human Rights Law Journal*, IX, 212 (1988). On the relation between the two general principles see Sir Gerald Fitzmaurice, *The Law and Procedure of the International Court of Justice*, Grotius, Cambridge, 524–33 (1986).
57 H. Lauterpacht, *The Development of International Law by the International Court*, Stevens, London, 172 (1958).

CHAPTER 9

The Convention
and international law

Like the general principles of law, international law is part of the legal background to the Convention and can therefore supply a vital reference point for the Court's judgments. Several articles of the Convention refer expressly to international law and so require the Court to employ particular principles in its decisions. Many articles deal with matters which are also covered by other treaties. Here, though there is no express link between the Convention and other sources of obligation, the latter frequently need to be taken into account. Finally, a human rights convention which contains both a statement of rights and arrangements for their enforcement is bound to raise issues of substance and procedure for which reference to general international law can sometimes provide the solution. International law, then, enters the Court's jurisprudence by a variety of routes. This chapter examines how this occurs and its implications for the development of the law.

General international law in the Court's decisions

Since the protection of human rights is a relatively recent development in international law and has been mainly brought about by treaty, the majority of references to general international law in the Court's case-law have concerned points of jurisdiction or procedure. In the *Belgian Linguistics* case, for example, the Court referred to the decision of the Permanent Court in the *Electricity Company of Sofia and Bulgaria* case[1] as support for the proposition that certain arguments put forward by the Belgian Government could not be dealt with as preliminary objections because they were intimately concerned with the merits.[2] And in the *Stögmüller* case when dealing with the question of what evidence could be taken into account, the Court observed that it was 'in accordance with national and international practice that a court should hold itself competent to examine facts which occurred during the proceedings and constitute a mere extension of the facts complained of at the outset', and noted that 'international judicial bodies have frequently held that compensation for damage resulting from an illegal act of a state must also cover damage suffered by the applicant party after the institution of proceedings'.[3]

In the *Belilos* case,[4] where the question was what effect, if any, should be given to a so-called 'interpretative declaration' which Switzerland had made to Article 6(1) of the Convention, the Court referred to the 1969 Vienna Convention on the Law of Treaties to establish the nature of the instrument. Pointing out that Article 2(1)(d) defines a reservation as 'a unilateral statement, however phrased or named, made by a State . . . whereby it purports to exclude or to modify the legal effect of certain provisions of the treaty in their application to that State', the Court decided that, on account of its content, the declaration must be treated as a reservation. This was an important ruling because it meant that the validity of the Swiss declaration depended on the criteria for making reservations set out in Article 64 of the European Convention, which, as noted earlier, it failed to satisfy.

The Court similarly relied on international practice in a number of early cases in which it established the scope of its authority to award just satisfaction under Article 50. Thus in the *Ringeisen* case the Court rejected the Austrian Government's attempt to narrow the scope of this provision, saying, 'it would be a formalistic attitude alien to international law to maintain that the Court may not apply Article 50 save on condition that it either rules on the matter by the same judgment which found a violation or that this judgment has expressly kept the point open'.[5] While in the *Vagrancy* cases it rejected Belgium's argument that a claim for just satisfaction requires the exhaustion of local remedies by pointing out that 'Article 50 has its origin in certain clauses which appear in treaties of the classical type . . . and have no connection with the rule of exhaustion of domestic remedies'.[6]

In the *Cruz Varas* case, on the other hand, the Court relied on treaty practice to justify a narrow interpretation of the powers of the Convention organs. The issue in that case was the scope of the Commission's power to indicate interim measures of protection under Rule 36 of its Rules of Procedure, and in particular whether such measures are binding. To answer this question the Court compared the Convention with the Statute of the International Court of Justice, the American Convention on Human Rights and the Treaty of Rome. Finding that these instruments all contain a specific provision relating to interim measures, whereas the European Convention does not, the Court held that, 'In the absence of a provision in the Convention for interim measures an indication given under Rule 36 cannot be considered to give rise to a binding obligation on Contracting Parties'.[7] The Court then reinforced this conclusion by adding that no assistance could be derived from general principles of international law since 'the question whether interim measures indicated by international tribunals are binding is a controversial one and no uniform legal rule exists'.[8]

It must be pointed out, however, that international practice is not always relevant. The Convention establishes a unique system and so the significance of any general rule must depend on its compatibility with this special character. In the preliminary phase of the *Lawless* case, for instance, the Commission invoked various precedents drawn from advisory proceedings at The Hague to support the argument that it could present the applicant's views to the Court. Although the Court upheld the submission in substance, it stated that it was 'not called upon to examine in detail the precedents invoked by the Commission with regard to the part to be played by the individual before an international judicial body' because 'though recognising their force, the Court must bear in mind the fact that none of the examples cited is that of an individual appealing against the action of his own government'.[9] Accordingly, 'the solution to this question must be sought in the special nature of the procedure laid down in the Convention'.

Similarly, in the *Irish* case the Court explained that the British Government had invited it to declare the issue of Article 3 moot and had relied in this connection on the decisions of the International Court in the *Northern Cameroons*[10] and *Nuclear Tests*[11] cases. The Court nevertheless rejected the submission on the ground that the responsibilities assigned to it under the Convention extended to pronouncing on the non-contested allegations.[12] Later in the same judgment, however, it had occasion to observe that:

The Court is not bound, under the Convention or under the general principles applicable to international tribunals, by strict rules of evidence. In order to satisfy itself, the Court is entitled to rely on evidence of every kind, including, insofar as it deems them relevant, documents or statements emanating from governments, be they respondent or applicant, or from their institutions or officials.[13]

Here, therefore, international practice was of greater assistance.

In addition to its possible bearing on procedure, international law can sometimes be relevant to substantive issues. Thus in the case of *H v Belgium*[14] three judges referred to the International Court's advisory opinion in the 1973 *United Nations Administrative Tribunal* case[15] to provide support for the Court's decision that to comply with Article 6(1) of the Convention a body which is concerned with 'rights' must function in accordance with ascertainable rules and support its decisions with adequate reasons. Similarly, in the *Lithgow* case, where there was considerable argument about how nationalised property should be valued, the applicants drew attention to international case-law indicating that valuation should take place at the vesting date. Although evidence of this kind is clearly relevant when the Court is dealing with issues such as nationalisation on which there is already an enormous amount of practice, the Court found the specific argument unconvincing, saying that not all the cases cited were apposite and that in any event international practice did not establish that the vesting date was the only proper basis of valuation.[16] In the *Golder* case, on the other hand, the Court was able to use the general legal position more constructively and as part of the elaborate justification for its decision that Article 6(1) impliedly confers a right of access to the courts, said, 'The principle whereby a civil claim must be capable of being submitted to a judge ranks as one of the fundamental principles of law; the same is true of the principle of international law which forbids the denial of justice.'[17]

One of the applicants' claims in the *Abdulaziz* case was that by failing to permit foreign husbands to join their wives in the United Kingdom, British immigration legislation failed to provide effective respect for family life and thereby violated Article 8. The Court, it will be recalled, rejected this argument on the ground that in the circumstances the measures complained of fell within the margin of appreciation.[18] The relevance of the case in the present context lies in the Court's observation that it had approached the case mindful of the fact that it was 'concerned not only with family life but also with immigration and that, as a matter of well-established international law and subject to its treaty obligations, a State has the right to control the entry of non-nationals into its territory'.[19] Subsequently, the Court made the same point when a claim was brought under Article 8 in relation to an alien's expulsion.[20]

This is a rare instance of the Court using the position under general international law to justify a restrictive interpretation of the Convention. The function of human rights treaties is, of course, to extend the obligations of the State beyond those imposed by the general law. Moreover, as we saw in chapter 4, the Court has rejected the suggestion that because the Convention deals with what have traditionally been regarded as matters of domestic jurisdiction, a cautious and conservative interpretation of its provisions is called for. Usually, therefore, the fact that general international law leaves a State free to deal with a given matter as it wishes, may be expected to carry little weight, and it is noticeable that the Court's recognition of traditional prerogatives has in practice not prevented it from imposing significant limitations on States' freedom of action, particularly in the field of expulsion.[21] In *Abdulaziz*, however, the Court was being asked to hold that Article 8 imposes positive obligations of a far-reaching kind in a very sensitive area. It is therefore not altogether surprising that it considered it appropriate to refer to the position under the general law as one of several factors relevant to its decision.[22]

References to international law in the Convention

Article 7(1)

This provision lays down that 'No one shall be held guilty of any criminal offence on account of any act or omission which did not constitute a criminal offence under national *or international law* at the time when it was committed.' The qualification is then elaborated in Article 7(2) which provides that this article 'shall not prejudice the trial and punishment of any person for any act or omission which, at the time when it was committed, was criminal *according to the general principles of law recognised by civilised nations*'. Unlike the provisions considered below, these references to international law have not yet been considered by the Court. However, as a link between the Convention and general international law which indicates the significance of such arrangements for the Court's activity, this aspect of Article 7 is worth briefly considering.

The object of including these references to international law, as the *travaux préparatoires* demonstrate, was to ensure that where a Contracting State uses its criminal law to punish those who committed atrocities during the Second World War, it will not be open to the accused to invoke the principle of legality, provided that the offence in question was criminal according to international law. Since the principle of individual criminal responsibility was applied by the Nuremberg and Tokyo War Crimes Tribunals, which specifically rejected the argument that this constituted retrospective punishment, provision for the punishment of war criminals in Article 7 is in principle unobjectionable. Indeed, like the reference to international law in Article 15 to be considered shortly, it may be regarded as a way of harmonising the legal position under the Convention with the situation in general international law.

The difficulty, however, is that the references to international law in Article 7 are in quite general terms and while it is clear that the various charges on which the defendants were arraigned at Nuremberg would fall within their scope, it is for the interpreter to decide how much further this part of the Convention extends. An example will illustrate the point. In the *De Becker* case[23] the applicant was punished by the authorities in Belgium for collaborating with the Nazis during the War. His claim that the law under which he was convicted violated the principle of legality was rejected by the Commission as manifestly ill-founded in the light of Article 7(2). But collaboration was not one of the charges at Nuremberg and does not appear to be either a crime involving individual responsibility under international law, or contrary to a general principle of law in the international sense. The correctness of the Commission's ruling may therefore be doubted.[24]

If the Court is called upon to decide the meaning of the references to international law in Article 7, it may therefore find itself having to decide how far international law has developed beyond the Nuremberg principles to cover new crimes. Where the conduct in question is the subject of international conventions, as with genocide and apartheid, then provided they have received the requisite international support, the issue will be reasonably straightfoward. However, in cases where the criminal act or omission is allegedly contrary to customary law, or reliance has to be placed on general principles, the decision will be more difficult and the Court's responsibility, bearing in mind that the fundamental value here is legality, a good deal more onerous.

Article 9 of the American Convention contains a provision almost identical to Article 7(1), while Article 15(2) of the Covenant on Civil and Political Rights is virtually the same as Article 7(2). It follows that in any decisions which may be required as to the scope of these references to international law in the Convention, the European Court may be assisted by interpretations of those instruments, as well as the views of the Commission. Conversely, the Court's rulings on this aspect of Article 7 will not only be a contribution to international criminal law, but can also be expected to influence the application of the other conventions.

Article 15(1)

This provision lays down that:

In time of war or other public emergency threatening the life of the nation any High Contracting Party may take measures derogating from its obligations under this Convention to the extent strictly required by the exigencies of the situation, *provided that such measures are not inconsistent with its other obligations under international law.*

The reference to international law here has the effect of preventing a Party from relying on Article 15 to release itself from obligations it may have in general international law or under other treaties.[25] However, there is another effect which is no less important. If a State adopts measures which are inconsistent with its other obligations, the effect of the proviso is to prevent it from relying on Article 15 to derogate from its obligations under the Convention. In other words, measures which are inconsistent with a State's other obligations are legally ineffective and in this respect exactly like measures which go beyond those 'strictly required by the exigencies of the situation'.

Because Article 15 is an emergency provision, it has so far been considered by the Court in only two cases. In both, moreover, the international law proviso was dealt with only briefly. In the *Irish* case the applicant government referred to this requirement as part of its case against the United Kingdom, but developed its argument by reference to other points. In dealing with this issue in its judgment the Court therefore said:

Article 15(1) *in fine* prohibits any derogation inconsistent with 'other obligations under international law'. There is nothing in the data before the Court to suggest that the United Kingdom disregarded such obligations in this case, in particular the Irish Government never supplied to the Commission or the Court precise details on the claim formulated or outlined on this point in their application of 16 December 1971.[26]

Earlier, in the *Lawless* case, where the Irish Government was itself the respondent, the Court examined the international law requirement *ex officio,* and again concluded that compliance was not seriously in issue.[27]

Although the Court has not had to address this aspect of Article 15(1) in any detail, its powers here are really very considerable. For in a case where argument on the issue is presented or a serious issue arises, the Court will need to establish exactly what the respondent's 'other obligations under international law' are. This will certainly mean examining its other treaty obligations, though the treaty in question may not otherwise be subject to compulsory international jurisdiction. Thus in subscribing to the Convention and accepting the Court's jurisdiction in matters pertaining to its interpretation and application, the Contracting States are also accepting its jurisdiction over a wide field of other matters, should these be relevant to Article 15.

As an extension of international jurisdiction this is somewhat analogous to the power of the Inter-American Court of Human Rights under Article 64 of the American Convention to give advisory opinions regarding the interpretation 'of other treaties concerning the protection of human rights in the American States'. In its first advisory opinion,[28] the American Court held that in principle *any* human rights treaty to which American States are parties can be the subject of an advisory opinion and justified this by saying that the purpose of its advisory role is 'to assist the American States in fulfilling their international human rights obligations' and adding that the object of the American Convention is to integrate the regional and the universal systems of human rights protection. Although Article 15 is confined to derogation in emergency situations and is not concerned with advisory jurisdiction, its effect, like that of Article 64, is to provide a means of integrating human rights obligations by giving the Court a competence to interpret and apply the provisions of other conventions.

As well as obligations under the United Nations Covenants and other human rights treaties, a State's 'other obligations under international law' include, of course, any relevant obligations under customary international law and any which arise by virtue of general principles of law.

Here, it has been suggested that 'the Strasbourg organs will not lightly go beyond the scope of conventional law, unless they can rely on clear international case law or an express consensus'.[29] This may well be so. It should be noted, however, that the law of human rights is an expanding subject which has already developed more quickly than might have been anticipated. The reference to international law in Article 15(1) is important not because there are ever likely to be a large number of emergencies in which it may have to be applied, but because in those exceptional situations in which it is relevant, the Court can assess the actions of the State in the light of the totality of its international obligations. In this way the Court is acting as something more than an organ of the Strasbourg system, and has both the powers and the responsibilities which a duty to judge States' developing international obligations entails.

Article 26

This lays down one of the conditions of admissibility of an application and provides: 'The Commission may only deal with a matter after all domestic remedies have been exhausted, *according to the generally recognised rules of international law.*'

This – the local remedies rule – as it is commonly termed, is a principle of customary international law which developed as part of the law governing the diplomatic protection of nationals. Its inclusion in the European Convention and other human rights conventions[30] reflects the function of the rule which is to enable a State to redress an injury through its own procedures before the issue reaches the international plane, thereby ensuring that international procedures are reserved for cases which can only be resolved by this means. In view of the wealth of practice which the application of the rule by courts and tribunals has generated over the years, it is not surprising that it was thought appropriate to include an express reference to international law in Article 26, nor that in their own decisions on the rule the Strasbourg institutions have made extensive use of this material.

Since the exhaustion of domestic remedies is a condition of admissibility, the major role in the interpretation and application of Article 26 has fallen to the Commission. It will be recalled, however, that in its decision in the *Vagrancy* cases[31] the Court held that the Commission's competence in matters of admissibility is not exclusive. Specifically, if the Commission rejects a respondent's claim that a case is inadmissible, it is open to the Court to reconsider the issue. As a result of this ruling, the Court has itself developed a substantial jurisprudence on Article 26. For the most part this closely follows the practice of the Commission which is, of course, far more extensive.[32] An outline of some of the issues the Court has considered will, however, indicate the distinctive features of its approach.

One of the first issues to be considered by the Court concerned the position of an applicant who brings a case to the Commission while a domestic appeal is pending. In the *Ringeisen* case the Austrian Government, invoking the rule in diplomatic protection as a parallel, argued that all domestic proceedings must be complete before an application is lodged. The Commission, on the other hand, argued that the non-exhaustion of domestic remedies does not prevent the lodging of the application, but only its examination by the Commission. The Court decided that it could not adopt either of these views because:

On the one hand, it would certainly be going too far and contrary to the spirit of the rule of exhaustion of domestic remedies to allow that a person may properly lodge an application with the Commission before exercising any domestic remedies. On the other hand, international courts have on various occasions held that international law cannot be applied with the same regard for matters of form as is sometimes necessary in the application of national law. Article 26 of the Convention refers expressly to the generally recognised rules of international law. The Commission was therefore quite right in declaring in various circumstances that there was a need for a certain flexibility in the application of the rule.[33]

Pointing out that in practice applications are frequently followed by additional documents the object of which is to fill gaps or clarify obscurities, the Court held that there was no reason why such supplementation 'should not relate in particular to the proof that the applicant has complied with Article 26, even if he has done so after the lodging of the application. When the Commission decides whether or not a case is admissible, its examination is directed necessarily to the application and the later documents considered as a whole'.[34] Thus the result of this ruling was, as the Court put it, that:

while it is fully upheld that the applicant is, as a rule, in duty bound to exercise the different domestic remedies before he applies to the Commission, it must be left open to the Commission to accept the fact that the last stage of such remedies may be reached shortly after the lodging of the application but before the Commission is called upon to pronounce itself on admissibility.[35]

This is a telling decision because there is certainly evidence in the law of diplomatic protection to support the stricter interpretation advocated by the Austrian Government. However, the Court was evidently conscious of the fact that individual applications to Strasbourg often come from laymen who address themselves to the Commission without the benefit of legal assistance. In these circumstances it considered that a formalistic interpretation of Article 26 would lead to unfair consequences. Instead of applying the local remedies rule in a mechanical way, the Court therefore emphasised the flexibility of international law and in this way was able to take due account of the special character of the Convention.

The element of flexibility which the Court emphasised in the above cases is particularly important in cases concerned with continuing situations, such as detention on remand, which was in issue in *Ringeisen* and a number of other cases at about the same time. Thus in the *Stögmüller* case the Court observed that, 'international law to which Article 26 refers explicitly, is far from conferring on the rule of exhaustion the inflexible character which the government seems to attribute to it',[36] and went on:

Thus, in matters of detention while on remand, it is in the light of the circumstances of the case that the question is, in appropriate cases, to be assessed whether and to what extent it was necessary, pursuant to Article 26, for the detained applicant, who had exhausted the remedies before the Commission declared his application admissible, to make later on further appeals to the national courts in order to make it possible to examine, at international level, the reasonableness of his continued detention.[37]

This was another important ruling on the scope of Article 26. Though rare in cases of diplomatic protection, challenges to detention on remand are common under the Strasbourg system. These cases are therefore a further example of how the Court has sought to adapt the local remedies rule to meet the particular needs of the Convention.

In general international law an individual will not be regarded as having exhausted his local remedies unless it is clear that as far as possible the substance of his complaint has been raised in any domestic proceedings which he has brought. In the *Van Oosterwijck* case the Court applied the same principle. The applicant, a transsexual Belgian, after undergoing a sex-change operation brought proceedings in Belgium for the rectification of his birth certificate. When his claim was rejected he lodged an application against Belgium alleging that the status assigned to him by Belgian law violated various articles of the Convention. This was denied by the government, which also challenged the admissibility of the claim on the ground that by failing to plead the Convention in the courts and not appealing to the Court of Cassation, the applicant had failed to exhaust his local remedies. This objection was rejected by the Commission but upheld by the Court.

This was the first case in which the Court disagreed with the Commission on an issue of admissibility and the decision suggests that the obligation to put the relevant legal points in domestic proceedings is likely to be construed strictly. It is certainly no answer to say that the domestic court should have considered a neglected point on its own initiative. For as the Court observed: 'The fact that the Belgian courts might have been able, or even obliged, to examine the case of their own motion under the Convention cannot be regarded as having dispensed the applicant from pleading before them the Convention or arguments to the same or like effect.'[38]

It should be noted, however, that the applicant's obligation here is to raise his case 'in substance' before the national organs. This means that it is not always necessary to raise a particular point expressly. In the *Guzzardi* case, for example, which concerned the right to liberty in Article 5, the Court said that although the applicant had not specifically raised the question of his detention in the Italian courts, Article 26 'should be applied with a certain degree of flexibility and without excessive regard for matters of form'.[39] Since he had complained of matters which could be regarded as raising the question of detention 'in substance', he had provided the Italian courts with the opportunity of righting the alleged wrong which was the object of the local remedies rule in international law. In the Court's view he had therefore satisfied the requirements of Article 26.

Deciding whether a particular point has been raised 'in substance' where it has not been discussed specifically may be difficult and can sometimes be a source of disagreement. Thus in the *Cardot* case,[40] which involved the right to call witnesses guaranteed by Article 6(3)(d), a majority of the Court held that the issue had not been sufficiently brought to the attention of the French courts, whereas three judges agreed with the unanimous opinion of the Commission and considered that it had. In this case, however, it was also clear that the applicant had not sought to call the relevant witnesses at his trial and in view of this omission it was questionable whether the issue could have been considered by the Court of Cassation, even if the applicant had raised it. The Court therefore invoked as a further ground for its decision the principle laid down in the *Ambatielos* arbitration that 'It would be wrong to hold that a party who, by failing to exhaust his opportunities in the court of first instance, has caused an appeal to become futile should be allowed to rely on this fact in order to rid himself of the rule of exhaustion of local remedies'.[41]

It is also well established that to satisfy the local remedies requirement in general international law it is not necessary to exhaust every conceivable remedy, but only those that are available and sufficient. This qualification, which appears to have been the reason for including an express reference to international law in Article 26,[42] has been another prominent feature in the Court's cases. In *Campbell and Fell,* for example, which concerned a challenge to proceedings before a prison Board of Visitors, the Court held that one of the applicants was under no obligation to take proceedings by way of *certiorari* because at the time he had no reason to believe that this remedy was available and 'the existence of a remedy must be sufficiently certain before there can be an obligation to exhaust it'.[43] In the *De Weer* case,[44] on the other hand, where the applicant claimed that he had been denied a fair trial and access to the courts, contrary to Article 6(1), the Court rejected Belgium's argument that he should have applied to the *Conseil d'État* and undertaken proceedings for restitution because these remedies, though evidently available and unexhausted, would not have been sufficient to meet the substance of his claim.

In a number of cases the Court has held that the applicant is not required to use a particular procedure because to do so would be ineffective. A particularly important illustration of this is provided by cases in which the applicant's claim is based on a law or administrative practice, as opposed to injury attributable to individual acts or decisions. In such a case the local remedies rule will be inapplicable if there is no way in which the law or practice can be effectively challenged. This was the situation in the *Irish* case where the Court held that the claims which had been put forward under Article 3 could be examined in so far as they were based on a practice of torture or inhuman or degrading punishment. A leading member of the Court explained this conclusion as follows:

The rationale of any finding upholding the non-applicability of the domestic remedies rule where the complaint is about the existence of a practice, can only be based on the assumption that, normally, domestic forums, whether judicial or administrative, can only deal with concrete claims preferred by individuals on their own behalf, and cannot conduct roving enquiries into the existence of practices, for which special machinery would have to be set up such as (in the United Kingdom) a Royal or Parliamentary Commission, Departmental Committee of Enquiry, or other *ad hoc* body. . . . But of course such bodies are not part of the ordinary domestic forms of recourse available to the individual and whose jurisdiction he can himself invoke: the initiatives and decisions necessary for their creation must be governmental or parliamentary.[45]

As this passage makes clear, the Court's treatment of administrative practices is in no sense a departure from the principles governing the operation of the local remedies rule in international law, but rather an application of one of its conditions, that of effectiveness, in the special context of human rights.

Article 1 of Protocol No. 1

This provision protects what the Court has termed the 'right of property' and provides that 'Every natural or legal person is entitled to the peaceful enjoyment of his possessions. No one shall be deprived of his possessions except in the public interest and subject to conditions provided for by law *and by the general principles of international law*'. At first sight this may appear to be one of the most important references to international law in the Convention. As we have seen, the reference to international law in Article 26 occurs in a context where such recourse might be anticipated even without an express directive. Deprivation of possessions, on the other hand, is not a concept taken from international law and so including a reference to general principles here might be thought to be introducing a requirement, and providing the Court with an opportunity, which would not otherwise be present. This, however, assumes that the object of this part of the Convention is to extend the protection which international law affords to the property of aliens, to the property of nationals. If, alternatively, the Convention is read as simply preserving the rights of aliens, while allowing States to deal with the property of nationals subject only to the other requirements of Article 1, then the reference to international law is very much less significant.

Which of these approaches to Article 1 is correct was first considered in the *James* case in 1986. The applicants complained that as a result of leasehold enfranchisement in the United Kingdom they had been deprived of their possessions without adequate compensation. As part of their argument they maintained that although they were nationals, they were entitled to prompt, adequate and effective compensation in accordance with what they claimed were the general principles of international law. The Court, however, rejected their argument and held that whatever the international law standard might be, only aliens are entitled to its protection.

One justification for this conclusion rests on the text of the Convention. For, while acknowledging that there was force in the applicants' argument as a matter of grammatical construction, the Court held that it was:

. . . more natural to take the reference to the general principles of international law in Article 1 of Protocol No. 1 to mean that those principles are incorporated into that Article, but only as regards those acts to which they are normally applicable, that is to say acts of a State in relation to non-nationals. Moreover, the words of a treaty should be understood to have their ordinary meaning (see Article 31 of the 1969 Vienna Convention on the Law of Treaties), and to interpret the phrase in question as extending the general principles of international law beyond their normal sphere of applicability is less consistent with the ordinary meaning of the terms used, notwithstanding their context.[46]

If this reasoning is perhaps not entirely convincing, the Court was on firmer ground when it took into account the *travaux préparatoires* of the Convention as supplementary means of interpretation. Pointing out that an express reference to a right to compensation was contained in earlier drafts but later excluded, the Court explained that 'The mention of the general principles of international law was subsequently included and was subject to several statements to the effect that they protected only foreigners.'[47] Since this was later confirmed by a Resolution in which the Committee of Ministers approved the text of the Protocol and opened it for signature, the Court was satisfied that the *travaux préparatoires* did not support the wider interpretation for which the applicants contended.

Shortly after its ruling in *James* the Court was presented with the same issue in the *Lithgow* case[48] which concerned nationalisations carried out in the United Kingdom under the Aircraft and Shipbuilding Industries Act 1977. The Court dealt with the issue in exactly the same way and in identical language. Since both cases were decisions of the plenary Court, the point must now be regarded as settled. What is the significance of the approach the Court has chosen to adopt to this part of Protocol No. 1?

It may be thought that by interpreting the reference to the general principles of international law so restrictively the Court has rendered this part of Article 1 redundant. It is doubtful, however, if this view is accurate. As the Court has pointed out, the reference to international law in Article 1 can be seen to serve at least two purposes:

Firstly, it enables non-nationals to resort directly to the machinery of the Convention to enforce their rights on the basis of the relevant principles of international law, whereas otherwise they would have to seek recourse to diplomatic channels or to other available means of dispute settlement to do so. Secondly, the reference ensures that the position of non-nationals is safeguarded, in that it excludes any possible argument that the entry into force of Protocol No. 1 has led to a diminution of their rights.[49]

Since these are real, if limited purposes, it is difficult to agree that the Court's interpretation of Article 1 has made the reference to international law superfluous.

A more substantial point may be that drawing a distinction between the rights of aliens and those of nationals runs counter to the obligation under Article 1 of the Convention to secure its rights and freedoms to *everyone* within each Contracting State's jurisdiction, and the general principle of non-discrimination embodied in Article 14. However, the Convention already permits differentiation between nationals and non-nationals in certain circumstances, and Article 14 does not outlaw every form of discrimination, only those which have no 'objective and reasonable justification'. Moreover, as the Court observed in *James*:

Especially as regards a taking of property effected in the context of a social reform, there may well be good grounds for drawing a distinction between nationals and non-nationals as far as compensation is concerned. To begin with, non-nationals are more vulnerable to domestic legislation: unlike nationals, they will generally have played no part in the election or designation of its authors nor have been consulted on its adoption. Secondly, although a taking of property must always be effected in the public interest, different considerations may apply to nationals and non-nationals and there may well be legitimate reason for requiring nationals to bear a greater burden in the public interest than non-nationals.[50]

Whether the distinction is of practical significance depends on how much difference there is between the standard of treatment required by the general principles of international law and that called for by the Convention. On the question of compensation, generally a major issue where expropriation is concerned, the difference may not in fact be very great. In *James* and in *Lithgow* a number of members of the Court drew attention to the fact that the traditional standard of prompt, adequate and effective compensation has been strongly challenged, and the rival view that the standard is a flexible one is reflected in the increasing tendency of international arbitrators to award 'equitable' compensation.[51] How much the law has changed and whether it would be open to an industrialised State to pay less than the face value for expropriated property, are still matters of controversy. The trend, however, is clear and the fact that a move away from the traditional standard is occurring means that the protection of the general principles of international law is now less valuable than was once the case.

As far as the Convention standard itself is concerned, on the other hand, the Court has made it clear that in deciding whether a deprivation of property can be regarded as 'in the public interest' it will normally regard the provision of compensation as a major consideration. For although Article 1 does not expressly confer a right to compensation, 'compensation terms are material to the assessment whether the contested legislation respects a fair balance between the various interests at stake'.[52] Moreover, the standard of compensation called for is a sum bearing some relation to the value of the property, because 'the taking of property without payment of an amount reasonably related to its value would normally constitute a disproportionate interference which could not be considered justifiable under Article 1'.[53]

In the light of the clarification of the meaning of Article 1 by the Court and the trend just mentioned, it may be doubted whether the decision to deny nationals the protection of the general principles of international law is any longer of great practical significance in terms of the standard to be applied.

Although the differences between the Convention and international law may now be more apparent than real, there is one way in which drawing this distinction is certainly important. Interpreting Article 1 in a way which makes the general principles of international law relevant only to cases involving aliens, means that in the great majority of cases it is unnecessary for the Court to decide what those general principles require. This means that the Court is usually spared the task of grappling with a highly controversial issue of general international law. Instead of having to spend time trying to make sense of a mass of material deriving from arbitral, judicial and State practice, it is free to concentrate on developing the Convention standard. From the Court's perspective this is undoubtedly an advantage. On the other hand, precisely because the general law is so much in need of clarification, it may be thought unfortunate that the Court is not in a position to contribute to a solution.

The relevance of other treaties to interpretation

Although the task of the Strasbourg institutions is to interpret the Convention, light can often be shed on its meaning by comparing it with other treaties, and the Court has made extensive use of this assistance. The situations in which it has done so, and which provide further evidence of its resourcefulness in developing the law, fall into three types. When a provision needing interpretation was inspired by an earlier instrument dealing with the subject, the Court has naturally turned to the other treaty for guidance. When, on the other hand, the Convention omits certain rights guaranteed in another treaty, the Court may refer to the other treaty to justify an interpretation holding that a right is not protected. Finally, in cases falling into neither of the preceding categories, the Court may refer to another treaty to show that a particular interpretation is in harmony with other obligations in the human rights field.

Amplifying the Convention

A good illustration of the first situation is provided by the *Van der Mussele* case. There the Court was required to decide the meaning of the phrase 'forced or compulsory labour' which is used in Article 4, but not defined therein. Having also found that no guidance was to be found in the preparatory work of the Convention, the Court turned for assistance to the International Labour Organisation's Convention No. 29. This convention is expressly concerned with forced or compulsory labour and was, the Court found, the inspiration for Article 4. The Court then pointed out the 'striking similarity, which is not accidental, between paragraph 3 of Article 4 of the European Convention and paragraph 2 of Article 2 of Convention No. 29'. It went on:

Paragraph 1 of the last-mentioned Article provides that 'for the purposes' of the latter Convention, the term 'forced or compulsory labour' shall mean 'all work or service which is exacted from any person under the menace of any penalty and for which the said person has not offered himself voluntarily'. This definition can provide a starting-point for interpretation of Article 4 of the European Convention.[54]

Later in the judgment the Court again had recourse to the ILO Convention to demonstrate that the services which were the subject of the present proceedings, viz. a barrister's representation of his client, amounted to 'labour' for the purposes of Article 4(2). On this point the Court said:

It was common ground between those appearing before the Court that the services rendered by Mr Van der Mussele to Mr Ebrima amount to 'labour' for the purposes of Article 4 para 2. It is true that the English word 'labour' is often used in the narrow sense of manual work, but it also bears the broad meaning of the

French word *'travail'* and it is the latter that should be adopted in the present context. The Court finds corroboration of this in the definition included in Article 2 para 1 of Convention No 29 ('all work or service', *'tout travail ou service'*), in Article 4 para 3(d) of the European Convention ('any work or service', *'tout travail ou service'*) and in the very name of the International Labour Organisation (*Organisation Internationale du Travail*), whose activities are in no way limited to the sphere of manual labour.[55]

Similarly, when the Court considered whether there was in the present case 'the menace of any penalty', its application of this concept – derived, it should be noted, from Convention No. 29 – again looked to ILO practice. For having explained that if the applicant had refused to defend his client, he could have been struck off the roll of pupils or refused registration as an *avocat,* the Court ruled that: 'these prospects are sufficiently daunting to be capable of constituting "the menace of [a] penalty", having regard both to the use of the adjective "any" in the definition and to the standards adopted by the ILO on this point ("Abolition of Forced Labour": General Survey by the Committee of Experts on Application of Conventions and Recommendations, 1979, paragraph 21).'[56]

Although the ILO Convention exercised a major influence on the decision in this case, the Court, as we have seen, described its definition as a 'starting-point' for interpreting Article 4 and added that 'sight should not be lost of that Convention's special features or of the fact that it is a living instrument to be read "in the light of the notions currently prevailing in democratic States".'[57] The Court's intention to use Convention No. 29 as a guide, but not in an uncritical way, was underlined by its treatment of another point where it parted company with the earlier treaty. This was whether forced or compulsory labour requires that in addition to the labour being performed against a person's will, the obligation to carry it out must be 'oppressive' or its performance must constitute 'an avoidable hardship', be 'needlessly distressing' or 'somewhat harassing'. The Commission had imported these requirements into Article 4 on the basis of Convention No. 29. The Court, however, held that this was the wrong approach. Pointing out that the Commission's criterion is not stated in Article 2(1) of Convention No. 29, the Court explained that it 'derives from Article 4 and the following Articles of that Convention, which are not concerned with the notion of forced or compulsory labour but lay down the requirements to be met for the exaction of forced or compulsory labour during the transitional period provided for under Article 1(2) (see "ILO – internal minute – January 1966", paragraph 2)'.[58] In view of this difference the Court decided that another approach to Article 4(2) was appropriate, but agreed with the Commission's conclusion that there had been no transgression in the present case.

Indicative omissions

The second situation we must consider is really the converse of *Van der Mussele*. That is when another treaty clearly grants a particular right, but the Convention does not. In such a situation the other treaty may be seen as a reason for refusing to read the disputed right into the Convention by implication, or to interpret it in a way which would have the same effect as if the right had been mentioned. This is, of course, a particularly powerful argument when there is evidence that the right in question was considered for inclusion, but deliberately omitted.

The *Kosiek* case is a good illustration of this kind of reasoning. The applicant was dismissed from his civil service post for 'lack of allegiance to the West German Constitution' and claimed that the decision to dismiss him, which was based on his opinions and activities, violated his right to freedom of expression under Article 10. The Court dismissed the case on the ground that the basis of the applicant's claim was not freedom of expression, but access to the civil service which is not something that is guaranteed by the Convention. Contrasting the Convention with other instruments, the Court said:

The Universal Declaration of Human Rights of 10 December 1948 and the International Covenant on Civil and Political Rights of 16 December 1966 provide, respectively, that 'everyone has the right of equal access to public service in his country' (Article 21, para. 2) and that 'every citizen shall have the right and the opportunity . . . to have access, on general terms of equality, to public service in his country' (Article 25). In contrast, neither the European Convention nor any of its Protocols sets forth any such right. Moreover, as the Government rightly pointed out, the signatory States deliberately did not include such a right: the drafting history of Protocols Nos. 4 and 7 shows this unequivocally. In particular, the initial versions of Protocol No. 7 contained a provision similar to to Article 21 para. 2 of the Universal Declaration and Article 25 of the International Covenant; this clause was subsequently deleted. This is not therefore a chance omission from the European instruments; as the Preamble to the Convention states, they are designed to ensure the collective enforcement of 'certain' of the rights stated in the Universal Declaration.[59]

In his separate opinion in the *Golder* case Sir Gerald Fitzmaurice used the same type of argument to support his conclusion that it would be wrong to treat Article 6(1), which concerns the right to a fair trial, as impliedly conferring a right of access to the courts.[60] He pointed out that such a right is contained in Article 18 of the Bogotá Declaration which provides that 'Every person may resort to the courts to ensure respect for his legal rights.' In the Universal Declaration, however, this is rendered as 'Everyone has a right to an effective remedy by the competent national tribunals', a provision which corresponds to Article 13 of the European Convention which was not in issue in *Golder*. The provision in the Universal Declaration which corresponds to Article 6(1) is Article 10, which is in very similar terms and similarly confers no express right of access.

Fitzmaurice's opinion, which also referred to the International Covenant on Civil and Political Rights and the American Convention, is a good example of how the inclusion of something in another treaty can be used as a justification for reading the Convention narrowly, supported in this case by similar omissions in other instruments. The Court, it will be recalled, preferred a different approach and instead of examining the equivalent provisions of other treaties, emphasised the central place of the rule of law in the Convention and general international law. In this way the Court was able to arrive at the conclusion that a right of access to the courts should be implied into Article 6(1).

The *Golder* case demonstrates that other treaties are just one of several sources to which the Court may turn for guidance and are far from decisive. In a similar way, although the Court and individual judges have used the contrast between the Convention and other instruments as an aid to interpretation, they have also made the point that such differences should sometimes be regarded as more apparent than real. This was the position in the *Pretto* case which concerned the requirement in Article 6(1) that 'judgment shall be pronounced publicly'. One of the questions in that case was whether depositing a judgment in the domestic court's registry, with written notification of its operative provisions to the parties, but without a reading in open court, was enough to comply with the Convention. The Court noted that at first sight the terms of Article 6(1) appear stricter than those of the International Covenant on Civil and Political Rights which provides in Article 14(1) that a judgment 'shall be made public'. Although the Convention might seem to require judgments to be read out, the Court considered that in view of the long-standing European tradition of ensuring publicity by other means, so literal an interpretation was not required. It therefore decided that 'in each case the form of publicity to be given to a judgment must be assessed in the light of the special features of the proceedings in question and by reference to the object and purpose of Article 6 para 1'.[61]

A particularly interesting debate over the conclusions to be drawn from comparing the Convention with other treaty texts occurred in the *Soering* case. When deciding whether the extradition of the applicant to the United States could engage the responsibility of the United Kingdom under Article 3, the Court was urged by the respondent to attach significance to the fact that in the 1951 Convention relating to the Status of Refugees, the 1957 European Convention on Extradition and the 1984 United Nations Convention on Torture, the risks involved in removing a person to another jurisdiction are addressed specifically, whereas the Convention on Human Rights is silent on the matter. According to the government this was good reason for absolving the Contracting States from responsibility, under Article 3, for the consequences of extradition.

The Court, however, rejected this argument and, far from accepting the government's view, used international treaty law to draw precisely the opposite conclusion. Thus the Court pointed out that the absolute prohibition of torture and inhuman or degrading treatment or punishment in Article 3 is to be found in similar terms in the Covenant on Civil and Political Rights and the American Convention on Human Rights and 'is generally recognised as an internationally accepted standard'.[62] As for the specific prohibition on extradition in the Convention on Torture and other instruments, this was held not to be significant because:

The fact that a specialised treaty should spell out in detail a specific obligation attaching to the prohibition of torture does not mean that an essentially similar obligation is not already inherent in the general terms of Article 3 of the European Convention. It would hardly be compatible with the underlying values of the Convention . . . were a Contracting State knowingly to surrender a fugitive to another State where there were substantial grounds for believing that he would be in danger of being subjected to torture, however heinous the crime allegedly committed.[63]

Contemporary developments

The third situation in which the Court has considered the relation between the Convention and other instruments has seen it using other treaties as evidence of the current state of human rights law. Thus in several cases the Court has justified a particular reading of the Convention by pointing out that its interpretation is entirely consistent with the treatment of the issue in another instrument which deals with the subject in greater detail. This use of other treaties has been particularly important in a number of cases involving trade union rights under Article 11, where the Court has interpreted the Convention in the light of the corresponding parts of the European Social Charter.

In the *National Union of Belgian Police* case, for example, the Court rejected the view that by virtue of Article 11(1) a State, as employer, is obliged to consult with a given trade union. The Court justified this conclusion by stating that 'while Article 11(1) presents trade union freedom as one form or a special aspect of freedom of association, the Article does not guarantee any particular treatment of trade unions, or their members, by the State, such as the right to be consulted by it'. It then went on:

In addition, trade union matters are dealt with in detail in another convention, also drawn up within the framework of the Council of Europe, namely the Social Charter of 18 October 1961. Article 6(1) of the Charter binds the Contracting States 'to promote joint consultation between workers and employers'. The prudence of the terms used shows that the Charter does not provide for a real right to consultation. Besides, Article 20 permits a ratifying State not to accept the undertaking in Article 6(1). Thus it cannot be supposed that such a right derives by implication from Article 11(1) of the 1950 Convention, which incidentally would amount to admitting that the 1961 Charter took a retrograde step in this domain.[64]

The following year in the *Swedish Engine Drivers Union* case[65] the Court similarly rejected the argument that the State as employer is under any obligation to enter into a collective agreement, citing in this connection Article 6(2) of the Social Charter according to which the Contracting States: 'undertake . . . to promote, where necessary and appropriate, machinery for voluntary negotiations between employers or employers' organisations and workers' organisations, with a view to the regulation of terms and conditions of employment by means of collective agreements', and making the same point about the prudence of the wording and its significance for the interpretation of Article 11(1).

Finally, in the *Schmidt and Dahlström* case the Court used the same reasoning to support its conclusion that Article 11(1) does not confer a right to strike. Recalling that 'the Convention safeguards freedom to protect the occupational interests of trade union members by trade union action, the conduct and development of which the Contracting States must both permit and make possible', the Court held that Article 11(1) leaves each State free to choose the means to be used. These may include recognising a right to strike, but need not do so. Then, with particular reference to the Social Charter, the Court said:

Such a right which is not expressly enshrined in Article 11, may be subject under national law to regulation of a kind that limits its exercise in certain instances. The Social Charter of 18 October 1961 only guarantees the right to strike subject to such regulation, as well as to 'further restrictions' compatible with its Article 31, while at the same time recognising for employers too the right to resort to collective action (Article 6(4) and Appendix). For its part, the 1950 Convention requires that under national law trade unionists should be enabled, in conditions not at variance with Article 11, to strive through the medium of their organisations for the protection of their occupational interests. Examination of the file in this case does not disclose that the applicants have been deprived of this capacity.[66]

In these cases, as in *Van der Mussele*, the Court used another instrument to shed light on the meaning of the Convention. In *Van der Mussele*, as we have seen, the Court used the ILO Convention to give substance to a concept, 'compulsory labour', the meaning of which was unclear. In the Article 11 cases, on the other hand, the Court's purpose was not to flesh out an undefined concept, but to demonstrate that the interpretation put forward by the applicant would have extended States' obligations beyond those imposed by the Social Charter. The Court therefore used the

Charter to demonstrate that while its interpretation of Article 11 might appear somewhat restrictive, a wider reading would be unjustified since the Contracting Parties, when given the opportunity to confer such rights in the Social Charter, had consciously declined to do so.

Reference to treaties has also been significant in cases involving other articles of the Convention. Thus in the case of *S v Switzerland*, which concerned the right to confidential communication with counsel, the Court noted that this right is not expressly guaranteed in Article 6(3)(c) and contrasted this with Article 8(2)(d) of the American Convention on Human Rights. It pointed out, however, that in a European context the right in question is guaranteed in Article 93 of the Council of Europe's Standard Minimum Rules for the Treatment of Prisoners and also in Article 3(2) of the 1969 European Agreement Relating to Persons Participating in Proceedings of the European Commission and Court of Human Rights. In the light of these instruments the Court was able to conclude that 'an accused's right to communicate with his advocate out of hearing of a third person is part of the basic requirements of a fair trial in a democratic society'[67] and as such inherent in the Convention.

A similar approach can be seen in certain cases involving freedom of expression. In the *Müller* case[68] the Court held that a claim relating to the confiscation of paintings was covered by Article 10 and pointed out that Article 19(2) of the Covenant on Civil and Political Rights expressly mentions information and ideas 'in the form of art', although the Convention does not. In the *Groppera Radio AG* case, on the other hand, one of the issues was whether the licensing of broadcasting which is authorised in Article 10(1), must satisfy the various conditions laid down in Article 10(2), or whether it is entirely a matter for the State's discretion. The Court decided that the first interpretation is correct and supported its conclusions by referring to the discussions which had taken place when Article 19 of the Covenant, which does not refer to licensing, was being drafted.[69]

Interpreting the Convention by reference to comparable provisions in other instruments is more than a useful technique. For it seeks to ensure that human rights law develops consistently – indeed, that it is possible to speak of 'human rights law' at all, and not simply the provisions of particular conventions. It should be pointed out, however, that the aim of interpreting the Convention in a way which is consistent with other instruments will not always produce agreement. If inspiration is sought in instruments which are themselves open to more than one interpretation, any difference of opinion is naturally likely to result in different views as to the meaning of the Convention.[70]

Problems can also arise when treaty law is used to justify a particular interpretation as part of the Court's policy of interpreting the Convention as a living instrument. There is no difficulty when another treaty deals with a relevant matter and is generally accepted. In the *Engel* case, for example, the Court was on solid ground when it justified military disciplinary penalties which varied according to rank by observing that 'Such inequalities are traditionally encountered in the Contracting States and are tolerated by international humanitarian law'[71] and referred to Article 88 of the Geneva Convention on Prisoners of War. When, however, treaties are used which are not so well accepted, this kind of argument is less convincing.

Thus in the *Marckx* case the Court referred to the evolution of domestic law 'in company with the relevant international instruments'[72] towards removal of discrimination against illegitimate children and in the light of these developments held that Belgium had violated the Convention. However, reference to the instruments in question points to a weakness in this reasoning. When the *Marckx* case was decided in 1979 the 1962 Brussels Convention on the Establishment of Maternal Affiliation of Natural Children and the 1975 European Convention on the Legal Status of Children born out of Wedlock had been signed by less than half the members of the Council of Europe. Moreover, each convention had been ratified by only four States. Furthermore, the 1975 Convention permits States to make reservations with a direct bearing on one of the points in issue.

The Court recognised all these points but held that 'this state of affairs cannot be relied on in opposition to the evolution noted above'. It then went on:

Both the relevant Conventions are in force and there is no reason to attribute the currently small number of Contracting States to a refusal to admit equality between 'illegitimate' and 'legitimate' children on the point under consideration. In fact, the existence of these two treaties denotes that there is a clear measure of common ground in this area amongst modern societies.[73]

This, it may be thought, is somewhat circular reasoning. Although agreement on a convention text is certainly some evidence of opinion on an issue, signature and *a fortiori* ratification can scarcely be treated as insignificant formalities. If, as in this case, the question is whether opinion has developed to the point where a principle can properly be regarded as one of international obligation, support for the principle should be tested by considering the status, not merely the existence of treaties on the subject, since that is the clearest possible evidence of governments' readiness to assume the obligation in question.

In the *Inze* case in 1987 the Court again invoked the 1975 Convention, this time to support the conclusion that an Austrian law which placed special restrictions on the right of a person born out of wedlock to inherit a farm was inconsistent with Article 14 of the Convention, taken in conjunction with Article 1 of Protocol No. 1. By this time the Convention had been accepted by nine States, one of which was Austria. The Court was therefore justified in citing it to support its view that 'very weighty reasons would . . . have to be advanced before a difference of treatment on the ground of birth out of wedlock could be regarded as compatible with the Convention'.[74] There is, however, an obvious difference in the weight which can properly be given to a treaty before and after its acceptance. To make the mere existence of a treaty text the crucial factor, as the Court did in *Marckx*, and to place the onus on those who wish to deny its significance, is thus to run the risk of adopting an evolutive interpretation of the European Convention which may be premature.

Notes

1 P.C.I.J., Judgment of 4 April 1939, Series A/B No. 77.
2 Series A, No. 5 p. 18.
3 Series A, No. 9 p. 41.
4 Series A, No. 132
5 Series A, No. 15 para. 18.
6 Series A, No. 14 para. 16.
7 Series A, No. 201 para. 98. It should be noted, however, that nine judges dissented on the ground *inter alia* that the absence of an express provision relating to interim measures 'does not exclude an autonomous interpretation of the European Convention with special emphasis placed on its object and purpose and the effectiveness of its control machinery', dissenting opinion of Judge Cremona and others, para. 5.
8 Judgment, para. 101
9 Series A, No. 1 p. 15.
10 [1963] I.C.J. Rep., 15.
11 [1974] I.C.J. Rep., 253 and 457.
12 Series A, No. 25 paras. 152–5. For discussion see chapter 3.
13 *Ibid.*, para. 209.
14 Series A, No. 127, joint concurring opinion of Judges Lagergren, Pettiti and Macdonald.
15 [1973] I.C.J. Rep., 162.
16 Series A, No. 102 para. 134.
17 Series A, No. 18 para. 35.
18 See chapter 7.
19 Series A, No. 94 para. 67.
20 See the *Moustaquim* case, Series A, No. 193, and the *Vilvarajah* case, Series A, No. 215. In the former the Court went on to reject a claim that the applicant had been discriminated against because he was not an EC national, saying that as regards the preferential treatment of such nationals, 'there is an objective and reasonable justification for it as Belgium belongs, together with those States, to a special legal order' (para. 49).
21 Thus the Court's recognition of a State's right to expel aliens did not prevent it from finding a violation of Article 8 in the *Moustaquim* case and a number of others.

22 In addition to the cases mentioned in the text the Court also referred to general international law in the *Groppera Radio AG* case, Series A, No. 173, and the *Autronic AG* case, Series A, No. 178, in order to determine whether restrictions on broadcasting contained in Swiss legislation were 'prescribed by law' for the purposes of Article 10(2).

23 Series A, No. 4.

24 See P. van Dijk and G. J. H. van Hoof, *Theory and Practice of the European Convention on Human Rights* (2nd ed.), Kluwer, Deventer, 365–7 (1990).

25 This would in any case be precluded by Article 60 which provides that nothing in the Convention is to be construed 'as limiting or derogating from any of the human rights and fundamental freedoms which may be ensured under the laws of any High Contracting Party *or any other agreement to which it is a party*'.

26 Series A, No. 25 para. 222.

27 Series A, No. 13.

28 *'Other treaties' subject to the Consultative Jurisdiction of the Court*, Advisory Opinion No. OC–1/82, *International Legal Materials*, XXII, 51 (1983).

29 Van Dijk and van Hoof, *Theory and Practice*, 555.

30 The requirement of exhaustion of domestic remedies is also to be found in the American Convention (Article 46(1)(a)), the African Charter (Articles 50 and 56(5)) and the International Covenant on Civil and Political Rights (Article 41(c)) and its Optional Protocol (Articles 2 and 5(2)(b)). On the last see P. R. Ghandhi, 'The Human Rights Committee and the right of individual communication', *British Year Book of International Law*, LVII, 201 at 232 (1986); and D. McGoldrick, *The Human Rights Committee*, Clarendon Press, Oxford, 187–97 (1991).

31 Series A, No. 12 and see chapter 3.

32 An excellent review of the early jurisprudence of the Commission is to be found in A.A. Cançado Trindade, *The Application of the Rule of Local Remedies in International Law*, Cambridge Studies in International and Comparative Law, Cambridge U.P., Cambridge (1983).

33 Series A, No. 13 para. 89.

34 *Ibid.*, para. 90.

35 *Ibid.*, para. 91.

36 Series A, No. 9 p. 42.

37 *Ibid.*

38 Series A, No. 40 para. 39. Contrast *B v France*, Series A, No. 232C where the decision in *Van Oosterwijck* was distinguished.

39 Series A, No. 39 para. 72.

40 Series A, No. 200, see paras. 32 to 36 of the Judgment.

41 *Reports of International Arbitral Awards*, XII, 122, quoted *ibid.*, para. 34.

42 See Trindade, *Local Remedies*, 6.

43 Series A, No. 80 para. 61.

44 Series A, No. 35.

45 Series A, No. 25, separate opinion of Judge Sir Gerald Fitzmaurice, para. 10.

46 Series A, No. 98 para. 61.

47 *Ibid.*, para. 64.

48 Series A, No. 102.

49 Series A, No. 98 para. 62, but see F. G. Jacobs, *The European Convention on Human Rights*, Clarendon Press, Oxford, 165–6 (1975).

50 *Ibid.*, para. 63.

51 See, for example, *Libyan American Oil Co. (LIAMCO) v Libya* 62 I.L.R., 140. Cf., however, the jurisprudence of the Iran–United States Claims

Tribunal supporting the right to 'full compensation' in cases of expropriation and nationalisation. See J. A. Westberg, *International Transactions and Claims Involving Government Parties: Case Law of the Iran–United States Claims Tribunal*, International Law Institute, Washington D.C., 228–39, 249–50 (1991). For general discussion of this issue, see P. M. Norton, 'A law of the future or a law of the past: modern tribunals and the international law of expropriation', *American Journal of International Law*, LXXXV, 474 (1991).

52 *James* case, Series A, No. 98 para. 54.

53 *Ibid.*

54 Series A, No. 70 para. 32.

55 *Ibid.*, para. 33.

56 *Ibid.*, para. 35.

57 *Ibid.*, para. 32.

58 *Ibid.*, para. 37.

59 Series A, No. 105 para. 34.

60 Series A, No. 18, separate opinion of Judge Sir Gerald Fitzmaurice, para. 43.

61 Series A, No. 71 para. 26.

62 Series A, No. 161 para. 88.

63 *Ibid.* The government also raised the question of the relation between the Convention and the obligations of the United Kingdom under extradition treaties, but this question, which is of great practical importance, was only dealt with briefly by the Court. See C. Van den Wyngaert, 'Applying the European Convention on Human Rights to extradition: opening Pandora's box?' *International and Comparative Law Quarterly*, XXXIX, 757 (1990); and C. Warbrick, 'Coherence and the European Court of Human Rights: the adjudicative background to the *Soering* case', *Michigan Journal of International Law*, XI, 1073 (1990).

64 Series A, No. 19 para. 38.

65 Series A, No. 20.

66 Series A, No. 21

67 Series A, No. 220 para. 48. See further on this point the *Campbell* case, Series A, No. 233.

68 Series A, No. 133.

69 Series A, No. 173 para. 61. However, a different view was expressed by Judge Pinheiro Farinha who considered that it was 'unacceptable to reason on the basis of the drafting history of a later instrument drawn up within a different community (the UN), not within the Council of Europe', concurring opinion, para. 4.

70 Thus when interpreting the reference to 'torture' in Article 3, the Court in the *Irish* case referred to Article 1(2) of General Assembly Resolution 3452(xx), whereas Judge Zekia, adopting a wider interpretation, relied on Article 1(1). See also on this point the separate opinions of Judges Matscher and Evrigenis.

71 Series A, No. 22 para. 72. In the subsequent *Autronic AG* case the Court similarly supported its decision that Switzerland's control of satellite broadcasting was over-restrictive by referring to the recent European Convention on Transfrontier Television and pointing out that several States had already authorised the reception of uncoded broadcasts from satellites, without arousing protests (Series A, No. 178 para. 62).

72 Series A, No. 31 para. 41.

73 *Ibid.* See also the *Johnston* case, Series A, No. 112 para. 74, where the Court referred to the Preamble of the 1975 Convention.

74 Series A, No. 126 para. 41.

CHAPTER 10

Ideology and international human rights law

At the beginning of this book we said that its aim was to identify issues of method and function relevant to the international judicial process generally, and specifically to the role of adjudication in the development of an international law of human rights. Having examined the work of the European Court in a number of particular aspects, it is now time to consider what the Court's work as a whole has to tell us about these issues.

In the light of what has been said earlier, two propositions will be put forward in this chapter. First, we shall argue that the case-law of the European Court demonstrates that the extent to which the decisions of an international tribunal develop the law depends in large measure on which of two general judicial ideologies the members of the court subscribe to. These ideologies will be called 'judicial restraint' and 'judicial activism'. Secondly, we shall argue that when an international court develops the law, the direction in which it does so is again influenced by judicial ideology, only this time ideology pertaining to the subject matter of the particular court's jurisdiction. In the case of the European Court, that subject matter is human rights and the judicial ideologies we shall examine will be termed 'tough conservatism' and 'benevolent liberalism'.[1]

General judicial ideologies

There is one issue which every court must deal with in the course of its work. Not every decision will raise it and the treatment of it may not be consistent from case to case. But how the court responds to the issue, when it arises, has a vital bearing on its activity. The issue is whether the court is to adopt the ideology of judicial restraint, or the ideology of judicial activism, or to be more precise, where on the continuum between these polarities the court chooses to locate its decisions at a given time.

Analysis of judicial behaviour in terms of restraint and activism was first applied to domestic courts, but is no less relevant in the international sphere. Because the European Court is an international tribunal, the considerations favouring restraint or activism are not identical in all respects to those which are relevant in municipal law. In the same way, because the Court's work is focused on the interpretation and application of a treaty, rather than on legislation or the common law, manifestations of these ideologies, in practice, assume a particular form.[2] As we shall see, however, considering the Court's decisions from this perspective provides an important insight into its work.

Judicial restraint

The ideology of judicial restraint takes as its premise the proposition that the judge's job is to apply law, not to make it. Of course, a court must normally be prepared to decide every case which comes before it, and even the proponent of extreme restraint will concede that in applying the law to novel situations, new law will inevitably be made. Believers in restraint do not deny that courts sometimes make law. What they maintain, however, is that, subject to this inescapable feature of the judicial process, courts should, to the greatest degree possible, confine themselves to applying the law as its exists, and leave its development, modification and alteration to the political process where it properly belongs.

For the advocate of judicial restraint, deciding cases is seen as a process of interpreting and applying rules which others have laid down for the regulation of society and the courts. He therefore attaches great importance to what has appropriately been termed the 'rule-book',[3] that is, the set of authoritative materials traditionally regarded as comprising the law. Moreover, since he is conscious that his own authority is limited, he not only regards the rule-book as sacrosanct, but also considers that it should be construed strictly. It follows that in cases of doubt he is likely to conclude that a particular matter is not covered, since a contrary conclusion might be seen as overstepping the bounds of his authority.

Although, as we have mentioned, the believer in judicial restraint will admit that an element of legal development occurs as a natural part of the judicial process, his concern for the rule-book makes him uncomfortable with doctrinal innovation. When this occurs, he is therefore likely to begin by opposing it on the ground that no one knows where it may lead; then, if that is unsuccessful, he will seek to restrict its growth by subjecting the new doctrine to the same strict construction as he employs elsewhere. In this way he can achieve two objectives: the judicial role remains circumscribed and, at the same time, innovations acquire defined boundaries, making them suitable for inclusion in the rule-book.

Because his ideal image of the law is of a clear set of rules for the judge to apply, the believer in the ideology of restraint sets considerable store by precedent. Following previous decisions promotes legal certainty, but, more importantly, is legitimate because this material has become part of the rule-book and can therefore properly be regarded as 'law'. In contrast, considerations of policy, (or even worse, politics), are not part of the law and have no part in the judge's decision. Advocates of restraint thus react with great hostility to anything which can be regarded as 'politicisation' of the judicial process, or any attempt to suggest that moral, social or economic factors should play a part in decision-making. The law is sufficient unto itself and the judge's task is to apply it in accordance with its own internal logic.

The limited role which the advocate of restraint sees for the courts has as its corollary the belief that if the law is unsatisfactory in any way, the responsibility for putting things right rests with the legislature, or others with the necessary political responsibility. Judicial restraint, as an ideology, thus does not entail a belief that the law is perfect, simply that law reform is not an appropriate judicial function. To the extent that they accept that a degree of legal development is inevitable in any system of adjudication, believers in restraint will usually recognise that the court has a limited power to choose the more sensible solution. But the limits of this power are strictly drawn and do not encompass major legislative initiatives. It is therefore common to find supporters of restraint admitting that a particular decision is regrettable, while at the same time holding it to be inevitable on the ground that the law leaves no room for choice. 'Perhaps', they will say, 'the law should be changed, but this is not a matter for us to decide.'

Judicial restraint may therefore be summarised by saying that to the adherent of this ideology there is a fundamental distinction between legislation and adjudication. The judge's task is to apply the law; he is 'an outsider in the political process',[4] who should never think of himself as a legislator, but concentrate on the job in hand, which is resolving disputes in accordance with established rules.

Judicial activism

The ideology of judicial activism takes a diametrically opposed position. Where the ideology of restraint emphasises following the rules, the ideology of activism emphasises using and developing them to achieve results. So to the activist, what the court decides is more important than how it decides it. Again we must be careful not to distort the activist's position. Few supporters of activism would wish to argue that results are all that matter, or that method is entirely irrelevant. Activists know that judgments have to be explained and that the judicial role imposes limits on the kinds of decisions which can be justified. Compared with believers in restraint, however, activists interpret constraints on the judicial role very liberally, and since they regard it as part of the judge's job to produce an appropriate result if at all possible, elements which others think conclusive are treated as simply factors in the equation.

Since the activist is keen to consider what the law ought to be, he regards established rules and principles as essentially a means to an end. Regarding himself as endowed with the authority to seek the result he would like, the activist has no instinctive preference for strict construction. If such a construction will produce the desired result, then it will be adopted. Otherwise it will not. Thus in doubtful cases instead of concluding that something is not covered, the activist will decide if he thinks it ought to be covered and construe the rule appropriately.

The activist's interest in results makes him a natural supporter of doctrinal innovation. He not only sees new doctrines as an aid to result manipulation, but, as new ideas are developed, is eager to exploit their potential. Instead of worrying about whether new doctrines are necessary, or how they will fit into the rule-book, the activist sees innovation as essential to what he would regard as the judge's job: doing justice in individual cases and, more generally, keeping the law up to date.

It follows from the activist's general outlook that his attitude to precedent reflects his attitude to the rest of the rule-book. In this he resembles the believer in restraint, but whereas the latter treats both as controlling, the activist is less deferential and, as regards previous decisions, is likely to be highly selective. By the same token, the extra-legal factors which collectively go under the name of 'legal policy' and which the restrained judge eschews, play a major part in the activist's decisions. Activists regard the idea of applying legal rules without regard to policy as at best an illusion and at worst an evasion of responsibility. They do not regard law as autonomous and believe that to do his job properly, the judge has to recognise this.

Because the activist sees the courts as having a significant legislative role, he does not accept that they are helpless in the face of rules which are obviously unsatisfactory. The activist is, of course, aware that courts must operate with the legal material they are given and that the primary responsibility for legislation lies elsewhere. The key point, however – and this more than anything else is what distinguishes activism and restraint as judicial ideologies – is that the activist is not prepared to regard the legislative responsibility of other bodies as exclusive. Not only is he aware that change can often be achieved more quickly by judicial action, he also considers that such initiatives are expected. In short he sees his job as both to apply the law and, where necessary, to make it.

It would therefore be accurate to say that to the activist courts are part of the political process and adjudication always a political act. Since deciding cases involves making choices about matters of fundamental importance, the activist considers this should be acknowledged and the process performed with a recognition of what is at stake. The activist, then, sees law as much more than a matter of rules. While recognising that the judge cannot ignore the law which has been laid down, he considers that as part of his job he must be ready to develop and, if necessary, change it.

General judicial ideologies in the Court's jurisprudence

The tension between restraint and activism in the work of the Court is most evident in cases in which a majority judgment reflecting one ideological tendency is opposed by a judge, or judges, championing the other. Since the Court, with varying degrees of emphasis, has generally adopted an activist approach towards the Convention, some of the clearest statements of judicial ideology are to be found in dissenting judgments articulating the case for restraint. This is not invariable, how-ever, and sometimes the position has been reversed. Cases which feature dissenting judgments of either tendency are not, of course, the only ones in which general judicial ideology is significant. As cases in which the Court is unanimous rarely expose ideological assumptions in such an illuminating way, however, it is the former which we shall concentrate on in the present discussion.

The contrasting assumptions of the two general judicial ideologies may be seen very clearly in the *Irish* case. It will be recalled from chapter 3 that when the British Government submitted that the issue of torture and inhuman or degrading treatment had become moot, the Court rejected the argument on the ground that its judgments 'serve not only to decide those cases brought before the Court but, more generally, to elucidate, safeguard and develop the rules instituted by the Convention.'[5] In a separate opinion Sir Gerald Fitzmaurice agreed that the Court was entitled to decide the case, but held that the justification for this was based on its relationship with the Commission and was therefore much narrower. He took particular exception to the reference to a power to 'develop' the law and suggested that by using this language the Court was 'acting out the consequences of a doctrine which it has itself propounded and decided to abide by, but which is neither propounded nor imposed upon it by the Convention.'[6]

Here, then, is the basic distinction between the two ideologies, one asserting a power to develop the law, the other denying it. It is, however, interesting to note that Sir Gerald drew a distinction between what he termed the 'natural development that always occurs as an inevitable corollary of the legitimate interpretative process properly belonging to the judicial function' and 'development as a conscious aim . . . a quasi-legislative operation exceeding the normal judicial function'.[7] As already noted, advocates of restraint can accept a degree of development as unavoidable. What they object to, as Fitzmaurice indicated, is a deliberate legislative posture.

Whether the Court has anything more than a marginal role in legal development is naturally a question with a vital bearing on interpretation. The view that it has not, and that to avoid exceeding its function the Court must interpret the Convention strictly has been put forward in many different contexts. Thus in the *Airey* case Judge Vilhjálmsson observed that 'The war on poverty cannot be won through broad interpretation of the Convention' and concluded 'without much hesitation but admittedly with regret'[8] that in view of the language of Article 6(1) the applicant had no right to legal aid. Similarly, in the *König* case Judge Matscher held that the autonomous concept of 'civil rights and obligations' in Article 6(1) requires close attention to domestic law and suggested that the Court in its approach was 'going beyond teleological interpretation and venturing into the field of legislative policy'.[9] And in the *Tyrer* case Fitzmaurice held that the concept of degrading treatment in Article 3 requires a strict interpretation and suggested that to include birching or other practices which modern opinion considers undesirable, 'would mean using the Article as a vehicle of indirect penal reform, for which it was not intended'.[10]

In these cases an approach to interpretation based on restraint confronted an approach by the majority based on far-reaching applications of, respectively, the effectiveness principle, the notion of an autonomous concept, and interpretation of the Convention as 'a living instrument', all activist devices. The same disagreement can be seen in other areas of interpretation. Thus in the *Golder* case those who held that a right of access to the courts was not implied in Article 6(1), took the view that it was not a necessary inference. This they considered essential because, as Fitzmaurice put it:

There is a considerable difference between the case of 'law-giver's law' edicted in the exercise of sovereign power, and law based on convention, itself the outcome of a process of agreement, and limited to what has been agreed, or can properly be assumed to have been agreed. Far greater interpretational restraint is requisite in the latter case, in which, accordingly, the convention should not be construed as providing for more than it contains, or than is necessarily to be inferred from what it contains.[11]

This passage points very clearly to the assumptions behind the ideology of restraint in its international application and, not surprisingly, leads to the conclusion that the Convention must be given a 'cautious and conservative' interpretation in which any serious doubt must 'be resolved in favour of, rather than against the government concerned'.[12] The same sentiment also produces an emphasis on the *travaux préparatoires* as the best evidence of the Contracting States' intentions, and an emphasis on precedent, both of which can be seen in Sir Vincent Evans's dissent in the *Campbell and Cosans* case.[13] The Court uses the *travaux* and refers to precedent too, but in accordance with its general posture of judicial activism, has done so more selectively.

Contrasting attitudes towards doctrinal innovation can also be seen in the cases. Thus in the *Le Compte* case Judge Matscher criticised the Court's innovative description of when a 'dispute' relates to a 'civil right' for the purposes of Article 6(1), saying:

This is not the right language either for providing the Contracting States with guidance on the adaptation of their law to the requirements of the Convention institutions, or for enlightening persons protected by the Convention on an application's prospects of success. In short, it makes no contribution to legal certainty, a principle which has often been invoked, and rightly so, in the Court's judgments.[14]

Similarly, the three judges who dissented in *Golder* made the point that implying a right of access to the courts creates a need to define it and said that the absence of such a definition (which they did not regard the Court as competent to provide) was bound to create uncertainty.

Relating the issue of innovation to the future decisions of the Court, Sir Gerald Fitzmaurice, in a comment exemplifying the doctrinal conservatism of a believer in restraint, then said:

Once wide interpretations of the kind now in question are adopted by a court without the clearest justification for them based solidly on the language of the text or on necessary inferences to be drawn from it, and not, as here, on a questionable interpretation of an enigmatic provision, considerations of consistency will thereafter make it difficult to refuse extensive interpretations in other contexts where good sense might dictate differently; freedom of action will have been impaired.[15]

The fears expressed here, that innovation will create uncertainty and at the same time acquire its own force as precedent are typical of the arguments used to support restraint. Although in neither of the cases mentioned did the arguments prevail, both aspects of Article 6(1) are still subject to considerable uncertainty, a fact which the dissenting judges would say confirms their doubts and their activist colleagues would probably regard as the unavoidable price of legal development.

One of the main tenets of the ideology of restraint, that courts are concerned with law, not policy, has already been touched on and was further explained by Fitzmaurice in his separate opinion in the *National Union of Belgian Police* case. Challenging what he saw as excessively broad readings of Articles 11 and 14, he said that he was not opposed to a 'reasonably liberal' construction of the Convention:

But this is a different matter, and quite different from the subservience to policy that seems to have been advocated in recent argument before the Court in which the speaker terminated his remarks by stating: 'I conclude by saying that law is always the instrument of policy' . . . such a conclusion is dangerous unless carefully qualified – for if taken literally and generally, it would seem to justify the excesses of courts of law in the carrying out of the policies of some of the worst tyrannies in history. In my view the integrity of the law requires that the courts should apply it neither as the instrument, nor as the contriver, of policy, but in accordance with their own professional standards and canons.[16]

The view that courts are not concerned with policy, leads naturally to the conclusion that if there are gaps in the law, filling them is a legislative task which must be left to the proper authorities. Thus, in discussing the scope of Article 6(1) in the *Le Compte* case, Judge Matscher said:

The present judgment, like the *König* judgment as well for that matter, is, of course, prompted by the worthy intention of affording to the individual pro-tection against interferences by public, professional or social authorities in an especially important area like the exercise of a profession. The fact that the Convention is defective in this respect is a point that I myself have emphasised on numerous occasions. But according to my view of the judicial role, it is no part of the functions of an international court to give recognition to rights which the authors of the Convention did not intend to include therein. This unsatisfactory situation cannot therefore be validly rectified by means of judicial interpretation, and this is all the more so because such an interpretation threatens to upset the Convention system in one of its most sensitive sectors; rectification can be effected only by the legislature, in other words by the Contracting States, who should take steps to amend the Convention.[17]

Similarly, when rejecting the Court's use of the principle of legal certainty in the *Marckx* case, Judge Pinheiro Farinha said 'The Court has jurisdiction not to redraft the Convention but to apply it. Only the High Contracting Parties can alter the contents of the obligations assumed'.[18] And when dealing with the scope of Article 3 in the *Irish* case, Fitzmaurice, who dealt with the problem in these kinds of cases in more detail than can be quoted here, said:

The real dilemma that faced the Commission and the Court in the present case, and which would face any tribunal trying to apply Article 3 with some sense of proportion and objectivity, is that the Convention contains no prohibition cover-ing intermediate forms of maltreatment that clearly fall short of, or only doubtfully attain, that degree of severity, which could, without evident exagger-ation, justify classifying them as inhuman, or as amounting to torture. . . . The Convention is obviously defective in not providing for lesser forms of ill-treatment. . . . If the Parties to the Convention should now wish to go beyond what they originally provided for, it is for them to do so by amendment of the Convention, not for a tribunal whose task is to interpret it as it stands.[19]

In all these cases the Court rejected the arguments of those favouring restraint and adopted an activist interpretation. Needless to say, its reasons for so doing have left the doubters unconvinced. The issue here, which goes to the heart of the judicial function, is the Court's competence vis-à-vis the Contracting States. On the one hand, the view that the Court has a duty to take action; on the other, the view that the range of activist arguments and techniques are 'typical of the cry of the judicial legislator all down the ages' and that when the Court is presented with a hard case 'it is for the States upon whose consent the Convention rests, and from which consent alone it derives its obligatory force, to close the gap or put the defect right by an amendment – not for a judicial tribunal to substitute itself for the convention-makers'.[20]

The debate over whether it is any part of the Court's task to develop the Convention is one way in which different views of the relationship between the Strasbourg organs and the Contracting States have proved significant. Another, of course, is the margin of appreciation. Here the question of authority is not so much whether the Court may legislate to fill a gap, as how far it may compel States to treat a particular matter in a uniform way. Like the previous issue, however, this question of 'European standards' relates to the scope for judicial legislation and so generates an identical division of opinion. In the *Brogan* case, for example, where the majority found that the United Kingdom had violated its obligations under Article 5(3), Judge Martens dissented on the ground that it was desirable for the international judge 'to adopt an attitude of reserve' on this issue because national authorities had 'acquired a far better insight into the requirements of effectively combating terrorism and of protecting their citizens than an international judge can ever hope to acquire from print'.[21]

As we have seen in chapter 7, some members of the Court favour a broad margin of appreciation in which much is left to national discretion; others favour a more interventionist approach. The wide margin of appreciation, supported as it is by a combination of strict construction of the Convention and the argument that only the national authorities are competent to make the necessary political assessment, is a typical product of the ideology of restraint. The narrow margin, and the more radical view of some commentators that the very existence of the concept is an obstacle which should be done away with, are equally typical of exponents of activism. The Court, as has been seen, has applied the concept with close attention to the context. Sometimes, as in the cases on Article 15, it has recognised a broad margin and supported this with arguments based on the State's responsibility for political decisions; sometimes it has taken an activist approach and emphasised the extensive nature of its own competence. Both types of cases, not surprisingly, have often split the Court along ideological lines.

Nor is the question of the scope of the Court's authority confined to its

relations with the Contracting States. As we saw in chapter 3, the Court
has sometimes had to consider issues of competence relating to its role
vis-à-vis the Commission. Here, a general attitude of restraint, illustrated
by the Court's unwillingness to interfere with the Commission's regulation of its procedure, contrasts sharply with the activist decision in the
Vagrancy cases,[22] where the Court asserted its competence to examine
certain issues of admissibility. It will be recalled that this ruling was
opposed by several judges on the ground that admissibility is the
exclusive prerogative of the Commission. This argument, emphasising
that the existence of another responsible body had the effect of excluding
the Court, is another reflection of the ideology of restraint and was, of
course, rejected. It will be recalled, however, that though the Court has
established its competence to examine issues of admissibility, it has not
ignored considerations pertaining to the special function of the Commission, but sought to recognise them by applying the general principle of
estoppel.

The point just made highlights a general aspect of the Court's
jurisprudence of some importance. Whenever the Court has given the
Convention an activist interpretation, whether in the procedural or the
substantive field, it has had to take account of arguments counselling
restraint. Conversely, on the less frequent occasions on which the Court
itself has followed a restrained approach, the urge for judicial activism
has never been far away. It would be misleading to suggest that, caught in
this ideological tension, the Court has invariably sought the middle way.
For as between the two approaches, the argument for activism has
frequently prevailed. What is clear, however, is that the ideologies of
restraint and activism concern basic aspects of the judicial process which
it would be foolish to ignore. The Court and its judges, whatever their
general orientation, are obliged to take both into account in their
decisions.

Specific judicial ideologies

The general ideologies just considered tell the international judge how he
should see his role but provide no specific guidance as to what he should
do. They are therefore like a sign which flashes 'walk' or 'don't walk', but
conveys no sense of direction. To supply this, an ideology related to the
particular area of law is needed, and so in this section two such specific
ideologies, which we shall term 'tough conservatism' and 'benevolent
liberalism', will be described.

Tough conservatism
The ideology of tough conservatism is a blend of two elements: it is

conservative and it is tough. The conservative element is concerned with the preservation of existing institutions and attaches great importance to history, tradition and established social values. Conservatives therefore believe strongly in the family, conventional morality as regards, for example, sexual conduct, and State institutions like the monarchy and parliament. Because the ideology of conservatism is so concerned with preservation, a high value is placed on property rights, on order and on the institutions associated with order, such as the courts and the police. By the same token, criminals, subversives and the State's external enemies are all perceived as threats, justifying vigorous counter-measures. Some conservatives, indeed, regard any deviant or eccentric conduct in the same way, seeing it as a threat to traditional values and consequently dangerous. While many do not go so far, their espousal of tolerance is likely to be tinged with an underlying disapproval of anything at variance with the 'normal', reflecting an identical conservative instinct.

The emphasis which conservatism places on established practice and maintenance of the status quo means that conservatives are slow to recognise the need for change and rarely anxious to encourage it. Con-servatives recognise, of course, that change does occur, but believe that in general it is better if it is gradual and comes from within a society or group, rather than being imposed from outside. This is, no doubt, partly because they believe that change from within will be slower, but also because with an appreciation of our limited understanding of the process of social change, conservatives know that schemes undertaken with the best of intentions may turn out to have all kinds of unexpected conse-quences.

Another reason why conservatives have little faith in social engineering is that they have a view of human nature which suggests to them that even though change may sometimes be desirable, it is doubtful if the changes which would really be important can ever be successfully achieved. Thus conservatives not only want most things to go on in the same old way, as regards everything which relates to the basic human instincts, they expect them to do so and believe that nothing is likely to change very much whatever is done. This could easily become a formula for total inaction, but for many conservatives, at least, it does not do so because, as part of their belief in human fallibility, conservatives recognise that power is always likely to be abused. From this it follows that if things are to be preserved, political power, especially, must be subject to control. Thus, while conservatives support order and authority, they also believe strongly in the rule of law, seeing this as an essential way of protecting not only property and a way of life, but also life itself.

The other aspect of tough conservatism is its element of toughness. Tough conservatives believe that most people are capable of looking after themselves and should be encouraged to do so. This does not mean pretending that everyone is equally capable, or allowing the weak to be trampled on, but means accepting that there are limits to what the State ought, or can be expected to do in protecting people from suffering. Tough conservatives know that life in general is not fair and believe that instead of spending time and effort deploring this and trying to change things, everyone is happier if this state of affairs is accepted. It follows that they expect people to be able to take a few hard knocks without complaint and may even believe that, within limits, suffering strengthens character. Since they also believe that the individual is responsible for his actions and so has some control over his destiny, they have little sympathy for criminals or other social deviants, who when they are punished, are regarded as bringing this upon themselves. This attitude is naturally reinforced by the high value which tough conservatives place on order and conformity.

One could therefore sum up tough conservatism by saying that those who subscribe to this ideology are generally happy with the way things are, have no great faith in either the merits or the practicality of schemes for improvement and consider that in so far as it is necessary to recognise something as a social problem, the best way of dealing with it will often be to leave it alone.

Benevolent liberalism

This ideology, like tough conservatism, has two facets, a liberal facet and a benevolent facet. The liberal facet takes as its starting point the value of the individual. Every person is regarded as unique and possessing a potential which the liberal wishes to see fully developed. Whereas the ideal world of the conservative is one in which everyone's behaviour conforms to the standard pattern for people of his group or class, the liberal welcomes diversity. Unusual behaviour is seen not as a threat, but as a contribution to a rich tapestry of action and self-realisation which the liberal wishes to see encouraged.

The liberal's emphasis on individuality produces a characteristic attitude towards authority and established institutions. Whereas the conservative sees these as central and almost as ends in themselves, for the liberal they represent irksome restraints on the individual's realisation of his potential. Thus the conservative's respect for the courts, the police, and the law is replaced by the liberal's perception of the apparatus of state power as inherently oppressive and his belief that the proper attitude to authority is mistrust and scepticism. Although liberals believe that fears of anarchy, which haunt the conservative, are greatly exaggerated, the liberal is not an anarchist. He does not deny that the State is a necessary institution and has its uses. The difference between the conservative and the liberal as regards the question of authority is therefore essentially a matter of assumptions. The conservative believes that authority is beneficial, but knows that it can be abused; the liberal believes that authority is pernicious, but realises that it is necessary.

The liberal's emphasis on self-realisation makes for an attitude towards change which is exactly opposite to that held by the conservative. Since the liberal sees morality and the law as reflections of the past (which they generally are), he wants them changed to reflect the current state of affairs. He is quite happy for this to be done deliberately and recognises, moreover, that bringing the rules of society up to date cannot be a once and for all operation, but will need constant action. He is happy with the idea of this and, as with the conservative's espousal of the opposite position, his sentiment reflects his view of human nature.

The liberal believes that things can and ought to be improved because he has faith in the human ability to solve problems and believes that people can be changed. Problems which the conservative attributes to human nature, the liberal is more likely to see as the product of social circumstances. He therefore has a tendency to see people as the victims of society and is a strong believer in their banding together to bring about social change.

The benevolent aspect of benevolent liberalism is bound up with the role of the State in achieving the liberal's goals. The conservative, as we have seen, sees the State's job as to hold the ring and let the individual get on with his life. The liberal, on the other hand, sees the State as the best way to bring about the kinds of changes he wants and so wishes it to play a much more active role. The value which liberals place on the individual puts fairness and equality high on their agenda and the State is expected to take steps to bring this about by, for example, outlawing discrimination. The benevolent liberal would like to minimise all forms of suffering and far from regarding it as inevitable, considers that, wherever possible, it should give the individual a claim on the community's resources. Benevolent liberals, therefore, place great emphasis on rights, but the rights which are emphasised, though obviously similar to those recognised by conservatives in many respects, also differ from them in a number of ways. Where the conservative sees property as fundamental, the liberal is likely to attach more importance to trade union rights, or other means of collective action. More generally, civil and political rights, which are what rights mean to a tough conservative, are likely to be treated by the benevolent liberal as no more important than social and economic rights. The significance of civil and political rights is not denied – the liberal strand of the ideology sees to that. By virtue of the benevolent strand, however, the conception of rights is broadened.

Benevolent liberalism could therefore be summed up by saying that those who support this ideology are not at all happy with the way things are, and believe that change is essential if the individual's worth is to be recognised. They also regard the task of social improvement as never-ending and see State action as having a central role in virtually all aspects of the individual's welfare.

Specific ideologies in the Court's jurisprudence

As we did when considering general ideologies, we shall concentrate here on cases in which either or both of the ideologies we are considering have been articulated. Before we do so, however, a word of caution may be in order. Just as the followers of restraint and activism treat adjudication differently, but have some beliefs about the judicial role in common, so when considering specific ideologies we need to remember that the members of the Court share a belief in the western democratic tradition. Within that broad ideological consensus there is room, as we shall see, for sharp disagreement between tough conservatives and benevolent liberals, but given the common ideological commitment, we should not expect to find it in every case.

In view of the emphasis which conservatives place on order, discipline and security and the rather different priorities approved by liberals, it is not surprising that cases involving these kinds of issues are among those in which ideological differences have proved significant. In the *Engel* case, for example, several judges disagreed with the Court's decision that soldiers subject to military discipline enjoy full protection of their right to personal liberty under Article 5. Thus Judge Bindschedler-Robert said that when establishing the scope of Article 5(1):

Account must be taken of the nature of military service and the role of disciplinary law in instilling and maintaining discipline which is a *sine qua non* for the proper functioning of that special institution, the army. It is not enough to adopt, as does the Court, a narrow concept of deprivation of liberty; what must be borne in mind is the whole system of disciplinary law. Military discipline calls in particular for speedy and effective measures and penalties, adapted to each situation, and which, therefore, the hierarchical superior must be able to impose.[23]

Similarly, Judges O'Donoghue and Pedersen, though recognising that Article 5 was relevant, held that the measures in question could be justified under Article 5(1)(b) because military personnel are under a special obligation by virtue of their disciplinary code 'the maintenance of which is vital to the very continued existence of an armed force and quite different from any other body or association which purports to exercise a measure of discipline over its members'.[24]

In another case involving Article 5 the issue was crime, rather than discipline, but the same tension is apparent. In *Guzzardi*, as we saw in chapter 4, the majority adopted a broad interpretation of Article 5 and held that the confinement of the applicant on a small island infringed his right to personal liberty. This conclusion, which is a good example of judicial activism in the cause of benevolent liberalism, was challenged by those who, favouring a more restrained approach, supported their position with arguments characteristic of tough conservatism.

Judge Matscher, for example, held that action taken by the authorities must always be viewed in context. While this did not mean that the Court could condone violations of the Convention, it did mean that:

certain measures which, from the viewpoint of the Convention, might be seen as open to considerable criticism in a so-called normal situation are less open to criticism and can be considered as being in conformity with the Convention when there is a crisis overshadowing public order and notably when rights of others, which are also guaranteed by the Convention, are being threatened by the activities of certain dangerous and anti-social elements. Such a crisis was obtaining in Italy at the time when the present case began.[25]

Emphasising that in the light of the threat posed by the Mafia, Italy should be seen as 'a democratic State struggling to protect the rights of the general public',[26] he held that the Court should have exonerated Italy either by interpreting the concept of personal liberty more narrowly, or upholding the government's actions under Article 5(1)(c).

Several judges made similar points, drawing attention to the applicant's dangerous character and his subsequent imprisonment for kidnapping. They also suggested that the conditions of his detention on the island were less severe than might be gathered from its description in the judgment. Finally one member of the Court observed that the award of compensation to the applicant carried the case into 'cloud-cuckoo land',[27] a view which may well have been shared by other judges.

Reservations about the Court's approach to law and order were also expressed in the *Ciulla* case,[28] where Judges Valticos and Matscher suggested that the preventive detention of a man charged with numerous drugs offences could be justified under Article 5(1), in the *Ezelin* case in which Judge Matscher identified the question as 'whether, in the permissive society of today, a member of the Bar can still be required to behave with "discretion" ',[29] and in the *Moustaquim* case, where Judges Bindschedler-Robert and Valticos drew attention to 'the danger of misusing the concept of interference with "family life" in cases concerning the prosecution and punishment of criminal activities'.[30] These tough conservative sentiments were, however, all contained in dissenting opinions. As in *Guzzardi* the majority adopted a more liberal view.

Cases which challenge the response of governments to terrorism bring out the same tensions. Thus in the *Brogan* case[31] seven members of the Court considered that as the applicants had been arrested under the 1984

Prevention of Terrorism Act, the United Kingdom should not be held to have violated their rights under Article 5(3). Likewise, in the case of *Fox, Campbell and Hartley*,[32] three judges denied that a distinction should be drawn between 'reasonable suspicion' and 'genuine suspicion', when a person is arrested as a suspected terrorist and complains of a violation of Article 5(1). These opinions, like the dissenting opinions in *Guzzardi*, reflect a concern for general security which stands in contrast to the priority given to individual rights in the Court's judgments. In *Brogan*, moreover, three of the majority maintained that the judgment was too limited and argued that the vagueness of the relevant legislation meant that there was also a violation of Article 5(1). The contrast between the arguments used to support this liberal interpretation of the applicants' rights and those employed by the judges who dissented provides a clear demonstration of the range of ideological positions of members of the Court.

In the *Irish* case there was more agreement than in *Guzzardi*, or *Brogan*, but on the crucial issue of Article 3 views were expressed which reflect opposing ideological positions. The Court, it will be recalled, held that in the way they were employed, the 'five techniques' of interrogation amounted to inhuman and degrading treatment. Several judges, however, considered it should have gone further and characterised them as torture. These opinions with their emphasis on the applicants' suffering and the ingenious cruelties of the modern State, move further in the direction of benevolent liberalism than the judgment. Sir Gerald Fitzmaurice, on the other hand, took the opposite position and, maintaining that the effect of the five techniques had been exaggerated, held that far from constituting torture, they did not even amount to inhuman or degrading treatment. He was not saying that such methods of interrogation are unobjectionable, merely that they should not be regarded as contravening Article 3. The ideological underpinnings of his position are not difficult to identify, however. Not only is there a clear link with the same judge's dissent in *Guzzardi*, but the hint that the infliction of torture may sometimes be justified morally, if not legally,[33] is a glimpse of tough conservatism in its starkest form.

A similar disagreement over Article 3 occurred in the rather different circumstances of the *Tyrer* case. The majority decided that the birching of a juvenile in the Isle of Man constituted 'degrading' punishment. Fitzmaurice, however, disagreed and, as in the *Irish* case, did so not because he supported the disputed practice, but because he assessed it quite differently. The key points in his view were that the victim was a juvenile and that corporal punishment is not usually regarded as degrading when applied to juveniles. In a passage reflecting the quintessence of tough conservatism, he said:

I have to admit that my own view may be coloured by the fact that I was brought up and educated under a system according to which the corporal punishment of schoolboys (sometimes at the hands of the senior ones – prefects or monitors – sometimes by masters) was regarded as the normal sanction for serious mis- behaviour, and even sometimes for what was much less serious . . . . these beatings were carried out without any of the safe-guards attendant on Mr Tyrer's: no parents, nurses or doctors were ever present. They also not infrequently took place under conditions of far greater intrinsic humiliation than in his case. Yet I cannot remember that any boy felt degraded or debased. Such an idea would have been thought rather ridiculous . . . indeed, such is the natural perversity of the young of the human species that these occasions were often seen as matters of pride and congratulation – not unlike the way in which members of the student corps in the old German universities regarded their duelling scars as honourable – (though of course that was, in other respects, quite a different case).[34]

The ideological propensities with which we are concerned can also be seen in a number of cases involving the family.[35] A particularly good example is provided by the *Marckx* case which concerned the handling of illegitimacy in Belgian law. The decision that Belgium had violated the Convention in various ways was criticised by a number of judges, including Fitzmaurice who, in a wide-ranging dissenting opinion, dis- agreed on virtually every point. Much of his judgment is taken up with arguing the case for a strict construction of the Convention and may be regarded as a plea for judicial restraint. Associated with this general ideological position, however, is another reflecting tough conservatism. Thus Fitzmaurice held that the applicants were not a 'victims' for the purposes of Article 25 because their only injury was 'formal, nominal, remote or trivial'[36] and considered that the case fell outside Article 8 because that provision was concerned with the 'domiciliary protection' of the individual against police raids and the like, not with 'the civil status of babies'.[37] Finally, if the Convention was applicable, he considered that the need to give social change time to occur called for a wide margin of appreciation.[38]

There was an echo of the controversy in *Marckx* in the *Johnston* case. When dealing with the issue of illegitimacy in the latter case the Court followed its earlier decision and held that the disabilities of a child who was illegitimate on account of his parents' inability to end an earlier marriage involved a breach of Article 8. This decision was unanimous. However, whereas one judge wished that the Court had included in its judgment a statement expressing support and encouragement for the traditional family,[39] another considered that it should have declared 'that the legal situation of a child born out of wedlock must be identical to that of a child of a married couple and that, by the same token, there cannot be, as regards relations with or concerning a child, any difference between the legal situation of his parents and of their families that depends on whether he was the child of a married couple or a child born out of wedlock'.[40]

A sharper difference in approach can be seen in the case of *F v Switzerland* where the question was whether a temporary prohibition on remarriage could be justified in the case of a man who had already been married and divorced three times. Eight judges considered that it could on the ground that the Swiss authorities were entitled to consider that the restriction 'was justified in order to protect not only the institution of remarriage but also the future spouses of a person who, as the Swiss courts had established, had grossly violated fundamental conjugal rights'.[41] Nine judges, on the other hand, held that the restriction constituted a violation of the applicant's right to marry under Article 12. As regards the position of the applicant's intended fourth wife, the majority, far from seeing the ban on remarriage as a means of protection, stated that she 'could consider that she was personally and directly wronged by the measure' and concluded that 'given that she was neither under age nor insane, her rights were in no way protected by the measure in question'.[42]

Here then are two quite different views of the marital relationship: one as a traditional institution important enough to justify punishing those who abuse it and protecting potential victims; the other as an arrangement between consenting adults which people should be free to enter at their own risk. Such differences of approach have implications beyond the particular subject matter of *F v Switzerland*, being also related, for example, to the issue of whether the Convention can be read as guaranteeing the right to a divorce, and its bearing on a transsexual's right to marry. Plainly it does not follow that all of these issues have to be resolved in the same way.[43] Human rights decisions are not as simple as that. It is clear nevertheless that in relation to marriage and the family, as with issues of law and order, specific ideology does influence a judge's decision.

As might be expected, some of the clearest examples of conflict between tough conservativism and benevolent liberalism are to be found in cases concerned with sexual morality. Thus in the *Danish Sex Education* cases Judge Verdross based his disagreement with the majority's conclusion that there had been no violation of Article 2 of Protocol No. 1, on what he saw as a fundamental distinction between factual information on human sexuality and 'information concerning sexual practices, including contraception'. Whereas the former is morally neutral, the latter, Judge Verdross said, 'even if it is communicated to minors in an objective fashion, always affects the development of their consciences'.[44] It followed from this in his view that parents who objected to it were entitled to regard compulsory sex education as a failure to respect their right to ensure education and teaching in accordance with their religious convictions.

The Court's view that the State is entitled to warn children against phenomena it views as disturbing and to enable them 'to take care of themselves and show consideration for others in that respect',[45] is, of course, a classic statement of benevolent liberalism. Judge Verdross's view, on the other hand, that parents can invoke 'a well established Christian doctrine whereby anything affecting the development of children's consciences, that is, their moral guidance, is the responsibility of parents',[46] is an equally clear statement of tough conservatism.

A similar division of opinion is to be found in the *Dudgeon* case. The majority, it will be recalled, decided that the criminalisation of homosexual conduct in Northern Ireland violated Article 8, finding that the case concerned 'a most intimate aspect of private life'[47] and 'an essentially private manifestation of the human personality'.[48] Although the Court was careful to say that its decision did not imply approval of homosexuality, the thrust of the judgment emphasising, on the one hand, the undesirability of constraints on the individual's activity and, on the other, the decriminalisation of homosexuality in most member States, is a clear example of benevolent liberalism.

In contrast, the arguments put forward by the judges who dissented in this case are filled with tough conservatism. Judge Zekia began by noting that 'Christian and Moslem religions are all united in the condemnation of homosexual relations and sodomy'[49] and that 'All civilised countries until recent years penalised sodomy and buggery and akin unnatural practices.'[50] He then went on to emphasise the respect due to the majority where they 'are completely against unnatural practices'[51] and, in particular, their right to bring up their children in accordance with their own religious and philosophical convictions. Judge Matscher drew attention to the fact that the disputed law was not enforced, doubted whether the applicant had actually experienced any 'fear, suffering and psychological distress' as a result of it and pointed out that what he 'and the organisations behind him' really sought was not freedom to live his private life, which he already had, but a charter 'declaring homosexuality to be an alternative equivalent to heterosexuality'.[52] Judge Walsh, who dealt with the moral issue in some detail, distinguished between 'curable' and 'incurable' homosexuals, then said:

The rule of law itself depends on a moral consensus in the community and in a democracy the law cannot afford to ignore the moral consensus of the community. If the law is out of touch with the moral consensus of the community, whether by being either too far below it or too far above it, the law is brought into contempt. Virtue cannot be legislated into existence but non-virtue can be if the legislation renders excessively difficult the struggle after virtue. Such a situation can have an eroding effect on the moral ethos of the community in question. The ultimate justification of law is that it serves moral ends.[53]

In the *Cossey* case the position was reversed and the most liberal sentiments are to be found in the minority opinions. There the majority decided that certain limitations on the rights of transsexuals under English law had not infringed the applicant's rights, but eight judges maintained that there had been a violation of Article 8 and four considered that the measures in question also violated Article 12. As noted in chapter 7, the approach adopted by the minority judges bears a close resemblance to that accepted by the Court in the cases on homosexuality. Thus three judges referred to the 'growing awareness of each person's own identity and of the need to tolerate and accept the differences between human beings',[54] and Judge Martens after describing the applicant as belonging to 'that small and tragic group of fellow-men who are smitten by the conviction of belonging to the other sex'[55] observed that 'human dignity and human freedom' underlie the Convention and are concepts which 'imply that a man should be free to shape himself and his fate in the way he deems best fits his personality'.[56]

Of course, not all cases connected with sexual morality generate such controversy. In the *Handyside* case,[57] as we have seen, the Court upheld action against an allegedly pornographic publication, while in the *Müller* case[58] it declined to hold Switzerland in violation of Article 10 for confiscating obscene paintings and punishing the artist. It should be noted, however, that in *Handyside* Judge Mosler denied the necessity for the restriction in question, while in *Müller* Judge Spielmann adopted a similar position and Judge De Meyer dissented on the issue of confiscation. Thus even in cases where there is a broad consensus, strongly held views may produce disagreement.

The converse of the point just made is, however, also something to be borne in mind. In other words, divisions within the Court on issues of this type are not necessarily a reflection of sharply opposed specific ideologies. In the *Norris* case,[59] which like *Dudgeon* concerned homosexuality, the argument of the six judges who dissented was not that this activity merited prohibition, but that the applicant lacked the status of a 'victim' because the law in question was not enforced. Similarly, although the majority rejected the applicant's argments in *Cossey*, the judgment, like the earlier judgment in *Rees*, displays considerable sympathy for the plight of transsexuals. It is therefore a mistake to think of cases which touch on sensitive issues only in terms of a possible conflict between specific ideologies and to overlook the way in which the effect of liberal or conservative sentiment on a decision is bound up with general judicial ideology. As this is the key to understanding the significance of judicial ideologies in practice, the relationship between general and specific ideologies must now be considered.

The ideological field and the development of human rights law

The specific ideologies of tough conservatism and benevolent liberalism relate to the general ideologies of restraint and activism in two ways. First, a judge who is an activist will be guided by his specific ideology in deciding how the law should develop. Secondly, a judge who favours judicial restraint will find himself applying tough conservative values, or benevolent liberal values, according to which ideology is reflected in the Convention. Thus, the decisions of the Court and of individual judges may be seen as reflecting one of three approaches: activism guided by tough conservatism, activism guided by benevolent liberalism, and restraint.[60]

In the light of the examples we have considered, it might be thought possible to classify individual judges and the Court itself according to this scheme. In the case of the Court this is possible and, subject to the qualifications which must attend all large generalisations, it can be said that the evidence points to a tendency towards activism guided by benevolent liberalism. In the case of individual judges, however, the exercise is less valid.

Apart from the fact that evidence of any judge's ideological propensities is limited and depends on the number and length of his individual opinions, judges are sometimes inconsistent and can change their minds. Even more important is the point that no one feels equally strongly about everything. Thus, a judge who is in general a supporter of restraint may adopt an activist posture when he is presented with an issue touching on an aspect of his specific ideology which is particularly sensitive. In *Young, James and Webster*,[61] for example, where the Court adopted an activist approach to Article 11, Sir Vincent Evans, who generally favoured restraint, voted with the majority, perhaps because he saw the right not to join a trade union as a tough conservative value worth promoting. Similarly Judge Martens, who has put forward persuasive arguments in favour of judicial restraint on several occasions,[62] made a no less powerful case for common European standards in the *Cossey* case.

When considering the position of individual judges it should also be noted that not only does the intensity of ideological commitment vary with the issue and the individual, but the kinds of questions which come before the Court can often be analysed in more than one way. It is not necessary to be a tough conservative to support the decision in *Young, James and Webster*, since freedom of non-association reflects liberal, as well as conservative, instincts. In the same way, there may frequently be room for more than one view as to how much judicial activism a particular decision represents. We have treated *Young, James and Webster* as a significant example of activism because the Court relied on the 'substance' of the concept of freedom of association to minimise the effect of the *travaux préparatoires*. The dissenting judges saw the decision in the same way, but treaty interpretation being a less than exact science, not all the judges in the majority would necessarily agree with our analysis. Of course, when a judge wants to do something, he may fail to recognise the true significance of his actions, but that is not really the point. Activism and restraint, like conservatism and liberalism, are useful, but not self-evident, categories, and therefore should not be thought of as more precise than they really are.

It follows that instead of trying to classify individual judges according to their ideological tendencies, it is more useful to see members of the Court as caught within a field of ideological tensions with positions ranging from extreme activism to extreme restraint on one axis, and from tough conservatism to benevolent liberalism on the other. Looking at the Court's jurisprudence in this way not only brings out the underlying issues in individual cases, but also enables one to see more precisely why the decisions of a court which is dealing with human rights issues are always likely to be controversial.

Where the tensions within the ideological field are to be found at a given moment depends on a number of factors. One is the particular types of cases which the Court is required to consider. The significance of this point should not be underestimated. The Court, for example, has never been asked whether permitting abortion is a violation of Article 2, or prohibiting racist literature is contrary to Article 10, or to pronounce on any number of other radical conservative causes. The dearth of opinions espousing conservative activism, compared with the numerous decisions endorsing liberal activism, may therefore stem, at least partly, from lack of opportunity.

A second factor which determines where ideological tensions will be significant is the extent of consensus on what we have called the western democratic tradition. As noted earlier, tough conservatism and benevolent liberalism have many values in common. As a result, whether a disputed law or practice is 'a good thing' is usually a much less significant question than whether the Court can do anything about it. In other words, because the judges are more agreed about the content of human rights than about the nature of the judicial process, the activism/restraint axis is, in practice, more important than the conservatism/liberalism axis.

The third factor which influences the pattern of the ideological field is the human rights rule-book. We have already explained that since supporters of restraint are committed to following the rule-book, their decisions will tend to reflect its orientation. The ideological content of the Convention therefore seems very significant. This is so, but in a more subtle way than might be thought. The language of the Convention is, of course, important. No one could suggest that it permits torture, slavery, arbitrary imprisonment or any number of other things which are expressly prohibited. On the other hand, the Convention is couched in very broad terms and many of its provisions are qualified. It is therefore not difficult for tough conservatives and benevolent liberals to find in it support for their respective positions and, as we have seen, both have done so. The Convention, then, can certainly be thought of as reflecting the area of consensus, but taken by itself, is compatible with either specific ideology.

The Convention, however, no longer stands alone. The human rights 'rule-book' is the Convention together with the case-law in which it has been applied. This has had the effect of developing the Convention and investing its provisions with ideological significance. In terms of the pattern of tensions in the ideological field such development is extremely important. In 1975 supporters of judicial restraint could argue that Article 6 did not confer a right of access to the courts. When the Court, in a notable piece of judicial activism, held in *Golder* that it did, the argument shifted to one about the scope of the right. Similarly, as soon as the Court held in *Marckx* that an effective respect for rights may impose positive obligations, a debate opened up as to when such obligations exist. Supporters of restraint can seek to limit these developments, but, committed as they are to respect for the rule-book, including precedent, they cannot reverse them without becoming activists.[63] Thus as the Court's jurisprudence develops, the effect is to shape the rule-book and hence shift the ground for the next battle between activism and restraint. A tough conservative supporter of restraint could therefore consider himself engaged in a constant struggle to prevent benevolent liberal activists from conquering new territory for use as a bridge head in the next stage of the human rights campaign.

This brings us to the fourth and final factor relevant to the ideological field: the question of natural affinities between general and specific judicial ideologies. It will not have escaped attention that in our earlier discussion some of the strongest advocates of restraint appeared as supporters of tough conservatism, and, though the evidence is less striking, a similar correspondence can be seen between activism and benevolent liberalism. When the main features of the respective ideologies are recalled, this correspondence is not surprising. If we crudely characterise conservatism as the ideology of leaving things alone and liberalism as the ideology of getting things done, the affinities of conservatism and restraint and liberalism and activism are obvious. This is confirmed when we also consider their respective attitudes towards authority, society and the position of the individual. In each case the assumptions underlying conservatism will generally point to restraint; those underlying liberalism, to activism.

The above observations hold good in general but must be seen against the background of our earlier discussion. There is nothing which says that tough conservatives always have to favour judicial restraint and, given a particularly sensitive issue, or the opportunity to mount a general offensive to roll back the frontiers of liberalism, conservatives might exhibit activist tendencies which would have liberals pleading for restraint. In the same way, the alliance between activism and liberalism depends very much on the state of the rule-book. To the extent that liberal values have already been injected into the Convention through the Court's case-law, activists need only be activist in respect of new issues. Moreover, since not all liberals subscribe to the motto 'onwards and upwards' with the same fervour, at some point a liberal activist may decide he is content with what has been achieved and no further activism is appropriate. At that point, while still an ideological liberal, he is ready to join the supporters of judicial restraint.

The relevance of this discussion of judicial ideologies to the methods and function of international adjudication and to the specific issue of human rights law is not difficult to see. Activism and restraint raise questions about the nature of the judicial process which confront courts everywhere. The treatment of this issue in the European Court, though clearly bound up with the special character of the Strasbourg system, holds lessons for all international tribunals, featuring, as it does, both penetrating discussions of principle and a wide-ranging jurisprudence exploring the techniques and limitations of judicial law-making in practice. On the development of human rights law specifically, we have been able to see something of what the Court has achieved and, more importantly, how it has achieved it.

To extrapolate sensibly from the Court's experience requires two things. First, a recognition that the law of the Convention is still developing. In studying the Court's work we are therefore dealing with a process as much as a product. Secondly, it must be appreciated that, though all human rights tribunals face similar problems, what we have called the ideological field within which the European Court operates is unlikely to correspond precisely to anything found elsewhere. The terms of the various human rights conventions are not identical, the specific ideologies we have considered have different counter-parts in other regions of the world, and so on. All this having been said, however, the Strasbourg system remains the most developed scheme of international human rights protection, and the Court the most active judicial organ in the field. It would be remarkable if, after more than a quarter of a century of activity, the Court had not contributed something to international legal culture. In our submission it has done far more and, through an ever-growing jurisprudence, has provided a remarkable demonstration of the role which courts can play in the elucidation and development of international law.

Notes

1 On the use of the term 'ideologies' in the context of judicial decision-making see J. N. Adams and R. Brownsword, 'The ideologies of contract', *Legal Studies*, VII, 205 (1987).
2 See C. C. Morrisson, *The Dynamics of Development in the European Human Rights Convention System*, Nijhoff, The Hague, ch. 1 (1981). Also 'Judicial activism and judicial self-restraint in the European Court of Human Rights', *Human Rights Law Journal*, XI, 57 (1990).
3 Adams and Brownsword, 'Ideologies', 206.
4 Morrisson, *Dynamics of Development*, 4.
5 Series A, No. 25 para. 154.
6 *Ibid.*, separate opinion of Judge Sir Gerald Fitzmaurice, para. 7.
7 *Ibid.*, para. 6.
8 Series A, No. 32, dissenting opinion of Judge Thór Vilhjálmsson.
9 Series A, No. 27, separate opinion of Judge Matscher, para. A.
10 Series A, No. 26, separate opinion of Judge Sir Gerald Fitzmaurice, para. 14.
11 Series A, No. 18, separate opinion of Judge Sir Gerald Fitzmaurice, para. 32.
12 Fitzmaurice, *ibid.*, para. 39.
13 Series A, No. 48.
14 Series A, No. 43, partly dissenting opinion of Judge Matscher, para. 3.
15 Series A, No. 18, separate opinion of Judge Sir Gerald Fitzmaurice, para. 37.
16 Series A, No. 19, separate opinion of Judge Sir Gerald Fitzmaurice, para. 10.
17 Series A, No. 43, partly dissenting opinion of Judge Matscher, para. 1.
18 Series A, No. 31, partly dissenting opinion of Judge Pinheiro Farinha, para. 4.
19 Series A, No. 25, separate opinion of Judge Sir Gerald Fitzmaurice, paras. 15–17.
20 Series A, No. 18, separate opinion of Judge Sir Gerald Fitzmaurice, para. 37(c).
21 Series A, No. 145B, dissenting opinion of Judge Martens, para. 12. See also the same judge's call for restraint from the Court in procedural matters in the *Borgers* case, Series A, No. 214A, and Judge Storme's view in that case that if the fundamental principles of a fair trial are protected, 'the historical and sometimes unusual traditions of each judicial system fall outside the scope of the review of the European Court of Human Rights', dissenting opinion, para. 11.
22 Series A, No. 12.
23 Series A, No. 22, separate opinion of Judge Bindschedler-Robert, para. 1.
24 *Ibid.*, p. 55, joint separate opinion of Judges O'Donoghue and Pedersen. It is interesting that a number of judges took the opposite point of view and criticised the Court's approach as insufficiently liberal.
25 Series A, No. 39, partly dissenting opinion of Judge Matscher, para. 2.

The development of international law

26 *Ibid.*
27 *Ibid.*, dissenting opinion of Judge Sir Gerald Fitzmaurice, para. 13.
28 Series A, No. 148, dissenting opinion of Judge Valticos, joined by Judge Matscher.
29 Series A, No. 202, dissenting opinion of Judge Matscher. The conclusion was that he could be so required.
30 Series A, No. 193, dissenting opinon of Judges Bindschedler-Robert and Valticos. See also the reservations concerning the Court's approach to a different aspect of Article 8 expressed by Sir John Freeland in his partly dissenting opinion in the *Campbell* case, Series A, No. 233.
31 Series A, No. 145B.
32 Series A, No. 182.
33 Series A, No. 25, separate opinion of Judge Sir Gerald Fitzmaurice, para. 33, note 19. See also the same judge's separate opinion in the *Tyrer* case, Series A, No. 26 para. 5.
34 Fitzmaurice, *Tyrer* opinion, *ibid.*, para. 12.
35 In addition to the cases referred to in the text see also the *Airey* case, Series A, No. 32, where Judge O'Donoghue discussed the history of marriage law in Ireland, and the *Johnston* case, Series A, No. 112, where Judge De Meyer dissented on the ground that the exclusion of any possibility of civil dissolution of a marriage in Ireland was 'inflexible' and 'draconian' and a violation of Articles 8, 9 and 12.
36 Series A, No. 31, dissenting opinion of Judge Sir Gerald Fitzmaurice, postscript, para. 3.
37 *Ibid.*, para. 7.
38 *Ibid.*, para. 29.
39 Series A, No. 112, declaration by Judge Pinheiro Farinha.
40 *Ibid.*, separate opinion of Judge De Meyer, Section III para. 1.
41 Series A, No. 128, joint dissenting opinion.
42 *Ibid.*, judgment, para. 36.
43 Judge De Meyer, for example, was one of the dissenting judges in *F v Switzerland*, but in the *Johnston* case argued that Article 12 should be interpreted to include the right to a divorce.
44 Series A, No. 23, separate opinion of Judge Verdross.
45 *Ibid.*, para. 54.
46 *Ibid.*, p. 31.
47 Series A, No. 45 para. 52.
48 *Ibid.*, para. 59.
49 *Ibid.*, dissenting opinion of Judge Zekia, para. 1.
50 *Ibid.*, para. 2.
51 *Ibid.*, para. 3.
52 *Ibid.*, dissenting opinion of Judge Matscher, section I(b).
53 *Ibid.*, partially dissenting opinion of Judge Walsh, para. 14.
54 Series A, No. 184, joint dissenting opinion of Judges Palm, Foigel and Pekkanen.
55 *Ibid.*, dissenting opinion of Judge Martens, para. 2.1
56 *Ibid.*, para. 2.7. Contrast the approaches towards transsexualism adopted in the dissenting opinions in *B v France*, Series A, No. 232C.
57 Series A, No. 24.
58 Series A, No. 133.
59 Series A, No. 142.
60 Cf. Adams and Brownsword, 'Ideologies', 217–18.

61 Series A, No. 44.
62 See Judge Martens' dissenting opinions in the *Brogan* case and the *Borgers* case, Series A, No. 214A.
63 See in this connection the revealing observation of Judge Thór Vilhjálmsson in para. 1 of his dissenting opinion in the case of *Thynne, Wilson and Gunnell*, Series A, No. 190.

TABLE OF CASES

INDEX